HOW TO DECORATE
FOR AND WITH ANTIQUES

[ABOVE] Dining room, Wentworth-Gardner House, Portsmouth, New Hampshire, 1760. Courtesy The Art Institute of Chicago. [BELOW] Entrance hall, Pierce Mansion, Portsmouth, New Hampshire, 1799. Courtesy The Art Institute of Chicago

HOW TO
DECORATE
for and with
ANTIQUES
by
ETHEL HALL BJERKOE

WITH DRAWINGS BY LYN WATSON

AVENEL BOOKS · NEW YORK

TO

MY HUSBAND

JOHN ARTHUR BJERKOE

WITHOUT WHOSE CONSTANT HELP
AND ENCOURAGEMENT I WOULD
ACCOMPLISH LITTLE

LIBRARY OF CONGRESS CATALOG CARD NUMBER 59-8256

COPYRIGHT MCML, MCMLIX ETHEL HALL BJERKOE

This edition published by Avenel Books,
a division of Crown Publishers, Inc.,
by arrangement with Doubleday & Company, Inc.

FOREWORD

SOMEONE has said "To love these old houses is not so much a matter of education but a matter of the heart." With knowledge and understanding, however, the love and pleasure in a beautiful home or a precious antique are surely greatly increased. Too often a home is furnished in one period or another without knowing why. Too often a fine antique is cherished for its monetary value in one case, for its esthetic value in another. I believe the owner will cherish both home and antique more when she knows the story back of each.

A home is one's castle, one's refuge, and the place where one is entirely oneself, usually without pretense, and nothing will disclose anyone so quickly and so completely as the home. It is only necessary to see a man and a woman in the environment they have created—and not just the drawing room—to take a quick glance at the books on their shelves and tables, to see the orderliness or disarray, the signs of individualism or conformity, and all the other evidences of their everyday life, to know pretty clearly what kind of people they are.

And so, departing from the custom usual in books on decorating or on antiques, I have portrayed the story, very simply, of the architectural and decorating periods in our country and have tried to depict the people living in them. I felt that if the homemaker could see the men and women of each era in their homes, could know a little of their lives, how they dressed, and how they reacted to the age in which they played a part, she would be able to go about the task of creating her own home with better understanding and with a keener pleasure in the antiques she had inherited or acquired.

FOREWORD

I have presented the theory of color and its uses in the home. I have summarized the stories of wallpaper, furniture, spinning, and weaving.

The Early American family described lived somewhere in Connecticut, a simple pioneer family. For the Colonial period I have chosen Portsmouth, New Hampshire, as the place to be described in detail, since this was one of the outstanding towns of those years in New England, with its beautiful houses, its royal governors, and its courtly social life. Salem, Massachusetts, the richest town of its size in America around 1800, is the setting selected as the background for the Federal period. Samuel McIntire and so many of the shipowners and merchants who made Salem known the world over lived there. The Victorian period is treated with less detail than the other three, since it was a time of rapid change and one in which taste in architecture and decorating declined generally.

Then, in order that information may be available regarding the many wonderful old houses in New England open to the public and which may be studied in conjunction with this book of mine, I have added an appendix compiled by the New England Council with the assistance of the Society for the Preservation of New England Antiquities, the Boston Museum of Fine Arts, and the State Development Commission of Connecticut. I wish to take this occasion to thank them for their kindness in permitting me to use these data.

I am grateful to many in Connecticut for their help: Mr. Harold de Groff, West Hartford; Mr. Williams Haynes, Stonington; Mrs. John Avery Ingersoll, Hartford; Colonel Vincent Miller, Woodbury; Mrs. Katharine Prentis Murphy, Westbrook; and Mrs. Martin W. Wright, Centerbrook.

I wish also to thank Mr. Samuel Chamberlain, Marblehead, Massachusetts; Mrs. Arthur Taylor Gillette, Dorset, Vermont; Mr. Karl A. Dickinson and Mrs. Leon D. H. Teal of the Cape May County Historical Society, Cape May Court House, New Jersey; Mr. Frederick J. Griffiths, Director, and the Board of Regents of Gunston Hall, Lorton, Virginia; Miss Anna K. Cunningham and the Division of Archives and History, New York State Education Department, Albany, New York; the Art Institute, Chicago; the Essex Institute, Salem, Massachusetts;

FOREWORD

the Marblehead Historical Society, Marblehead, Massachusetts; the New Hampshire Historical Society of Concord; the Preservation Society of Newport County, Newport, Rhode Island, and the Webb House, Wethersfield, Connecticut.

The Massachusetts Historical Society kindly permitted me to quote the description of the Ipswich house contained in their *Collections* for 1865.

I desire also to express my appreciation to the Thomas Strahan Co. for the use of illustrations of two of their many fine reproductions of old wallpapers; to Richard E. Thibaut, Inc., for the illustration of one of their reproductions of lovely old stenciled walls; and to W. H. S. Lloyd Co., Inc., for the illustration of "Italian Scenery." The original for this paper was discovered in a home in Woodbury, Connecticut, many years ago, purchased by Lloyd's and reproduced.

And to all those who have helped consciously or unconsciously I wish to express my appreciation. It might have been but a word that started a train of thought that developed some part of the book. It might have been a charming color combination or an interesting use of an accessory seen in some house I was permitted to visit. It might have been a simple gesture of encouragement. For all these I am grateful.

ETHEL HALL BJERKOE

CONTENTS

Part One
VIGNETTES

Introduction	17
Color	28
Wallpapers	39
Stenciled and Painted Walls	51
Spinning, Weaving, and Other Handicrafts	53
Furniture	61

Part Two
BACKGROUNDS
THE FOUR ARCHITECTURAL AND DECORATING PERIODS

Early American—to 1720	91
Colonial—1720–1790	112
Federal—1790–1830	140
Greek Revival—1820–1850 (Overlapping Federal and Victorian)	153
Victorian—1830–1880	159

CONTENTS

Part Three

TODAY'S INTERIORS

The Early American Home of Today   167

How to Create a Colonial Interior   189

Contemporary Federal Style of Decorating   202

Victorian as We Like It   212

APPENDIX   221

BIBLIOGRAPHY   237

INDEX   243

ILLUSTRATIONS

Dining room in Wentworth-Gardner House, Portsmouth,   Frontis
   New Hampshire

Entrance hall in Pierce Mansion, Portsmouth, New Hampshire   Frontis

Fireplace in home of Williams Haynes, Stonington, Connecticut   12

An Early American interior today   12

Parlor, Connecticut Valley Tavern, c. 1750   13

Bedroom, New England, c. 1750   13

Living room, Cape Cod cottage, c. 1750   13

Exhibition room in White House Tavern, Newport, Rhode Island   14

Dining room in New Hampshire Historical Society, Concord,
   New Hampshire   14

Living room in home of Mrs. Katharine Prentis Murphy, Westbrook,
   Connecticut   15

Dining room in the Pingree House, Salem, Massachusetts   16

Shaw memorial bedroom, Pingree House   16

Palladian Room in Gunston Hall, Lorton, Virginia   88

Victorian interior in the period   90

Victorian interior today   90

Wallpapers   166

Dining room in Webb House, Wethersfield, Connecticut   166A

Drawing room in Lee Mansion, Marblehead, Massachusetts   166A

Bedroom in Sir William Johnson Hall, Johnstown, New York   166B

Matthews Room in Cape May County Historical Society Museum,
   Cape May Court House, New Jersey   166B

Lower front hall in the Pingree House   218

Entrance hall, Gideon Tucker House, Salem, Massachusetts   218

I

Vignettes

[ABOVE] Fireplace in home of Williams Haynes, Stonington, Connecticut, showing rare trimmer arch. Courtesy Frank J. Raymond. [BELOW] An early American interior today. Courtesy Colonel Vincent Miller

[TOP] Parlor, Connecticut Valley Tavern, c. 1750. Showing English Windsor chair with central splat and American Windsor with writing arm. Courtesy The Art Institute of Chicago. [CENTER] Bedroom, New England, c. 1750. Courtesy The Art Institute of Chicago. [BOTTOM] Living room, Cape Cod cottage, c. 1750. Courtesy The Art Institute of Chicago

[ABOVE] Exhibition room, White Horse Tavern, Newport, Rhode Island, restoration of a seventeenth-century inn. Woodwork painted old red; walls cream. Curtains, table cover, and cushions of red homespun. Banister-back chairs, oak gate-leg table. An outstanding Early American interior. Presented by Mrs. Katharine Prentis Murphy, Westbrook, Connecticut, from Prentis Collection. Courtesy the Preservation Society of Newport County, Newport, Rhode Island [BELOW] Dining room, Prentis Collection, New Hampshire Historical Society, Concord, New Hampshire. Unpainted pine paneling from a Massachusetts house built c. 1730. Plaster walls and hand-woven woolen hangings mustard brown that approximates paneling color. Early Kouba rug. New England banister-back chairs 1680-1720. Pine dresser with rare pewter. Courtesy New Hampshire Historical Society

Living room, home of Katharine Prentis Murphy, Westbrook, Connecticut. Woodwork unpainted, plaster walls mustard brown. Hangings of crewel embroidery. Furniture of New England provenance 1680-1730. Chairs attributed to Gaines, Portsmouth, New Hampshire. Large portrait by John Smibert. Early pair of portraits of Winslows of Plymouth. Courtesy Mrs. Murphy. Photograph by Gottscho-Schleisner

[ABOVE] Dining room at the Pingree House, Salem, Massachusetts. Courtesy The Essex Institute. [BELOW] Shaw memorial bedroom, Pingree House, Salem, Massachusetts, done in robin's-egg blue. Saraband and Bokhara rugs. Courtesy The Essex Institute

INTRODUCTION

A WELL-KNOWN decorator once said to me, "Every woman at heart is a decorator." I shall let you decide whether he was right or wrong. In any event, I know there is scarcely a woman today who is willing to turn her home over to the professional decorator and give him carte blanche. In the first place, she realizes she will lose all the pleasure and satisfaction she would have if she did the decorating herself. The professional decorator has a very important place in the scheme of things as an adviser. He can save the homemaker much time and energy by advising as to sources for necessary items, but in every case the final decision should be that of the homeowner herself. In my opinion, it is much better for a home to be less perfect from a trained decorator's point of view and be one in which the family feels comfortable—much better for it to be in keeping with the tastes and needs of those who live in it—than for it to be a correct example, let us say, of Early American or Federal.

Do you think you must furnish your home in a completely traditional manner? Not at all. You can bring into it the furnishings and atmosphere of the past, but these must be in keeping with the times in which we live. A successfully decorated and furnished home will always be a center of happy living, and that is the main requisite.

If you are planning a new home or if you are rejuvenating the one in which you are living, your first decorating problem is to decide which style trend you wish to follow. Shall it be Early American, Colonial, Federal, or Victorian? You may decide to try Modern. The selection of one definite style trend will give unity and character. This does not mean there will be no overlapping of style trends and that you must adhere to one period exclusively. It does mean, however, that whatever finds its way into the home from an earlier or later period or from a foreign country will be in key with the general scheme.

The Early American setting of our ancestors is not the Early American of today; neither is the Victorian decorating style of yesteryear that of the Victorian of today. We have added electric lighting, plumbing, and central heating; these have made great changes in our decorative schemes. We have learned much about the use of color and the value of comfort. Living everywhere has become more informal since we no longer can get or afford many servants. Seldom is a house built today in the elaborate style of the French châteaux so popular in America a hundred years ago. They were and still are beautiful. The building and furnishing of them were jobs left entirely to the most expert of architects and decorators —jobs much too complicated for the uninitiated. It is impossible to live in them comfortably without a staff of servants. Today many of the large, impressive houses are being bought for schools and clubs while others are being torn down to save taxes. And we moderns make ourselves comfortable and happy in less pretentious surroundings, beautiful in their decorative schemes, their furnishings, their accessories; all expressing the modern need for combined beauty, comfort, and convenience. In the past the beautifully decorated home was almost without exception the home of the wealthy, but today it is no surprise to find beauty and comfort in a reconverted barn or a Quonset hut. It all depends upon the homemaker.

In this introduction we shall discuss briefly the four major architectural and decorating periods—Early American, which begins with the settlement of various colonies to 1720; Colonial, 1720 to 1790; Federal, 1790 to 1830; and Victorian, 1830 to about 1880. This discussion will give a very brief over-all picture of each period and a very slight comparison with its counterpart today. That accomplished, we shall discuss color, wallpapers, fabrics, and furniture making as it developed in the new country.

Part Two will be devoted to the backgrounds of the four periods:

the houses, the interiors, the furnishings, and the accessories. Part Three will be concerned with the problems of decorating a home today in each of the four periods—the walls and their coverings, the floors and floor coverings, draperies and curtains, furniture, accessories, lamps, and the very important selection of color.

These four architectural and decorating periods will be considered primarily as they developed in New England, where many houses of all periods may be studied today. All divisions in these four periods are somewhat arbitrary and any year taken as the beginning or ending of a period must be an average rather than an absolute date. In the early settlement of New England there was a definite time lag between widely separated sections owing to lack of easy communication, and between various parts of the country as a whole there was also a similar time lag.

For many years there has been much interest in the old houses of New England, and measured drawings of many of the best of them have been made by competent architects. These are available to anyone wishing to build in this manner and tradition. The antique furniture and accessories of New England are eagerly sought by people from all over the country. Although California, Texas, Kansas, Oregon, and other states far distant from New England have each developed a house type, they also have untold numbers of beautifully built houses in the New England tradition, furnished with New England antiques.

EARLY AMERICAN—TO 1720

The Early American period must not be confused with the Colonial, which immediately followed. The first houses in the New England colonies were primarily shelters. Generally they consisted of one room with a huge chimney place. In this room the family lived and died. In it they ate and slept, spun and wove. In it the children were born and the ill were cared for.

In the early days of the colonies a tax levied by England, dependent upon the number of stories in a house, influenced somewhat the building size. Window glass was also taxed, and this affected the windows; perhaps not so much as the necessity of keeping out the winter cold. So windows were small and often filled with oiled paper or isinglass instead of glass. Later the settler's one-room house was enlarged by the addition of a room above, by a second room unit on the opposite side of the chimney stack, or by a lean-to. The fireplace furnished the only heat.

The furniture was of the simplest. If brought from England, it was of oak. If made in the colonies, it was simply constructed of pine, maple, birch, hickory, whitewood, or even of several woods in one article. Whatever was available was used. This furniture made by the carpenters and joiners of the colonies followed in design that which they had known at home in the mother country but was simpler and cruder. The colonists had pottery, coarse china, pewter, fire utensils of iron, copper, and brass, spinning wheels, hand-woven coverlets and rugs, and the very necessary bed warmer.

Today a home decorated in the Early American style will have simple and sturdy furniture, much of it from the country furniture of later periods. In it there will be Windsor or banister-back chairs; the later Hitchcock chairs and Boston rockers; tavern, trestle, gateleg, butterfly, or simple drop-leaf tables; settles, dressers; hooked, braided, or loom-woven rugs; pewter, old iron, and brass; pottery; and simple lamps. There will be little of the oak of the period, since this has found its way into museums and private collections. A home furnished in this period style is interesting, informal, colorful, and comfortable.

The walls of such a room should be paneled or paneled and plastered. The woodwork may be left unpainted with a wax finish. The plastered walls may be left in their natural grayish white or they may be painted. Or the woodwork may be painted one of the appropriate colors with the plastered walls unpainted, painted, or covered with one of the brightly colored small-patterned wallpapers. If the woodwork and walls are treated differently, then all woodwork—paneling, baseboard, window frames, and beams—should be treated alike. The floor should always be a little darker than the woodwork.

Only the simplest of curtains should be used. Doubtless the early settlers did not use curtains, but today you may use cottage draw curtains of chintz or calico, crewelwork, or simple white organdy or Swiss. The colors used should be the crude primitive ones: red, green, mulberry, yellow, and blue. Today's concession to modern needs will be the addition of comfortable sofas and chairs, but these must be in harmony with the other furnishings. I doubt if anyone would consider using broadloom carpeting in an Early American type home, unless, perchance, it was one of those reproducing the early hooked-rug designs. Old hooked, braided, or loom-woven rag rugs should be used. If the floors are badly stained, they should be painted, but do not use a paint simulating wood tones. Here is an opportunity for individual selection. Many beautiful colors are proper, including reds, greens, blues, beiges, grays, yellows, and black. With one of these as the base color the floor may be grained, stenciled, or spattered with other colors.

Woven hangings, simple mirrors, and Chinese painted mirrors may be used. Currier and Ives prints are charming in these homes. Although these are the products of early nineteenth-century mass production in this country, some of the drawings were done by excellent artists, and these lithographs produced for the common people of the times are very dear to the heart of innumerable collectors. Primitive paintings, usually by unknown artists, framed samplers, and botany prints may also be used. The rooms should be colorful with the bright, rich colors of the period and comfortable and cheerful with their sturdy furniture with its warm wood colorings.

In this type of home one should use old oil lamps electrified or a lamp made from some simple piece of pottery, pewter, or some early wooden article. It is well to refrain from bizarre effects except in so-called playrooms. Very often ceiling and side lights are not desirable in these early rooms. Many people use both with success. Perhaps I am opposed to ceiling lights without justification, but too often have I suffered from having to sit at a dinner table with a glaring light from above.

Lampshades should be of gingham, old red tablecloths, chintzes of small design, calico, unbleached cotton dyed the desired shade, parchment (opaque or translucent), wallpaper, or Chinese tea-leaf paper.

In a dining room of this period one's imagination may have more lati-
tude because a separate room for eating was quite unusual in the days of
the early settlers. Doubtless the room will be small with a low ceiling.
The furniture may be a dresser, a simple pine or cherry table, Windsor,
painted, ladder-back or banister-back chairs. A tavern table may be used
for serving. Simple French Provincial furniture goes well in this type of
room. Rugs may be similar to those in the living room, and the general
atmosphere created in the two rooms, as throughout the entire house,
should be akin. The china used in this Early American dining room may
be Chinese Canton, pink luster, early Staffordshire, stoneware, or even
the plain, colorful modern pottery; and there will be more pewter than
silver.

In the bedrooms of the Early American home there may be very little
difference from those of the later Colonial bedroom, except traditionally
there should be less sophistication in the former. The furniture would be
of pine, maple, cherry, or other light wood, whereas mahogany would be
the wood often used in the Colonial bedroom. Wallpapers, accessories,
curtains, and floor coverings are all simpler and the coloring somewhat
more primitive in the Early American than in the Colonial bedroom.
Here again the general effect should harmonize with the other rooms.

COLONIAL PERIOD—1720–1790

The Colonial period follows the Early American and covers the years
between 1720 and those immediately following the Revolution. In this
period we find the English colonists building their simplified version of
the English manor houses along the coastline from Maine down. In the
cities Colonial versions of the English town house were constructed.
These were an American adaptation of the English Georgian house and
even the simplest had good proportions and dignity. These are the houses
with beautiful paneling, elaborate fireplace systems, and many other
features so admired today.

As the houses of this Colonial period were built during the early

Georgian period, maple, cherry, walnut, and mahogany in the Queen Anne and Chippendale styles were used in furnishing them, with some survivals from the former William and Mary and Jacobean furniture styles. Some of this was imported from England but much was made in the colonies from native woods and from mahogany brought home from the Indies in sailing vessels. Many beautiful and exotic treasures came from China in the late years of this period, brought home by the sea captains and the men in the crew. During this period the better type of houses and their furnishings had much formality about them and are quite distinct in character from the Early American homes. Yet one finds carry-overs from the first period into these homes—a carry-over that makes for interest.

With the beginning of this second period of American decoration, during the years from 1720 until just after the Revolution, Colonial life became richer and more comfortable. Each boatload of colonists brought furniture and accessories from home, there was constant communication between the mother country and the new, and any new fashion in England was soon found in America, allowing always for the usual time lag. Houses became more elaborate, casement windows were replaced by double-hung sash windows, structural beams were no longer left exposed, and more attention was given to the mantelpieces, the doors and windows, the room trim, and the paneling. A frequent treatment of a room during this period was the use of paneling on the chimney wall and wallpaper on the other three walls. Generally there was a dado or at least a dado cap or chair rail.

Mahogany soon became the fashion with the cabinetmakers, and although walnut was used particularly along the Delaware River, there was no walnut era, per se, in America as in England. These were the days of William Savery of Philadelphia, who made the finest highboys ever seen; of John Goddard and the Townsends of Newport, Rhode Island, who made the unique block-front secretaries, desks, and highboys. Besides these men there were many expert craftsmen who copied well the designs of Chippendale, the important name in furniture design in England at the time. In addition to the beautiful highboys, lowboys, and desks, the Colonial cabinetmakers were producing tall clocks, chests-on-chests, tables of all kinds, fine chairs, and sofas. As the furniture became more elegant so did the fabrics used to upholster it and for hangings. There was no lack of fine damasks, brocatelles, needlework, silks, or chintzes. These were imported from England, France, and China. Floor coverings ranged from hooked and braided rugs to costly Orientals and Aubussons.

Much lustrous ringing glassware was imported from Waterford, Cork and Dublin in Ireland, and Bristol in England. The precious china came from many parts of the world: Lowestoft and Canton from China; Worcester, Leeds, Spode, Copeland, and Liverpool as well as many others from England; and fragile bits of soft paste from France and Germany.

Colors became softer within the house. Woodwork was painted a gentle gray, various shades of green, primrose yellow, robin's-egg blue, a grayed blue, and sometimes rich dark colors such as chocolate brown and the rosy red of old bricks. Wallpapers were Chinese, scenic, floral, and architectural. Sometimes the walls were stenciled or painted with pictures by itinerant artists instead of papered.

Everything Chinese brought home by the sea captains and crewmen in the China trade was accepted eagerly and fitted well into the Colonial home, even as it does today. There was hardly a mansion along the sea-coast of New England that did not contain many wonderful things from China, and even the simplest home had some treasures brought from Cathay by some relative. This was even more true in the period that follows. Mentally and culturally the New Englander of those days was a cosmopolitan. It may be difficult for a first- or second-generation American, or for one whose heritage has been entirely in some other part of our country, to understand the inbred love of Chinese art in New England, but this is part of our inheritance; not an acquired affection by any means, but the love of familiar things.

Directly after the Revolution the common people in some parts of New England were in dire straits. Conditions for them were often intolerable. In fact they were difficult for most people. In the years immediately following the cessation of warfare there were insurrections in New Hampshire and Massachusetts. Household slaves and indentured servants became fewer except in the coast towns, where trading with the Far East and shipbuilding flourished.

The Colonial period was the most truly elegant and beautiful in the houses constructed, in their decoration and furnishings, and in the costumes of both men and women. While the Federal period saw a lessening of the rococo of the Colonial period and a marked progression toward the simplicity and refinement of Adam and his followers, life did become less gracious in many ways.

FEDERAL PERIOD, 1790–1830

The Federal period which began in 1790 continued until 1830. In America the Revolution was over. With the Declaration of Independence, the sympathy of the colonists turned to France. Nevertheless, they continued to be influenced by England in building and decoration.

In American homes of this period paneling disappeared and the plastered walls were papered or painted in some cool color. Pale gray, a soft shade of rose, Adam green, or light buff were in great favor. White also came into vogue for the painting of woodwork. It was in this period that Chinese, scenic, and landscape wallpapers, as well as those with medallions and other designs commemorating the American and the French fights for independence, reached their greatest popularity.

The influence of the Adam brothers of England was seen in a new simplicity without and within the house. Decoration in pairs, as introduced by Adam, was popular: a pair of sofas, a pair of mirrors, a pair of tables, et cetera. This gave a balance to the room that was both restful and symmetrical. The entire trend in furniture was toward lighter and more cheerful woods. Although mahogany remained fashionable, it was often inlaid with satinwood or other light-colored wood in a formal manner. Much of the furniture was made by trained cabinetmakers who had come to America for this purpose.

Salem in 1800 was acknowledged to be the wealthiest city of its size in America, and her wealth and growth were expressed in her beautiful houses built by Samuel McIntire during the years 1781 to 1811. More than twenty homes for Salem's wealthy merchants and sea captains were constructed and decorated by him. He probably drew the designs himself, kept an eye on the building, and did much of the exquisite carving on doors and mantels.

About 1812, following the new war with England, Americans were swept by a wave of patriotism and everything possible was decorated with the American eagle. About 1820 the temple-like buildings of the Greek Revival in architecture became fashionable and remained so popular until the middle of the century that it appeared at the time to be developing into a national building style.

As an adaptation of the French Empire we had the so-called American Empire. As the years advanced, furniture of this type became more and more massive. Much of it is so cumbersome that it has never become so popular with today's decorators and homemakers as the later early Victorian. By 1830 most of the Colonial traditions were forgotten, and taste in building and decoration was at a very low ebb. In the next period, however, it reached an even lower stage of decadence.

VICTORIAN PERIOD, 1830 TO ABOUT 1880

The Victorian period covers the years from the end of the Federal to about 1880. It was a time of easy money, of great industrial development, of rapid expansion westward, of the bitterness and suffering growing out of the war to abolish slavery, and of petty pretentiousness with overelaboration, fussiness, and bad taste generally in decoration, building, dress, and even in manners. Then came a revolt against all this lavishness and uncouthness, and many people turned to the more simple missionstyle furniture of the artcrafters, the oatmeal wallpapers, and the accessories of this colorless style. Later came a trend to early crude modernism, now developing into a definite American modern which is not really modern at all.

During the early years of the Victorian period an effort was made to revive Gothic forms in both building and decoration. The vine-clad cottage with latticed windows, peaked gables, and steep roofs appeared and was beloved by the romantic souls inspired by the "Gothic novel" and Ruskin. As the period came to a close in giddy and dazzling bewilderment, the beautiful furniture of the past was often replaced by the new golden oak of Grand Rapids or the mission style of the artcrafters.

During this confused half century interior walls were usually covered with wallpaper in strong, heavy colors—deep red, blue, green, or muddy brown—tapestry-like wallpaper, or reproductions of colored and embossed leather. Colored glass windows were popular. Floors were covered with deep-pile carpets, loud florals, or newly imported Orientals. The wood trim of rooms was often of golden oak, mahogany, black walnut, cherry, or birch. Windows were swathed in heavy draperies with elaborate swags or valances, always with glass curtains and sometimes with a second pair of elaborate lace curtains. Pictures and photographs covered all available wall space. Lace, embroidery, and antimacassars embellished the furniture. Black walnut and horsehair were popular.

Out of this welter of overadornment we can pick some things that are good, particularly from the early years of the period, and a room decorated in the Victorian style can be charming—charming in our way of doing it, not in the style of the period itself.

COLOR

WHAT IS IT?

THE creation of a home has been one of the chief preoccupations of woman for centuries. In this work of creation an understanding of color and design is of more importance than the mere possession of money, important as that is. And yet woman, generally, has been taught little about the principles of color. It is often a source of wonderment to me how successful the majority of untutored women are in using color; possibly through intelligent observation; perhaps through unconscious psychological and retinal nerve reactions. It is well known that it is not necessary to study color harmony to be influenced by it, since color sensation is instinctive. Color harmony is in our eyes and this has its psychological effect upon us. How closely color affects our everyday life is being more and more clearly demonstrated by physicists and psychologists.

In creating a home, a woman expresses and discloses herself. It is her selection and arrangement of what goes into it that give it beauty and charm, not the amount of money she spends in its embellishment. A limitless bank account may permit her only to demonstrate bad and confused judgment. No home should be a slavish copy of another; neither should it look like a shopwindow. It should be a setting for those who dwell in it—a background reflecting but not overshadowing them. It should be a place in which they can relax and be themselves. Even vibrant people have difficulty competing with strong colors all the time, so the home should not be decorated like a night club or a stage setting. It should have a personal quality about it that reflects the woman particularly but that will be expressive of the entire family. And at the basis of this personal quality will be the color scheme.

It is not possible in a small section of a book such as this to discuss color and its uses in the detailed manner the subject demands. However, I shall attempt to give the fundamentals underlying the use of color, and if an interest is aroused, the reader will find many books listed in the Bibliography for further study.

Great strides have been made since the seventeenth century when Sir Isaac Newton demonstrated that sunlight passed through a prism could be broken up into a continuous gradation of color called the spectrum. Since then many color theories and color systems have been proclaimed. Hermann L. F. Helmholtz (1821–94) made many studies regarding the nature of light, and these led to more comprehensive systems. Many of the color theories disagreed with one another. The physicist who sees color as light uses a system based on one set of primaries and secondaries; whereas the chemist, who considers color as pigment, uses a system based on pigment colors.

In 1905 Albert H. Munsell developed a workable color system with three color dimensions—hue, value, and chroma. This system is based on ten hues—yellow, yellow-green, green, blue-green, blue, blue-purple, purple, red-purple, red, yellow-red—and ten gradations of each hue, and is widely used today. It enables decorators and manufacturers to name definite colors in a way that is readily understood by all. Many decorators and manufacturers use beautiful words to designate different colors, such as "shocking pink" or "fuchsia," but since these names mean at least slightly different shades or tints to different people, the situation becomes more and more complicated for the bewildered home decorator.

One of the latest contributions to the study of color has been made by Louis Cheskin, technical director of the Color Research Institute of America and the author of two books on color. He confirms that there have always been disagreements about the primary colors and maintains that the latest studies made since the breaking down of the atom prove that the true primary colors are green-blue, magenta-red, and yellow. He claims that with these three primaries plus white and black it is possible

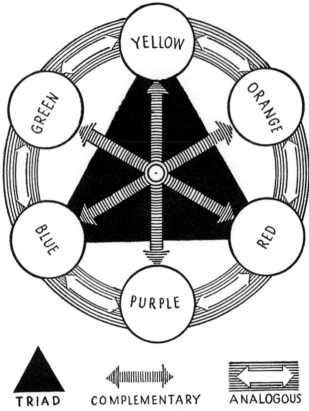

TRIAD   COMPLEMENTARY   ANALOGOUS

PRIMARY COLORS: Red, blue, yellow. SECONDARY COLORS: Orange, purple, green. ANALOGOUS HARMONY: Colors which adjoin one another on the spectrum. COMPLEMENTARY HARMONY: The color obtained from mixing two primaries. TRIAD: A balanced group of three colors selected at equal intervals on the color wheel.

to mix 1,296 colors, and that anyone with a formula and these five colors will be able to mix any desired color.

To make the approach to the understanding of color and its use in the home as simple as possible I shall resort to definitions that will give a concise meaning to the terms generally used. I would suggest that everyone buy a color wheel, as this will be of the greatest help in the assembling of color combinations.

Afterimage or Aftermirage: Complementary colors are seen by one optic nerve. For instance, the eye has an optic nerve for red and green. A second optic nerve sees blue and yellow; a third black and white. A co-ordination of two nerves enables the eye to see mixed colors. After the eye has been stimulated by looking at one color for about thirty seconds, the afterimage in the complementary color is seen.

This complementary color is that of the physicist and not of the chemist. For instance:

> Red will cause an afterimage of blue-green.
> Blue-green will cause an afterimage of red.
> Blue will cause an afterimage of yellow.
> Yellow will cause an afterimage of blue.
> Green will cause an afterimage of purple.
> Purple will cause an afterimage of green.

ANALOGOUS HARMONY: When two or more consecutive colors of the spectrum, such as blue and green, are used, we call it analogous harmony.

ADVANCING OR ACTIVE COLORS: Yellow, red, orange. Green is moderately so.

COLOR DIMENSIONS:

1. *Hue*. The quality which distinguishes one color from another is called hue. Each section of the color wheel is a hue. It is easiest understood as the name of a color, such as red.

2. *Value*. The lightness or darkness of a color—the amount of light it reflects—is called its value. When white is added to a color it becomes a *tint*, a color higher in value than its spectrum value. When black is added, it becomes a *shade*, a color lower in value than its spectrum value.

3. *Chroma*. The strength or weakness—intensity—of a color is called chroma. Chroma represents the amount of purity or fullness of a hue.

COMPLEMENTARY COLOR. By mixing any two primary colors, a color is obtained which is complementary to the third primary pigment.

PIGMENT COMPLEMENTARIES. Red and green; yellow and purple; blue and orange.

COMPLEMENTARY HARMONY. This is obtained when a color and its complementary are used, such as green and red.

COOL COLORS. *See* receding and passive.

MONOCHROMATIC OR DOMINANT HARMONY. When one color is used

throughout its shades and tints it is called monochromatic or dominant harmony.

PRIMARY COLORS. A primary color is a basic color. Every known color is obtained from these three. By mixing all three pigment primaries, a gray is obtained. Pigment primaries are red, blue, and yellow.

RECEDING OR PASSIVE COLORS. Blue and purple. Green is moderately advancing.

RELATED COLORS. Those colors which adjoin one another on the spectrum are related colors.

RETINAL STIMULATION. Physiologists have discovered that there are four primary colors known as the physiological primaries: red, green, blue, and yellow. In our eyes we have three sets of retinal nerves. One set is sensitive to the red-green rays, one to the blue-yellow rays, and the third controls the sight of black and white. These nerves co-ordinate in seeing other color mixtures.

SECONDARY COLOR. A color that results from the mixing of two primaries is called a secondary color.

SPECTRUM. When the colors in light are broken up so that they fall upon a background in their fullest intensity, the result is known as a spectrum. The six colors are purple, blue, green, yellow, orange, and red.

A TERTIARY COLOR. When a primary color is mixed with a secondary color, the resulting color is called a tertiary. It will vary in accordance with the proportions used.

A TRIAD. A balanced group of three colors selected at equal intervals on the color wheel is a triad. This can be easily seen if it is noted that the first color forms a triad with those two colors into which its complementary may be split.

WARM COLORS. *See* advancing and active.

COLORS—HOW THEY AFFECT YOU

Can you picture living in a world devoid of color, where everything appears as it does in a gray-and-white photograph? If this were so, people themselves would be as colorless and as alike as so many clams. Only within a short period of time has it been proven by scientists that colors have a definite effect upon our nervous system. The art of primitive people employs pure colors, for primitive people and children are not attracted by tints and shades. Up to five or six years of age the normal child prefers red to any other color and is not at all attracted by pastels.

Most people find the warm, active colors stimulating and the cool, passive colors relaxing. Many believe that each color awakens a particular emotion in our minds. Others contend that memory, through an association of ideas, sometimes quite unconsciously, causes us to like certain colors and to dislike others. Tests have shown that this psychological reaction can often be traced to some early experience. In any event, certain colors have a definite emotional association for most people. In literature, in art, and in our everyday thoughts white is the symbol of innocence and joy; black of mourning and wickedness. We often link yellow with meanness and treason, as when we say that someone has a "yellow streak." Blue stands for constancy, as "true blue," while red is the most ardent of all the colors, standing in its worst sense for cruelty and sin. We have all read Hawthorne's *Scarlet Letter*, and most of us, I am sure, have sung the old hymn "Though Your Sins Be as Scarlet." Green is closely akin to blue and may signify hope, but is more often used to express jealousy, as "green with envy." Purple is a symbol of royalty, "born to the purple," but it may also be reminiscent of a decadent period—the "mauve decade."

One not especially sensitive to color may not realize the peculiarly irritating properties of certain colors and color combinations to some people. Normal people react to color stimulation as to other stimuli and unconsciously surround themselves with both cold and warm hues; this combination gives a balanced stimulation. Depressed persons will invariably yearn for the warm, stimulating colors and will be more depressed if surrounded by a predominance of cool colors. They will feel better if their homes are decorated with colors from the red and yellow family with contrasts and accents only from the blue-green family. In like manner, very active people, who lead a stimulating existence, will tend to build their decorating schemes around the cool colors with accents from the red-yellow family.

Beatrice Irwin in *The New Science of Color* says that people demand one color or another in their surroundings, depending upon their state of being. She also says that colors are either physically, mentally, or spiritually stimulating, sedative or recuperative. Miss Irwin is of the opinion that the soul, the body, and the mind demand in the colors surrounding them the complement of their own state.

Today this idea is being followed in hospitals, in schools, in business, and in advertising as well as in homes. In mental hospitals depressed patients are put in rooms that are stimulating and manic patients in rooms done in the cool colors. A surgeon no longer works in a glaring septic white operating room, his eyes soon fatigued by the brightness of light reflected from tiled walls to shining instruments. Many operating rooms today are done in grayed green, a color soft and soothing to surgeons and nurses. If medical science has found the use of color schemes desirable, how important it is for homemakers to have some understanding of the value of color in the decorating of their homes.

COLOR—HOW TO USE IT

In selecting color for a home, the first two questions to be asked are "What decorating style trend do I wish to follow?" and "What color scheme is most suitable for a particular room and for those who will occupy it?"

In decorating a home as a background for antiques, a particular group of colors is indicated in each of the four general periods: Early American, Colonial, Federal, and Victorian. Today's style trends and inclinations have affected the use of these groups of colors but the colors themselves are still indicated. Since nothing would be accomplished by going into a discussion of these period colors in the present chapter, we shall discuss them in detail within each period section.

Before the home decorator reaches the question of a color scheme, she has, I am sure, made a decision as to which period style she will follow. Then she may study the different colors that have proven most suitable for that period and select those she prefers.

Since the living room will be used not only by the family but by visitors it is best to have it done in a complementary color scheme, or it may be desirable to use three or more colors. As these schemes combine both warm and cool colors, they will prove most satisfying to everyone. Bedrooms should be as restful and relaxing as possible. For this reason a color scheme not too brilliant and not too complex is desirable. Nowhere in the house will the individuality and personality of the occupant be so apparent as here. If desired, the dining room may be more formal than the other rooms, always remembering that the table should be the focal point of the room. A study or library should be decorated in a manner conducive to study. The books will be a strong focal point of color.

Each room created will have a definite personality. With thought and care the desired effect can usually be achieved. Each room should reflect in a greater or lesser degree those who occupy it. Often one will hear a homeowner complain that he does not like his home which has been done with great care and at much expense by a trained decorator. It is beautiful and follows all the decorating rules but it expresses the decorator and not the homeowner. The colors may be intriguing but they may be the wrong colors for him. The furnishings and accessories may be perfect in every way but not at all suitable for those who live in the rooms.

In using colors for decorating, pure colors are exciting; gray colors give a sophisticated effect; warm colors are stimulating; cool colors relaxing; dark colors stately and formal; light colors gay; related colors either warm or cool.

Decorating schemes are worked out by means of various color harmonies. The three most used are monochromatic or dominant harmony, analogous harmony, and complementary harmony. In dominant harmony, different tones of the same color are used, as in a room done in beige, tan, and brown. Analogous harmony is one that uses two or more consecutive colors on the color wheel, such as blue, green, et cetera. Both monochromatic and analogous color schemes may prove lacking in an interesting contrast of color qualities. Complementary harmony is obtained by combining a color and its complement, as red and green.

Probably more rooms are done in complementary colors than in the other harmonies, as they make for a balanced retinal stimulation and for an interesting variety and contrast. A room all warm or all cool, all active or all passive, unless done with the utmost skill, eventually becomes annoying. If two primary colors of equal value are used together in a scheme, the result may be confusing, since the contrast will be so sharp as to fatigue all the nerve endings. Hence there should be the right proportion of each color and its shades and tints. Generally, receding colors should be used for the large masses of background with active advancing colors for the small areas. Tints should be used generally for large masses of colors except when a dark background (shade) is used advisedly to achieve a certain desired effect.

If the background is light, there should be dark notes in the furnishings for interesting contrast. If the background is dark, furnishings and accessories in high value (tints) will effect a suitable contrast. Always remember that the proportions of contrast must be subtle and not equal. A light color will appear lighter against a dark background and a dark color will appear darker against a light background.

In general a room should progress from dark floors to somewhat lighter walls to lighter ceiling. It is becoming popular to have the ceiling—even in period decoration—a paler tint of the wall color rather than white. Unless desirable as a shock spot of color, accent colors should be repeated more than once at different levels. Occasionally it is interesting to have one spot of analogous color in a complementary color scheme if the accent is worthy of the job it has to do and sufficiently important for the job. For instance, in a living room done in reds and greens one might have a very simple, very beautiful turquoise-blue lamp of adequate size with a dark red shade. Or the shock accent could well be a proper-sized picture or wall hanging. Do not, however, have shock accents throughout the entire house. They may seem interesting at first but eventually become irritating.

In combining shades and tints of a color with other colors, it is well to remember that bright or pure colors on a dull ground of the same hue or of any hue not complementary—for example, a bright green on a dull green, on a dull blue, or on a dull yellow—will deaden the dull color. The dull color will also affect the brightness of the pure color. This reaction of colors is owing to the fact that the bright color throws its complementary color into the dull color. Thus a red will throw its complementary green into the green background, making it brighter, but a green thrown into a blue or yellow background would make it duller.

If a room is too large it can be made to appear smaller by using warm, intimate advancing colors. If it is desirable to make a room look larger, use the cool receding colors. If the ceiling is too high, use a warm advancing color, the value of the color depending upon how much the ceiling is to be brought down. If it is desirable to make the ceiling look higher without the use of striped paper or other mechanical trick, use a very high value of a receding color, such as blue. Avoid glossy finish on woodwork, walls, and furniture. In the kitchen especially, where walls of white glossy paint or enamel are apt to be found, the reflection of bright lights on these shining surfaces causes quick eye fatigue and may lead to cuts and burns.

In color, as in other features of home decoration, there should be unity in the entire house, particularly if the rooms are connected by open doorways. This color unity is not so necessary between one floor and another except that the hall decorating scheme on the first floor will undoubtedly be carried up to the second floor. Because of this there will be color transition. In the small house or apartment the use of the same color or slightly varying tones of the same color as backgrounds will give unity. An effect of monotony is avoided through the use of different colors in the accessories of adjoining rooms. Sometimes it is advisable to reverse the color schemes, that is, have the background color of one room as the accent color in the adjoining room, using different values of the colors for contrasting interest.

Graying colors is one of the simplest methods of keying. The transition from a room done in complementary colors with the warm color dominant to a room done in the same complementary colors with the cool color predominating is interesting and good decorating. For instance, the living room could have a background of grayed red of a very high value—practically a warm gray—with accessories in shades of blue-green and red. The connecting dining room could have a grayed blue-green background with yellow and mauve contrasts. The kitchen could have grayed-blue walls with red and yellow contrasts. A hall paper could pick up all these colors of blue-green, blue, red, yellow, mauve, and warm gray. A color scheme, however, should never be carried out so perfectly that it becomes monotonous and too studied; neither should it be so haphazard that it is confusing and irritating.

If a room is dark, it can be made to appear sunny by using a pale, warm yellow. If it is filled with sunshine in the summertime, it can be made to seem cooler by the use of grayed green. With a judicious use of color you can make your home do what you want it to do. Color is your servant. Make it work for you.

WALLPAPERS

As in the case of porcelain, gunpowder, and printing from wooden blocks, paper was an invention of the Chinese. According to Dagny Carter, a recognized authority on China, this invention occurred in A.D. 105. It may be assumed that shortly after this the ingenious Chinese were decorating this new paper with hand-painted pictures. Undoubtedly these first paintings were of birds and flowers and were used as wall hangings.

In the latter part of the thirteenth century Marco Polo spent many years traveling to and from China. Upon his return he wrote a book of travels describing all the wonders he had seen—wonders so fabulous that his fellow Venetians considered him a tremendous liar. Columbus, his mind filled with the fantastic stories of Cathay from reading Marco Polo's *Travels*, set sail from Italy in 1492 to find a westward route to China and discovered America. For years after this a search was made for a northwest water route through America. The result was the discovery of Hudson Bay.

In 1517 the Portuguese reached Canton under Fernando Perez de Andrade and established trading centers in several places. By the middle of the sixteenth century they were bringing back to Europe the products of China—products which in most instances surpassed anything known to Europeans at that time. In 1600 the British East India Company was chartered by Queen Elizabeth, and in 1602 the Dutch East India Company was chartered by Holland. At this time the only "foreign devils" permitted at Court by the Manchus were the Jesuits, who, upon their return to Europe, wrote and told of the fairy-tale country to the east.

With all these marvelous and exotic tales trickling into Europe and with an ever-increasing supply of porcelains, lacquers, silks, spices, pepper, nankeens, tea, and jewelry brought back by the Portuguese, Dutch, and English traders, wallpapers also became available. By the middle of the eighteenth century the fashion for everything Chinese had swept Europe, had traversed the Channel to England, where Chippendale was making some of his finest furniture in the so-called Chinese Chippendale, and from England had crossed the Atlantic to America, where the colonists were beginning to amass fortunes from this trading with the Far East and the West Indies.

The first papers from China were small rectangles about 12½ by 16 inches, similar in size to the tea-leaf paper which we can secure even today. Until the end of the eighteenth century all Chinese paper was hand painted. By 1750 the Chinese were painting landscapes in addition to the pictures of birds and flowers—landscapes flat, without perspective, but wonderfully and interestingly designed and executed.

FRENCH

By the end of the sixteenth century, the *dominotiers*, a guild of painters and papermakers, were established in France. The importation of Chinese papers had created a demand for patterned wall decoration, and the dominotiers produced papers with small hand-painted or stenciled patterns as well as those imitating marble, and were, without doubt, the actual originators of decorated papers to be applied to walls.

In 1620 Le François of Rouen introduced flock paper. This was an imitation of brocaded velvet. To produce this paper, finely cut wool or silk, called flock, was dusted on a design printed in size. The flock attached itself to this size and resulted in a raised design resembling the pile of velvet. Sometimes the process was repeated several times until the raised design attained the desired thickness.

About 1688 Jean Papillon, a Frenchman, was the first to make repeating pattern designs that would match on all sides when the separate sheets were pasted together. Thus Papillon may be considered the real inventor of wallpaper as we know it today. He carved his patterns in large wood blocks and by covering these blocks with different pigment colors could print any pattern in any number of colors desired.

Réveillon, a French stationer, established a wallpaper factory at Paris in 1752 as an answer to the increasing demand for cheaper types of wall coverings. At first he made the popular flock papers, but soon branched out into painted paper panels. Réveillon was a good craftsman himself and since he employed many of the best artists of the day, some of the most beautiful wallpapers ever produced were made at his factory. In 1784 he received an appointment from the King because of the high quality of his productions and his factory became a royal manufactory, where he employed at least three hundred workmen. During the French Revolution, on April 28, 1789, Réveillon's factory and warehouse were partially destroyed and he fled to England, where he died in 1795. Carlyle's description of the attack on this factory is an interesting one:

On Monday, the 27th day of April, Astronomer Bailly notices that the Sieur Réveillon, "extensive Paper Manufacturer of the Rue Saint-Antoine:" he, commonly so punctual, is absent from Electoral Committee;—and even will never reappear there. In those "immense Magazines of velvet paper" has aught befallen? Alas, yes! Alas, it is no Montgolfier rising there today; but Drudgery, Rascality, and the Suburb is rising! Was the Sieur Réveillon himself once a journeyman, heard to say that "a journeyman might live handsomely on fifteen sous a-day?" Some sevenpence halfpenny: 'tis a slender sum! Or was he only thought, and believed, to be heard saying it? By this long chafing and friction, it would appear, the National temper has got electric.

Down in those dark dens, in those dark heads and hungry hearts, who knows in what strange figure, the new Political Evangel may have shaped itself; what miraculous "Communion of Drudges" may be getting formed! Enough: grim individuals, soon waxing to grim multitudes, and other multitudes crowding to see, beset that Paper-Warehouse; demonstrate, in loud ungrammatical language (addressed to the passions too), the insufficiency of sevenpence halfpenny a-day. The City-Watch cannot dissipate them; broils arise and bellowings; Réveillon, at his wit's end, entreats the Populace, entreats the Authorities. Besenval, now in active command, Commandant of Paris, does, towards evening, to Réveillon's earnest prayer, send some thirty Gardes Françaises. These clear the street, happily without firing; and take post there for the night, in hope that it may be all over.

Not so: on the morrow it is far worse. Saint-Antoine has arisen anew, grimmer than ever;—reinforced by the unknown Tatterdemalion Figures, with their enthusiast complexion, and large sticks. The City, through all streets, is flowing thitherward to see: "two cartloads of paving-stones, that happened to pass that way," have been seized as a visible godsend. Another detachment of Gardes Françaises must be sent; Besenval and the Colonel taking earnest counsel. Then still another; they hardly, with bayonets and menace of bullets, penetrate to the spot. What a sight! A street choked up, with lumber, tumult and the endless press of men. A Paper-Warehouse eviscerated by axe and fire; mad din and Revolt; musket-volleys responded to by yells, by miscellaneous missiles, by tiles raining from roof and window,—tiles, execrations and slain men!

The Gardes Françaises like it not, but must persevere. All day it continues, slackening and rallying: the sun is sinking, and Saint-Antoine has not yielded. The City flies hither and thither; also, the sound of that musket-volleying booms into the far dining-rooms of the Chaussée d'Antin; alters the tone of the dinner-gossip there. Captain Dampmartin leaves his wine; goes out with a friend or two, to see the fighting. Unwashed men growl on him, with rumours of "*A bas les Aristocrates* [Down with the Aristocrats]": insult the cross of St. Louis! They elbow him and hustle him; but do not pick his pocket;—as indeed at Réveillon's too there was not the slightest stealing.

At fall of night, as the thing will not end, Besenval takes his resolution; orders out the Gardes Suisses with two pieces of artillery. The Swiss Guards shall proceed thither; summon that rabble to depart, in the King's name. If disobeyed, they shall load their artillery with grape-shot, visibly to the general eye; shall again summon; if again disobeyed, fire—and keep firing, "till the last man" be in this manner blasted off, and the street clear. With which spirited resolution, as might have been hoped, the business is got ended. At sight of the lit matches, of the foreign red-coated Switzers, Saint-Antoine dissipates; hastily, in the shades of dusk. There is an encumbered street; there are "from four to five hundred" dead men. Unfortunate Réveillon has found shelter in the Bastille; does therefrom, safe behind stone bulwarks, issue plaint, protestation, explanation, for the next month. Bold Besenval has thanks from all the respectable Parisian classes: but finds no special notice taken of him at Versailles—a thing the man of true worth is used to.

Before Réveillon's death in England, he arranged for the rebuilding of the factory and appointed Jacquemart and Bénard as his successors.

Although England set the fashion in many things for the colonists, France led in wallpapers.

After the Revolution in America and in France the entire character of wallpaper changed; even the colors became more somber. About this time scenic papers became important. These differed from the landscape panels in that they were intended to cover the walls of a room above a dado or chair rail in a continuous scene. They came in a sufficient number of strips to cover an average-sized room.

One of the finest examples of this type is the set known as *Les Amours de Psyche* (Cupid and Psyche), designed by Louis Lafitte—a designer to the King—and printed by Dufour in Paris in 1816. Twelve complete picture panels made up of twenty-six strips, each twenty inches wide, comprise the set.

And so through the years in France, under such men as Joseph Dufour, Jean Zuber, and others of their caliber, the making of wallpapers continued at a high standard. French designs even today are highly valued and are available from several importers in the United States.

ENGLISH

In 1692, during the reign of William and Mary, the first patent for making wallpaper was issued. In 1712, under Queen Anne, wallpapers were taxed at a penny per square yard. In 1714 this was increased 50 per cent and each rectangle bore a tax stamp. In 1714 "paper stainers" were also assessed an annual tax. In 1734 Langer took out a patent for making flock papers, claiming discovery of this method although it had been used by Le François in France as early as 1620. In 1746 John Baptist Jackson, probably the most important man of his times in England in the making of wallpapers, opened a factory in Battersea. Most of his designs were taken from Venetian and Roman landscapes, although he copied some French engravings. These were printed in oil from wooden blocks aided by a rolling press which Jackson had evidently invented. Two sets of his papers have been found in old American houses, one at the Lee Mansion in Marblehead, Massachusetts, carefully protected under glass.

In 1779 England forbade the importation of wallpapers, and this law remained in force until 1825. With its repeal, French papers flooded the English market.

From about 1800 wallpaper had been made in France in a long roll similar to that obtainable today. In England John Gamble had obtained patents for this invention in 1801 and 1803, but English manufacturers were not allowed to make paper in any size but the rectangles until 1830 because of the large revenue which the government received from the stamp tax on the small sheets. With the removal of this tax, the manufacture of wallpaper was less hampered and continued without spectacular designers until William Morris and his new creations in 1862.

AMERICAN

Wallpapers were not common in America until some years after the beginning of the Colonial period. The earliest were imported from England and France. Even the early Chinese papers arrived here by way of England or France. By the end of the Revolution French and English papers were to be found in many Colonial homes. After the Revolution many of the beautiful Chinese papers were brought home directly from China by the sea captains. These papers were often presented to the captains of the little American boats by the powerful "hong merchants," but it is doubtful whether the Chinese themselves used them as wall coverings in the way they were being used in Europe and in America.

Before the middle of the eighteenth century wallpapers were ordered by the individual house owners from the dealer in Paris or London, but by 1750 they were being carried by the merchants in all the larger towns, who advertised their new offerings upon the arrival of every boat from abroad. They were, however, very expensive, sometimes costing as much as $100 a room, added to which was the cost of hanging, also expensive.

In 1739 Plunket Fleeson of Philadelphia, in his shop At the Sign of the

Easy Chair, was advertising wallpapers made in America, but these were undoubtedly very crude, comparing in no way with the imported papers. In 1765 John Rugar of New York City was advertising domestic wallpapers, and soon others in Boston, Philadelphia, and Baltimore were doing the same.

Early paper was made entirely from linen rags, which accounts for its durability. It was originally hung with a specially prepared paste, the secret of which has long since been forgotten. Paper was so difficult to remove when this paste was used that the new paper was hung over the old, and it is because of this that later generations have discovered some of the beautiful old papers so well preserved that they could still be used after the later coats of paper had been removed.

About 1840 wallpapers began to be printed by machine on cheap paper and this was accompanied by a general decline in the quality of the designs. As a reaction against the horrible colors and designs of the late Victorian period, American walls took on a neutral monotone, whether papered or painted. Within the last few decades, however, homes are emerging from this colorless existence, and today it is possible to secure wallpapers reproduced from the choice old designs or in new patterns by competent designers.

HOW TO USE WALLPAPER

In selecting wallpaper for any room it is well to remember that the wall covering is undoubtedly the most important element in any decorating plan. Against it will be displayed all the furnishings of the room; against it you, your family, and your guests will be silhouetted. The most beautiful furniture and accessories will appear less beautiful and the most attractive people will lose some of their charm against an ugly background, whether it be paint or wallpaper.

The general color effect should follow the rules of color use as outlined in the chapter on color. However, in choosing wallpaper, additional care must be taken to avoid some very common mistakes. Here again your sense of the fitness of things and the keying of all parts of your decorating scheme will be of great help. Seldom would the least experienced home decorator choose for a living room a dainty floral pattern suitable only for a bedroom; nor would she be apt to use an architectural paper for a young girl's bedroom. An informal room needs an informal paper and a formal room demands a formal one. Gay chintz papers and pastel florals are naturally informal. Scenic, flock, architectural, large conventional designs, and landscape papers are generally formal. Any paper with a large, striking design is better in a formal room. It is also better in a hall or dining room not in constant use than in a living room, since with continuous association it tends to become irritating. The darker the background of a paper, the more prone it is to be formal, although at the moment there are being produced many small-patterned papers with dark backgrounds that are most interesting and that can be used in the most informal rooms.

A paper with wide vertical lines will give a formal effect and is excellent for the Federal type of home but would be entirely out of place in an Early American home. As in painted walls it is wise to allow your papered walls to determine the color scheme of the entire room.

Many people use plain or neutral wall coverings because they do not have the courage or the imagination to work out a decorating scheme with a patterned paper requiring perhaps a bit more intelligent thought and study, but when the proper result is accomplished it is much more individual and interesting. The plain neutral walls of our parents and grandparents are restful and relaxing, it is true, and some types of decorating demand them, but they were a reaction from the horrible Victorian walls of the late nineteenth century. Most of the beautiful Colonial interiors in the homes of our ancestors owed their loveliness to their wallpapers—wallpapers that were a very important part of the decoration and much beloved by their owners. Nothing is more correct or more suitable today than the fine reproductions of these early papers when decorating a home in the Colonial, Federal, or early Victorian tradition.

Since each decorating period has its own type of wallpaper as it has its own group of colors, we shall discuss the papers to be used for each period under the proper decorating section and here speak only of the general use of wallpaper.

Patterns will appear smaller on the walls and colors will look darker than they do in the samples. Stripes will make a room look higher; horizontal designs will lower the ceiling but they are also restful. Curved and broken lines suggest movement, but if too broken are fatiguing. In papering a room with dormers and with very cut-up wall space, use a small open pattern, very often using the same paper on the ceiling.

Many interesting things can be done with wallpaper. At times it is good decorating to have one wall done with a scenic paper or some other patterned paper and the other walls plain. All sorts of experiments have been tried and will be tried by different decorators. Some have been good and some have been bad. If you can afford to have your home redecorated often, it is possible that you may want to try some of these decorating schemes, but I can assure you that in most cases you will weary of them faster than you will of more conservative decorating. If you must experiment, do so in bathrooms, kitchens, or playrooms, and then, with a sure knowledge of your decorating ability and of your likes and dislikes, you can, if you choose, try your skill in more important rooms. But don't have this type of trick decorating all over the house. It is certain to be eye and nerve fatiguing.

In selecting a paper for any room that is in constant use do not select a pattern that fatigues the eye. Leave that for a room used for shorter periods of time. Never use a large scenic or a paper with a large pattern in a small room, or a small figured paper in a big room, unless in the latter case the figure is such that the paper gives the effect of a solid color.

It is not always easy for the most experienced decorator to visualize the effect of a wallpaper on a room from seeing a sample in a shop among hundreds of other samples. It is usually wise for anyone to take home a sample, or even a roll if this is possible, and try it against the wall for at least twenty-four hours to see it both by daylight and by artificial light. Some papers change entirely and for the worse in artificial light.

Paper hanging is not difficult if you have a little patience and the will to do it. In the earliest days paper was tacked to the walls. Later it was tacked to a canvas and the canvas attached to the walls. Sometimes today, if the walls are very bad, or if, as in some old houses, a wooden partition is to be papered, the wall is first covered with a material to prevent the paper from easily splitting. It is possible to buy a wallpaper tool kit from any of the large mail-order houses or from local dealers. This usually contains instructions for hanging paper. The necessary equipment is not expensive. It consists of a long table—seven- or eight-foot boards on sawhorses will do—a rotary trimming outfit containing a six-foot length of wood with a metal track, a trimmer with a steel wheel knife, and a six-foot zinc cutting strip. Then you need a paste brush, a smoothing brush, a good pair of library-type scissors, a plumb bob and cord line or level, if the walls are uneven, a good-sized paste pan, and a sense of humor. First remove all the old paper, scrape the walls smooth with a putty knife, fill in any holes and cracks with a good crack filler, and then give the walls a coat of size. Use a good quality of wheat paste and mix it until it is smooth and not too thick. The paste should spread easily but not drip. It is also a good idea to put a little size in the paste.

When cutting the lengths of paper have them match at the indicated spots on the edges and always cut your strips somewhat longer than absolutely necessary for the wall length to be covered. Very often the ceiling slants in old houses, and this extra length will take care of any such difficulties, particularly at the ceiling line. Until you near the end of the job, cut at least one double roll into lengths at a time. As you near the end, you can easily tell how many lengths are needed to finish.

After the paste has been applied to a length of paper, the two ends can be folded back to the center with the pasted side in, and then the edges cut off with the rotary trimmer. Leave the bottom third turned up until the top section has been fitted to the wall. This makes for easier handling. Always hang the paper from top to bottom and from left to right. Use the plumb bob and cord, or level, to make sure the first length is entirely straight or you may end up at a dizzy angle. Smooth the paper carefully on the wall. Any place not adhering tightly tends to dry and break open. If there is a wrinkle or if the paper is on the wall crooked, do not hesitate to peel the entire length off and start hanging it again.

After each length is attached to the wall to your satisfaction, the edges next to the ceiling and baseboard may be evened off. Paste spots from fingers or brush show up more easily on plain surfaces than on patterned paper. When such spots show, take a clean cloth and saturate it with clear water, tap the spots gently until thoroughly wet (do not rub), and when the paper is dry, the marks usually will have disappeared. If you think any of the paste has smeared the baseboard or other woodwork, wipe it off immediately with clean cloths. It dries in an ugly yellow-grained effect.

In the country most women do their own paper hanging. One woman told me with amazement of a city man who had a country home near her and who had attempted to paper a room. She said, "Can you believe it? He is a professor at a college and calls himself doctor, and yet he started to paper from the bottom of one wall and carried it right over the ceiling and down to the bottom of the other wall and could not understand why the paper did not look right!"

If you are figuring how much paper to buy, the following chart will be of help. Paper is never sold in single rolls although the price is quoted in single rolls. It is well to buy an extra roll in case you need some for later patching. And a word about patching. If you have to cover a spot with a patch, don't cut a piece of paper the exact size of the spot to be covered. A patch of this kind will always show. Instead, tear a piece of paper a bit larger than the spot to be covered with very uneven ragged edges, fit it well over the spot before applying the paste to it to judge if it matches well, then apply the paste to the patch and smooth it over the spot with the smoothing brush or a clean cloth. This kind of patch will never show.

WALLPAPER CHART

No. of feet
around the room   *No. of single rolls required*

Height in feet from floor to ceiling	8	9	10	11	12
28'	8	8	10	10	12
32'	8	10	10	12	12
36'	10	10	12	12	14
40'	10	12	12	14	16
44'	12	12	14	14	16
48'	12	14	16	16	18
52'	14	16	16	18	20
60'	16	18	20	20	22
64'	16	18	20	22	24
68'	18	20	22	24	26
72'	20	20	22	24	28
76'	20	22	24	26	28
80'	20	22	26	28	30
84'	22	24	28	30	32
88'	22	24	28	30	32
92'	24	26	28	32	34
96'	24	28	30	32	36
100'	26	28	32	34	38

Note: These figures are for solid walls. Any openings must be deducted.
Deduct one roll for every two average-size doorways.
Deduct one roll for every four average-size windows.

STENCILED AND PAINTED
WALLS

THROUGHOUT the New England states, sometimes in the most remote townships, one will come across a house in which stenciled or painted walls have been found. The earliest were discovered and described by Janet Waring in a fascinating book on the subject, and recently one of our large wallpaper manufacturers produced a set of wallpapers from stenciled wall designs found in some of the better known of these houses.

Miss Waring found the houses she describes not only in New England but also in New York State and farther west in Ohio, whither many settlers emigrated from New England. The earliest date assigned to any stenciled wall by Miss Waring was 1778, although most of the rooms described by her were apparently decorated during the first quarter of the nineteenth century.

In addition to stenciled walls one will find many houses in which the walls were freely painted with landscapes. In the majority of cases this work was done by itinerant painters who would often paint a room in return for lodging. In Gorham, Maine, there is such a painted room. The grandmother of the present owner told her that an itinerant peddler did the painting. He made his paints from roots and barks which he found in the woods, asked only for sour milk to set the colors, and painted the walls with a rather crudely executed landscape which has survived to the present day. Without doubt the stenciling and painting were done in lieu of the more expensive wallpapers of the time. Subsequently covered by paper, they were well preserved until later generations of the past few decades have uncovered them and now display them with much pride.

Four of the more famous houses with stenciled walls are

The Abner Goodale house in Marlborough, Massachusetts, built in 1778.

The Josiah Sage house in South Sandisfield, Massachusetts, built in 1803.

The Elisha Smith house in Stillwater, Rhode Island, built in 1726.

The Curtis Hickox house in Washington, Connecticut, built in 1789.

Several of my friends have recently stenciled walls in their own homes. These can be a definite addition to the individual interest of any home if the owner is interested in attempting them. They may be used in an Early American decorating scheme if a little all-over pattern in pure colors is used. For instance, the woodwork could be the old brick red or a blue, the walls dead white, and a small figured stencil pattern could be used in the brick red. In a Colonial or Federal interior you could use a stencil with a larger motif in an all-over design in keeping with the decorating style of these periods, or the walls could be plain with a stencil design around ceiling, doorways, and windows. This same type of decoration could be carried over into a Victorian interior, retaining the motif and the colors used in keeping with the period. In any event the wall would be painted the desired base color and allowed to dry thoroughly before the stenciling is undertaken. If a stenciling effect is desired without so much effort, the new wallpapers in stenciling designs may well be used. They come in several patterns and in many lovely background colors.

SPINNING, WEAVING, AND OTHER HANDICRAFTS

IN THE Early American period every farmer had his flax or hemp field and every home its spinning wheel. Many homes had looms, and often a lean-to was built to house these and their appurtenances while in some households the attic served for this purpose. By 1767 there was a weaving house at Mount Vernon, the home of George Washington, where linsey-woolsey, linens, and woolens were woven.

The first settlers, especially those of New England, knew both spinning and weaving, since these were domestic occupations to which they had been accustomed at home in the Old World. The homes of these early colonists did not lack for household linens, and many of them had damask or needlework table covers, printed East Indian cottons, loose cushions made of damask or Turkey work, and loomed rugs for their floors, but most of these decorative articles had reached America in the sea chests brought from the old home in England. In the first decades of the settlements life was too arduous for the women to experiment with any weaving except that most needed for everyday living, and it was not until after the Revolution that fabrics of an expert and sophisticated type were produced in the colonies. Then, too, in the early days of the period the settlers did not have the equipment or the skill to produce fabrics in other than the simplest weaves. The power loom was in use in England but knowledge of it was closely guarded by its possessors.

In the early days all the work that was necessary from the raising of the flax, hemp, or wool to the manufacture of the raw material into a finished article was done in the one household. Before long, however, there came into the economic life of the colonies the itinerant weaver, who traveled through the countryside, bringing his loom with him and remaining in the settlement until all the village weaving for the season had been completed.

In 1643 a factory was begun at Rowley, Massachusetts, the first textile factory in America, and this continued in operation until the early nineteenth century. A few years earlier some twenty families had arrived there from Yorkshire under the guidance of their minister, Ezekiel Rogers, bringing with them the necessary knowledge and experience for such an undertaking. Although the first products of this factory were of wool, soon it was making fabrics of flax and cotton as well. The establishment of this fulling mill was followed by others, although they seem to have been almost entirely within the boundaries of Massachusetts, with some few in Connecticut. Trumbull in his *History of Connecticut* says that "in 1713 there was but one clothier in the Colony." If this statement is true —and there is no reason to doubt it—this man was Abraham Fulford of Woodbury. Records of this town contain the following signed by forty-four inhabitants: "We, whose names are hereunto subscribed do hereunto grant Abraham Full-ford, a well-accomplished persin, both for combing wool, weaving and fulling cloth, if he so cause to cohabitt in this town, and be beneficial upon ye sd. accounts a ten acre accommodation in Woodbury, January 1700." Evidently Fulford accepted the offer because a deed was recorded in his name as of April 3, 1712.

Hemp was native to Virginia and flax grew well throughout the colonies, but wool was a matter of some very real concern to the settlers. Some woolen material was manufactured, however, for we know that as early as 1659 its export was prohibited so that the small supply might be conserved for home use. The lack of woolen clothing, however, was one of the greatest hardships borne by our Revolutionary soldiers.

An early attempt at the producing and weaving of silk was also made in the southern colonies. Mulberry trees grew in quantity in Virginia, and the Virginian colonists imported the finest silkworms available from Spain and Italy. As early as 1656 silk was sent to England from this colony, and somewhat later we hear that the King himself declared this silk to be the equal of the finest imported into England at that time.

Shortly after the first settlements were made we read in inventory after inventory lists of household linens which indicate that our early settlers had ample supplies, and soon the greater part of this was of domestic manufacture. Idleness and too much leisure were not considered necessary or desirable in those days. Then, every girl worked for her dower chest, weaving her sheets, her towels, her table linen, and her coverlets. This custom continued even through the Victorian period, when maidens worked diligently at their embroidering for their "hope chest," although by this time the weaving and spinning had largely disappeared as a domestic industry. Today, however, there is a growing revival of these handicrafts.

Some of the early pattern weaves exist today, although many have entirely disappeared. One of the most interesting collections of old linens will be found in the Henry Whitfield State Historical Museum in Guilford, Connecticut. Here you will see such weaves as "Rings and Chains," "Double Diamonds," "Honeycomb and Dimity," "M's and O's," "Herringbone," "Fish-eye," "Bird's Eye," and well known even today, "Huckaback."

In the early inventories we read of napkins, tablecloths, "hemppen cloath" by the yard, flaxen sheets, hempen sheets, "Dyeper" napkins, as well as of the more luxurious damasks, Turkey work, and laces. While the Pilgrim Fathers passed sumptuary laws in the early days of the settlements prohibiting finery for those of "mean condition, education, and calling," those of wealth and social position were permitted to wear "woolen, silk, and linen apparel" trimmed with "gold, silver, and thread lace." Inventories of this period in all the colonies, although perhaps to a greater extent in the southern settlements, are filled with such items as "a printed calico gown lined with silk," "waistcoats trimmed with lace," "holland sleeves with ruffles," "scarf of taffeta," "cornet and drawing caps with lace," "headbands with lace," "neckcloths with lace," "laced handkerchiefs," and "whisks" (deep collars usually trimmed with lace).

Unfortunately little of the lace and needlework of this period remains, but among the most treasured of what has come down to us are the old samplers, and these are most desirable, when properly framed, as decorative accents in our Early American and Colonial interiors.

In the inventories, also, are the names of many fabrics unfamiliar to us today. These include says, serges, darnicks, perpetuanas, carsays, camlets, paduasoys, tabbies, calamancos, palampores, and Turkey work. As a matter of interest we will record the meaning of some of these names.

Camlet: a woolen fabric, part silk and goat's or camel's hair. In America around 1790 it was a plain woolen material and was very popular in red, yellow, or green for draperies. It was often lined with silk.

Carsay: a twilled wool similar to broadcloth but lighter.

Darnick: a linen material used for hangings, similar to coarse linen diaper with check patterns.

Perpetuana: a smooth worsted weave with double or triple warp and single filling. Very popular in red.

Tabby: silk or woolen material similar to watered silk.

Turkey work: crude homespun made by drawing a woolen yarn through a coarsely woven fabric. Used for covering chairs and for cushions.

Coverlets were woven early in all the colonies as well as in New England, and those that have been preserved are much cherished today. They were woven in such intriguing patterns as "Sunrise on the Walls of Troy," "Bonaparte's Retreat," "Rich Man's Fancy," "Chariot Wheel," and "Cat Tracks."

Quilts were in such general use in the early settlements that they were not considered important enough to mention specifically in the writings of the period. As the women were released somewhat from the arduous task of constant spinning and weaving to fill the needs of their families, they spent more time in piecing and quilting. As the years passed, the quilting bee became one of the social events of the different communities. Sometimes quilting bees ran on for days into a regular house party, often sharing social honors with the house-raising parties. Proud is the person who has in her possession today, either by inheritance or purchase, some of these beautiful old quilts, whether pieced or patched, for they are truly works of art. The subject is too interesting, too stimulating, and too detailed to be attempted successfully in a few short paragraphs, so I urge you to read one or more of the very excellent books on the subject.

Rugs were a very necessary article of furnishing in the early home and were of several kinds. The loomed rug was produced in the same manner as the woolen material or the coverlets. The hooked rug belongs to America. While some would give it a Scandinavian origin, others believe it a folk development in Canada and the United States of ancient tambour embroidery. The weight of authority seems to be with the latter group. The designs in these hooked rugs were taken from objects and scenes known to the makers, and are in this way a documentary pictorial story although that was not the purpose for which they were made. The earliest were hooked upon a coarse linen material spun and woven at home from flax grown upon the place. Rugs with a burlap foundation are of fairly recent date. The earlier the rug the simpler the design, but geometric patterns were soon competing with crude scenes, and as the rugmakers became more proficient they attempted the beautiful florals in which the art of hooking reached the climax of workmanship. Today, however, these old rugs are not easily found and are cherished beyond price by their owners.

The braided rug, requiring less skill than the hooked, was another type made by our ancestors. Today this, too, is very popular for Early American and Colonial interiors.

The first aniline dye was made about the middle of the nineteenth century. Hence our early settlers made their own dyes. Indigo was one of the few mineral dyes which could be purchased from the itinerant peddler as was cochineal, which produced a beautiful scarlet.

A friend of mine, Doris Landry of Woodbury, has given me the directions for dyeing as used by her grandmother, Julia Hull of Roxbury, who married Sylvanius Markham of Woodbury. The bark or berries or roots were boiled in water until the desired color was attained. The liquid was then strained to remove the scum and other residue. The material to be dyed (either homespun or yarn) was wet thoroughly in clear water and then immersed in the dye and boiled until the desired degree of color was obtained. Salt was put into the dye and the material then boiled to set the color. If wool was to be dyed black, it was first boiled with some common field sorrel and then dyed with logwood and copperas. Oak bark also produced a black dye; hickory bark, yellow; chestnut or walnut, brown; pokeberry, purple; madder or sumach berries, reds and pinks; oak and maple, purple; goldenrod and alum with indigo, green; Duer's bugloss, a rich blood red; fustic and copperas, or onion skins boiled with alum, yellow. The resulting colors were soft and enduring. Homespun materials dyed with home-prepared dyes faded very little but the black usually turned an antique brown or greenish-blue and this is one proof of an old rug. It never shows a true black.

HOW TO USE FABRICS

In using fabrics it is important to keep in mind the basic rules of color and color harmonies as discussed in the chapter on color. In addition, it is necessary to remember the relationship between types of fabrics and the different decorating periods. Just as each period has its set of colors and color combinations, so does each period have suitable fabrics. This will be discussed in more detail under each period section.

The question often arises as to whether a figured textile may be used successfully with a figured wallpaper and whether more than one type of figured fabric may be used in the same room. In solving these problems, strive for a harmonious whole but always work for an interesting whole rather than a banal or monotonous one.

Today it is possible to secure materials that match the wallpapers, and this unity is often very pleasing. The old familiar rule of a plain-colored fabric with a figured wall covering and a figured fabric with a plain wall is always safe, but it is interesting to experiment at times and not always play safe—only experiment with intelligence.

When using a figured fabric with a figured wallpaper, use a small design in the fabric, a stripe or a plaid, if the wallpaper has a large design. If the wallpaper has a small pattern, it is usually better to use a large design in the fabric. Unless the fabric matches the wallpaper, it is best to have the design in fabric and in wallpaper unequal in size and in strength of coloring. In using a plain fabric with a figured wallpaper, do not use the obvious plain color at all times but search out a subtle color for the draperies and upholstery, using the proper color combinations for the period being achieved. It is also a good decorating idea to have at least one piece of furniture upholstered or slip-covered in the drapery material. When using fabric, consider the room to be decorated as a unit consisting of floor covering, wall and wall covering, furniture coverings, and draperies. With the basic rules regarding color harmonies and with the few simple rules above regarding pattern, you should be able to accomplish interesting results. It is not difficult.

MATERIALS IN USE TODAY

BROCADE This is used with the beautiful furniture of Chippendale, Hepplewhite, Sheraton, and similar types. It is a medium-weight fabric and is useful for draperies or on furniture not subjected to hard wear. It is rich in design, similar to the flock paper which attempted to reproduce it, and resembles embroidery on several background weaves.

BROCATELLE The designs in this fabric are similar to those in brocade but the material is much heavier. The figures are also more raised and resemble velvet. This fabric is used for heavy-weight upholstery and at times for draperies if the windows are large and demand a heavy material.

BURLAP This is a coarse, inexpensive, plainly woven fabric of hemp or jute. It comes in many colors and may be used for drapery or upholstery purposes with the simple type of furniture—never with the elegant.

CALICO This has changed little since our ancestors' day except in cost. When it was used for best dresses and lined with silk in the seventeenth century, it often cost as much as $30 a yard. It is a lightweight cotton fabric, and comes in a large range of colors. It is excellent for many decorative uses in our Early American interiors and in some of the Colonial interiors. It may be used for window curtains, draperies, upholstery, bedspreads, bed curtains, slip covers, and dressing-table skirts.

CHINTZ This is a firm cotton fabric of plain weave. It may be glazed or semiglazed. It comes in a large variety of colors, both plain and figured, and in many grades. It is one of the most useful fabrics. It is formal or informal, according to color and pattern, and is suitable for almost any room and any period, depending, of course, upon quality and treatment. It has a great variety of uses—comparable to calico in this respect.

CRETONNE A fabric of cotton or linen usually in large patterns. The use is similar to that of chintz, although cretonne is often more formal because of its designs.

CREWEL EMBROIDERY An excellent fabric for Colonial interiors and, on occasion, for Early American. It is usually of unbleached linen or cotton material embroidered with colored wool in tree, floral, and bird designs.

DOCUMENTARY PRINT Authentic reproduction of an old design in fabrics of various kinds. Sources of designs are *toiles de Jouy*, wallpapers, old calico designs, patchwork quilts, et cetera. Often the print is an authentic reproduction in both color and design. Again the design is used in different colorings from the original. The true collector prefers the first, but the second is often very desirable for the home decorator.

DAMASK Similar to brocade in design and use. Made of taffeta, linen, cotton, or wool, also in a satin weave on a taffeta ground.

HOMESPUN Coarse hand-woven fabric in linen, cotton, or wool. Power-loom material resembling the hand-woven material now available and useful for draperies and upholstery in our Early American or other informal rooms.

INDIA PRINTS The printed bedspreads, hangings, tablecloths, table squares, et cetera, printed in Indian or Persian designs on white or natural-color cotton backgrounds. Gay and colorful. Useful in Early American interiors.

TOILES DE JOUY The original toiles de Jouy were first made at Jouy near Paris, France. Printed cotton with designs of landscapes, classical scenes, pastoral groups, et cetera, usually in a single color on a white or natural background. The same designs are often used on wallpaper. Excellent for decorating any period except, perhaps, Victorian, depending upon color. In the Early American interiors, for example, the deep, pure colors would be desirable.

FURNITURE

IN ENGLAND AND AMERICA

As we take a backward glance at the development of furniture in England and America one interesting fact is apparent. Until the middle of the eighteenth century furniture styles received their designations from time periods or reigns, such as Gothic, Tudor, Jacobean, William and Mary, and Queen Anne. And then, for the short space of about seventy-five years, styles that developed into definite periods and schools were assigned the names of men—men who created or became identified with those styles: Chippendale, Adam, Hepplewhite, Sheraton, and, to a very much less degree, Duncan Phyfe in America. Then we return to the use of terms applied to the time period, as Regency, Federal, American Empire, and Victorian.

A second fact is self-evident. In furniture making, new styles, new schools, new periods evolve from preceding periods. This evolution is a steady progression with many a wandering off into pleasant byways but with the main highway as the chief line of development.

JACOBEAN, 1603–1689

In discussing furniture in the colonies it is not necessary for us to portray the Gothic or Tudor furniture of England. Suffice it to say that it was of oak, heavy, crude, with little artistic value and with few examples extant today outside museums. During the Tudor period we had the reigns of Henry VII, which began in 1485, then Henry VIII, Edward VI, Mary, and finally Elizabeth, whose reign ended in 1603.

The Jacobean period, which followed the Tudor, includes, in reality, several periods. It received its name from James I, who reigned from 1603 to 1625. Then came Charles I, who was executed in 1649. During these years the furniture was not unlike that of the preceding Elizabethan style. It was somewhat more subdued and a bit simpler, with fewer curves.

After the execution of Charles I there was the Commonwealth under Cromwell, who hated the aristocracy and the luxury they enjoyed. The

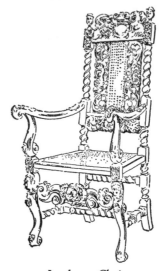

Jacobean Chair

Protectorate lasted from 1653 to 1660, and during it the furniture reflected the severity of the period. The general effect was forthright and straight. The bulbous legs of the Elizabethan and early Jacobean furniture went out of fashion; bun or ball feet remained, and underbracing was still used. Upholstery became more popular, and chairs had padded backs as well as padded seats, but the materials used were not colorful and leather was often selected for the purpose. The gate-leg table originated in England during this period.

With the Restoration in 1660 a revolt set in against the austerity of the Cromwellian period, and this was reflected in the furniture. Ornamentation became profuse, the legs of chairs were spiral turned, and there was much use of geometrical moldings. It was at this time that Grinling

Gibbon (1648–1721) appeared on the English scene, one of the outstanding wood carvers of all time. He was of Dutch origin, as were so many of the cabinetmakers and designers of this period in England.

Chairs were very ornate, with spiral legs and rails, an elaborately carved stretcher between the front legs, and a similarly carved back frame. Crowns to memorialize the return of the King, roses, acanthus leaves, and scrolls were used as decorative motifs by the carvers. Some chairs and settees were upholstered but without springs, as today. Day beds, banished by Cromwell, returned to new favor. The tall clock made its appearance shortly after the Restoration.

The furniture brought from England by the early settlers was of oak and of the early Jacobean period with its resemblance to the earlier Elizabethan. Foremost in importance was the chest in which could be packed belongings for the long sea voyage and which could be used later in the new home for storage. There were also tables, an occasional chair of some important elder, a few cumbersome oak cupboards, "forms" or benches, cooking utensils, some pewter, the mattress or pallet, the bed draperies and bed trappings. In the early days of the colonies the bed was simply a wooden frame of several kinds, and when the word "bed" is used in old inventories or wills, it refers to the bed pallet, draperies and coverlets, not to this wooden frame.

When the colonists began arriving in the new country in the tiny, heavy-laden boats, it is doubtful if among their number there were any cabinetmakers. Cabinetmaking in seventeenth-century England was a specialized job. There were, however, many of the very necessary carpenters and joiners. By 1675 these craftsmen in the New England colonies were making very good furniture, copying the English models of court chests, press chests, wainscot chairs, the Carver chair with its turned members and spindle back, slat-back chairs of various types, stools, benches, settles, small tables, and, after 1660, when the Roundheads (followers of Cromwell) fleeing England after the Restoration, arrived in the colonies, the Cromwellian chair with leather seat and back and the gate-leg table. During the last quarter of the seventeenth century the butterfly table made its appearance.

With the Restoration walnut became the popular wood in England, but oak still remained the favorite of the Colonial carpenter until mahogany came into general use in the early eighteenth century, at least ten years before it was used in England. Naturally walnut was used by the New England cabinetmaker, but maple, cherry, ash, hickory, oak, and elm were much more common, and pine was used almost universally for cottage furniture. Around Philadelphia and in some parts of the South walnut was used to a greater extent than it was in New England. Nevertheless, oak remained the principal wood for the making of furniture until the advent of mahogany, and there was no walnut period, per se, in America as in England.

When we say the colonists copied the English models, we must point out that there was a definite time lag of many years—sometimes as much as twenty-five to thirty—between style periods in the two countries. This is well understood when we realize the slowness of communication, constant though it was at this time, and that furniture was not brought over in quantities, especially in the northern colonies. In the southern colonies the time lag was always much less. The Queen Anne period, however, continued to be the major style until the advent of Chippendale, practically uninfluenced by the heavy, ornate furniture made in England between the Queen's death and the rise of the Chippendale style, except, perhaps, in Philadelphia. Even then the Colonial craftsmen did not give up the Queen Anne forms too easily. They liked this style and their clients continued to want it.

In this early period veneering was rare, but it was sometimes used. When attempting to assign a piece of veneered furniture to workmen on this side of the Atlantic or in England, it is safe to say that when the base is of pine it is American; when of oak, English.

One of the first contributions made by the Colonial craftsman to the usefulness of furniture was the addition of one or more drawers to the chest. This made it possible to find things more easily. It was no longer necessary to remove the entire contents when seeking some wanted article which was sure to be at the bottom. The next step was the replacing of the remaining top chest section with another drawer, and thus evolved the chest of drawers. We still have chests in which this top chest section has not been replaced by a drawer; these are known today as blanket chests. When for convenience the chest of drawers was placed upon a base, the beginning of the wonderful highboy of later periods was achieved.

At about this same time the desk developed slowly and gradually from the flat or slant-topped box in which the all-important Bible or valuable papers were kept. At first this box was set upon a base, also for convenience, and during the years this arrangement grew into the various types of desks and secretaries.

WILLIAM AND MARY, 1689–1702

Although William and Mary came to the throne of England in 1689, it is doubtful whether furniture of this style was made in the colonies much before the turn of the century, but once begun it persisted until well after Queen Anne's death in 1714. During this period the interiors of the colonists' homes became less severe. Life was a bit easier for the housewife; she could give some time to beautifying her home, and she wanted more comfort. It is possible that much of the furniture was made in the colonies while some was brought in by new settlers. It was still of oak but much lighter and more slender than that of the Jacobean period. Chairs were more comfortable and even looked so.

The Edict of Nantes had been revoked in 1685, and following this there was an influx into England of skilled Huguenot cabinetmakers and textile workers, and these excellent craftsmen had no little influence in improving the prevailing style. Then, too, William III was a Dutchman by birth and preferred the styles of his own country and of France. He made a Frenchman, Daniel Marot, his Minister of Works, and Marot became the leader of fashion in decoration.

At about this time the banister-back chair both with and without arms replaced somewhat the cane-backed chair, some of the furniture was painted to give bright spots of color within the house, the upholstered wing chair made its appearance, and there were many more day beds and settees, either upholstered or with loose cushions of color.

Outstanding characteristics of the William and Mary furniture are the turned legs with inverted cups and the serpentine-shaped stretcher. The double arched back was used on cabinets and settees. Chair backs were high and rounded at the top with carving. The cockleshell and acanthus leaf were both popular for this purpose. In addition to the banister-back chair there were other chairs, some caned and some upholstered. Chair legs were square, spiral, turned, or octagonal with hoof, claw, and ball

Banister-back Chair

or bun feet. Toward the end of the period the cabriole leg came in, the Spanish scroll was introduced, and block feet were used on chests. Most of these new features showed how great the Dutch influence was in England at this time.

From the Orient, by way of Holland, came the knowledge of lacquering, which became the vogue in England and continued with decreasing popularity until the end of the eighteenth century. This fad spread to the colonies and some of the work done before 1735 was very good. In Boston, as early as 1700, David Mason was advertising his ability to do this japanning as well as gilding, painting, and varnishing. However, this type of decorated furniture never became so popular in the colonies as in

England. There were, I think, two reasons, at least, for this. Had the vogue reached the colonies at the end of the eighteenth century, when the so-called China trade was at its height, it would have been accepted with great enthusiasm, as were all the other exotic wonders of Cathay. Early in the eighteenth century, however, the adoption of oriental products as a desirable and beloved addition to home furnishings had not begun. Then, too, lac has one quality peculiar unto itself. It dries best in a damp atmosphere and needs a certain amount of humidity to keep it in good

William and Mary Highboy

condition. In America, especially in the North, it disintegrates rapidly.

During this same period marquetry became a very important feature of furniture decoration, and some of the most beautiful examples were made at this time.

Highboys appeared about 1700 and rapidly became a favorite of Colonial craftsmen. The greater number were made with six trumpet-shaped legs with ball feet and flat cyma-curved stretchers. Occasionally the spiral-turned legs were used. Often we find a matching lowboy accompanying the highboy.

QUEEN ANNE, 1702–1714

Although Queen Anne came to the throne of England in 1702 it is doubtful whether the so-called Queen Anne furniture appeared in the colonies much before her death, and even then the acceptance and development of this new style proceeded slowly. This furniture marked the development from the heavy, underbraced style of the earlier periods to the designs of Chippendale, Hepplewhite, and Sheraton—a forward

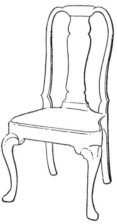

Queen Anne Chair

step in refinement and comfort. The Dutch influence, still potent at the beginning of the period, declined steadily, and, as it declined, workmanship improved.

The chair is probably the most representative piece of furniture of this period. The tall, uncomfortable chair of the previous eras was replaced by one of moderate height with a smooth cabriole leg, used with a Spanish foot and underbracing—survivals from the previous period. As the years advanced, however, the underbracing was abandoned and the cabriole leg became sturdier, to carry the extra weight, and was used with the claw and ball, the paw and the club foot.

In England at this period the furniture was almost entirely of walnut. In the colonies many other woods surpassed this in popularity although we find much fine furniture made of this wood around Philadelphia as well as some examples in New England. However, about three times as much furniture was made in oak, maple, cherry, fruitwoods, and pine as in walnut.

The carved cockleshell motif and the cabriole leg are characteristic of the furniture of the Queen Anne period. This leg was an adaptation of the S scroll or cyma curve (this curve is also found on aprons, mirrors, table tops, and chair backs) and had reached England by way of Holland from the Orient.

The cockleshell motif was used on the knees of the cabriole legs, as cresting of chair backs, in the middle of drawers and aprons. Chair backs were narrow, with solid fiddleback-shaped splat. Toward the end of the period the chair backs became more elaborate, as did furniture generally. Slats were usually veneered, a process introduced by the Dutch but now used in England for the first time in the making of chairs. Marquetry and inlay were no longer fashionable although lacquering was still occasionally used. As the period advanced, gilt gesso was used to decorate the backs and legs of some chairs and settees and fine gilding was popular. However, the cabinetmakers used veneering to a large extent to beautify their furniture, and the effects obtained from this use during the Queen Anne period have never been surpassed. The figured walnut veneers most commonly used were burl, oyster, and crotch. Wing chairs became more comfortable and much upholstery was used.

With the disappearance of the bed from the parlor it became the most important piece of furniture in the chamber, and during this period it had tall, slender posts supporting a tester.

In the early part of the period drop-leaf tables with cabriole legs replaced the former space-saving trestle and the gate-leg types. Candlestands, tea tables, folding card tables, wall mirrors, tall clocks, highboys, lowboys, desks, chests of drawers, many kinds of chairs, settees, and the roundabout chair with turned or cabriole legs were all important.

About 1725 Philadelphia cabinetmakers became interested in the Windsor chair. This, in England, was a development of a primitive stool and had been made in the Wycombe section of Buckinghamshire for hundreds of years. The body was of English yew and the seat of elm. In

America it was now made with the body of a combination of woods and the seat generally of pine. In both countries the seat was of the saddle type. Here the central splat of the English chair was discarded and the back was of several kinds, bow-back, hoop-back, fanback, and comb-back. This chair was cheap to make, was light and comfortable, and became very popular for the homes of the simple people, for public places, and for barber shops, for which there was a special type with dipped top rails. Another type developed in America had a writing arm with a box beneath the seat for paper and other supplies. The Windsor chair

Windsor Chair

fits well into the Early American home and in bedrooms and kitchens of the Colonial home, but it does not belong with the more formal furniture of the Colonial and Federal periods.

THOMAS CHIPPENDALE, 1718–1779

Around the middle of the eighteenth century there was an influx of good cabinetmakers into the colonies from England, some of whom settled in Pennsylvania while others remained in New England. This influx gave a new impetus to furniture making in America. At about the same time an additional boost was given by the appearance of Chippendale's catalogue entitled *The Gentleman and Cabinet-Maker's Director*.

A first edition of this appeared in England in 1754, but the third edition, appearing in 1762, seems to have been the popular one in this country. Although Chippendale had been working in England from about 1748, it was not until this catalogue became available to American craftsmen that furniture in this style was attempted here. The making of furniture entered a really great period, for Chippendale was the first cabinetmaker

Rhode Island Block Front Secretary

to lift it to a high peak of craftsmanship. He was not only a master cabinetmaker, he was a good carver, an excellent designer and adapter.

About 1760 Philadelphia was the most important city in the colonies, and located there was a group of craftsmen making very good furniture. This group copied the new designs in the *Director* with avidity, selecting, in most instances, the more elaborate. This "Philadelphia school" included such men as William Savery, Thomas Affleck, Thomas Tufft, Benjamine Randolph, and Jonathan Gostelowe. A second group, almost as famous and certainly so in the opinion of New Englanders, grew up around John Goddard of Newport, Rhode Island. Goddard had learned his trade with his father-in-law, Job Townsend, and was associated with John Townsend, a cousin by marriage. At one time John Townsend evi-

Philadelphia Highboy

dently set up business in Middletown, Connecticut, but appears to have returned to Newport at a later date.

The work of both the Philadelphia and Rhode Island groups included many reproductions (but with many changes of their own in design and construction) of the designs in the *Director* which seems to have been little more than a gathering together of all the popular furniture designs in England into a trade catalogue. These American cabinetmakers, however, did this reproducing with much skill, although changing and adding to the designs of Chippendale, so that we have the unique block-front desks, chests of drawers, and secretaries of Goddard and his Rhode Island group and the remarkable highboys of Savery and the other craftsmen in the Philadelphia school. The work of these two groups or schools differed from each other and both differed from the English designs. There is little affinity between the highboy as developed by the Philadelphia craftsmen and any piece of similar furniture of the period in England, nor does the block front of Goddard have any counterpart there.

Let not the word "reproduction" mislead you. In the days of Savery and Goddard a reproduction was the work of genuine craftsmen who added of their own artistry and skill to the designs in the *Director* and in other published books of designs, and today's collector in America is often willing to pay a much larger sum for a genuine Savery or Goddard than for an English piece of the same period. Authentic examples of the work of these famous Colonial cabinetmakers may be studied at the Boston Museum of Fine Arts in the outstanding Karolik collection; at the Metropolitan Museum of Fine Arts in New York City, in the American Wing; at the Yale Museum of Fine Arts in New Haven, in the Garvan collection; and in many other well-known museums all over the country.

Since we are speaking of the different Chippendale "schools" or groups we might as well mention the so-called "Irish Chippendale." It is the opinion of those who know furniture styles that this term is a misnomer, that "Irish Chippendale" was evidently not made in Ireland, that it is somewhat earlier than Chippendale, and that it found its way to Ireland from western England. The term seems to be applied only to the tables with a deep surface carved apron. One expert (George Leland Hunter, 1867–1927) says that he protested against this term some twenty years before his death but that many writers continue to use it *ad nauseam*.

Mahogany was the wood used for the furniture in the Chippendale manner, with some few pieces of walnut and simple pieces in maple— country Chippendale.

The *Director* did not introduce a new furniture era in England. It was a collection of different styles in use at the time. As in the past, these were a development of those of previous periods. It is interesting that no single design in the *Director* shows the claw-and-ball foot because this was popular in England at the time and much of the so-called Chippendale furniture makes use of it. The *Director* shows many different styles. Some were in the Gothic manner, others in the well-known Chinese

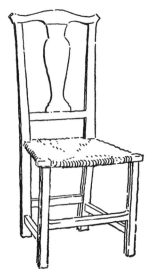

Chippendale Chair
New England Cottage Type

Chippendale Chair

Chippendale, many in the cabriole style, and others in which the square leg was used. Chippendale's French style was later than the publication of his catalogue, so no designs in this manner were included.

The Chippendale style chairs are most distinctive. The backs are approximately square with serpentine-shaped tops. Some have pierced splats, some are of interlacing scrolls, some ladder backs, and some the beautiful ribband backs. The cabriole leg was common in the Chippendale type of furniture as made in America. The straight leg was used on the Gothic and Chinese Chippendale as well as the usual straight square-leg style. A variety of feet were used: slipper, club, web, lion's paw, scroll, leaf, and dolphin as well as the claw and ball.

This style of furniture called Chippendale has infinite variety. Much is richly decorated with carving. All Chippendale furniture gives you a feeling of security and comfort as well as joy because of its beauty. Chippendale himself was influenced by all the fashion trends of the day and we find traces of these many whimseys in his designs—Gothic, Chinese, and French—but used and adapted with consummate skill.

In addition to the many types of chairs, remarkable secretaries, settees, sofas, desks, bookcases (a new idea in furniture), chests-on-chests, chests of drawers, highboys, lowboys, beds, and tables of many varieties—tilt, tripod, Pembroke, dining tables of several parts, pier tables, side tables —were made in this style.

As we have said, the American cabinetmakers copied many of the most rococo of Chippendale's designs, and in these we find some of the finest examples of American craftsmanship. This beautiful and opulent style continued in America long after the classicism of Adam had taken over in England with its most noted interpreters, Hepplewhite and Sheraton. Robert Adam—and his brothers—who exerted the greatest influence on architecture and decoration in England, and in America after the Revolution, was not a cabinetmaker, but he did design furniture for his extremely classical interiors, and both Chippendale and Hepplewhite made furniture for him from these designs. Chippendale's work merged into Hepplewhite's at the end of the period owing to this factor, although until his last years Chippendale was making beautiful furniture in his latest manner, the French.

In America Chippendale was the last great furniture style of the Colonial period. The influence of Hepplewhite and Sheraton was of little importance until after the Revolution, when we enter the Federal period.

ADAM BROTHERS
Robert Adam, 1728–1792

The last twenty-five years of the eighteenth century in England are often called "The Golden Age of Furniture," for during those few years we find a remarkable group of men—at least in the early part of the period—designing and making some of the most beautiful furniture the world has ever seen. Chippendale died in 1779 and Hepplewhite in 1786, but Sheraton lived until 1806, Robert Adam until 1792, and his brother James until 1794.

There were four Adam brothers—Robert, James, John, and William —the sons of an architect and builder of Scotland. In 1757 Robert returned to England after four years of study on the continent and in Italy especially. There he had become imbued with the classic ideal because of his intense interest in the excavations at Herculaneum and Pompeii. In 1758 he opened an office in London with his three brothers under the trade name of The Adelphi and soon became the most famous architect of his time, so famous that those years in which his influence was well-nigh supreme are called the Adam period.

Robert was foremost an architect, but when his beautifully classic houses were completed there was no furniture suitable for them, so he made designs for such furniture, often for special places within a given room. Since he was not a cabinetmaker, he employed others to do this work. He also planned the interior trim of his houses, the decorating, and the furnishings, so that an Adam interior possessed a perfect unity.

At first the furniture made for these houses built by Adam was of mahogany. Later, however, this became less popular than satinwood, harewood, and painted furniture, with much of the painting in the style of Angelika Kauffmann.

In the Adam designs, the cabinetwork was rectangular and the entire effect was one of great delicacy and charm. Legs were slender, either round or fluted, with turned feet, or tapered with spade feet. The Adam style made much use of oval and circular paterae: the classic urn and lyre; goats', lions', and rams' heads; the anthemia; the Greek fret and honeysuckle; swags; bellflower husks; egg-and-dart molding; and draped classic figures. Only the most elegant French brocade was used for upholstering.

Our debt to Adam is largely because of his classic influence on the Hepplewhite-Sheraton style, an influence which permeated the entire furniture trade in England after 1770. To him goes the credit for the shield-back chair, and the sideboard with doors and drawers as we know it today. His influence on architecture in our Federal period was very great, and this will be discussed in the chapter on that subject.

GEORGE HEPPLEWHITE, ?–1786

When we come to a discussion of the furniture styles known as Hepplewhite and Sheraton, it is well to remember that there is little difference between the two except in the chairs. The other pieces of furniture are much alike, and at times even the experts are unable to say which is Hepplewhite and which Sheraton. However, we shall not combine the two styles under one heading since it will be less confusing to study them as separate entities.

The date and birthplace of Hepplewhite are unknown. We do not know when he began work as a cabinetmaker. We know that he had a shop in Cripplegate, a section of London, and that he died in 1786. In 1788 his widow, Alice, published his *Cabinet-Maker and Upholsterer's Guide*. At that time she was carrying on the business under the name of A. Hepplewhite and Co. It is probable, however, that he had been working in London since about 1760 and that, like Chippendale, he had been constructing furniture from designs drawn by Adam for his classic interiors.

In the *Guide* (of which there was a second edition in 1789 and a third in 1794) Hepplewhite borrows freely from both Adam and the French. Louis XV of France died in 1774, and with his death the rococo style went out of fashion. In the France of Louis XVI, as in Adam's England, the classic ideal became popular, both countries influenced by the excavations at Herculaneum and Pompeii. This new classicism did not represent the classic ideal of early Greece and Rome. It bore the same relationship to them that an Early American interior today bears to an Early American interior of the seventeenth century. And so this classicism of Adam, Hepplewhite, and Sheraton is termed neoclassic.

Unlike the designs in Chippendale's *Director*, those in Hepplewhite's *Guide* were practical and technically accurate. In them the traditions of the earlier Chippendale style were carried on except in the chairs, in which there was a distinct difference. This difference was toward a lightness and gracefulness, and was owing to the influence of Adam and Louis XVI's France. Whereas the Chippendale had been sturdy and robust, the Hepplewhite was light and slender. Whereas Chippendale used much ornate carving, the new style used flat surfaces with inlay, painting, and veneering. Carving, when used, was light and classic in feeling. Hepple-

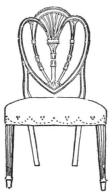

Hepplewhite Chair

white also made use of some of the lighter woods: satinwood, rosewood, tulipwood, and harewood.

Hepplewhite owed much to Adam, from whom he borrowed the shield-back chair, which is so characteristic of the Hepplewhite chair style, as is the interlaced heart. He did not, however, borrow any of the exaggerations of Adam's style, developing, instead, a type of furniture suitable for the homes of a rapidly growing middle class. For his chairs he also used the hoop-back, often with one or two depressions in the top; the oval back; and the kidney back popular in France at this time.

In the *Guide* those chairs marked "French" showed turned and cabriole legs. The stretcher was never used with the cabriole leg, but on rare occasions it is shown with the turned leg. This French style was not popular in America. Here the square tapered leg seems to have been the most common, used with or without the spade foot and with or without stretchers. At this time the various designers used the many types of legs almost indiscriminately.

Sometimes slip seats were used, but when the chair was upholstered, the material was carried well down over the seat rails. Occasionally the front of the chair was serpentine.

Hepplewhite's favorite motifs for decoration were wheat ears, bell-flower husks (borrowed from Adam), Prince of Wales feathers, honeysuckle, lyre, urns of various kinds, and the S curve. He was singularly free of those that were at all rococo.

Since the *Guide* was not published until 1788, it was not available to American cabinetmakers until some years after the Revolution. Doubtless some of the new-style furniture reached a few of the towns occupied by the British during the Revolution, but except in these cases it is doubtful whether much reached these shores before the turn of the century. The years immediately following peace were confused, and the growing irritation with England terminated in the War of 1812. In spite of all this, however, the English influence was still enormous. So the Hepplewhite style was very popular in the new Republic, but it was a style of the early nineteenth and not of the late eighteenth century.

The making of furniture in this style reached its highest development at the hands of the New England cabinetmakers, in New York and in parts of the South. No longer was the Philadelphia group, who had been supreme in the making of Chippendale, of equal importance. However, in America the Hepplewhite and Sheraton styles of furniture mingle and overlap until they have very little to distinguish them except in the chairs.

It was at this time that the sideboard as we know it made its appearance to replace the earlier side table. Undoubtedly Adam had designed the new type with drawers and doors, and without question it had been developed and improved by Thomas Shearer, one of the group of English cabinetmakers (and a very good one), contemporary with Hepplewhite and Sheraton. It is also true that it was popularized by Hepplewhite because of its inclusion in his *Guide*, which had such a wide circulation both in England and in America.

THOMAS SHERATON, 1750–1806

One will often hear it said that the square tapered leg with the spade foot is Hepplewhite and the round fluted leg Sheraton. This is largely true of furniture made in America at this time, but it is also true that Sheraton made furniture with the square tapered leg and that Hepplewhite at times used the round fluted leg. In this neoclassic period in England Adam, Hepplewhite, Sheraton, and the other designers used, as desired, the various types of legs.

Hepplewhite-Sheraton Type Serpentine Front Sideboard

Sheraton was the last of the great designers of the eighteenth century in England. And yet he lived and died in poverty. Most of the furniture bearing his name was made by others.

Thomas Sheraton was born at Stockton-on-Tees in 1750. He had been a drawing master, a preacher, and a cabinetmaker before he reached London, about 1790. It is probable that before coming to London he had largely completed *The Cabinet-Maker and Upholsterer's Drawing Book*, which he published in 1791. This was another catalogue for craftsmen of all the leading designs of the day. For the first edition Sheraton secured some five hundred subscriptions, apparently himself making a door-to-door canvass. The designs in this *Drawing Book* are freely borrowed from

Adam, Hepplewhite, and Shearer. In making his selections, however, Sheraton avoided the curve in favor of straight lines, and his chairs have slender, tapered legs, usually round, and often reeded, the backs largely rectangular. In some of his designs, however, the square tapered leg is shown, and in his later years some of his tables were designed with spiral turned legs.

Sheraton's designs all show classic dignity and restraint. His most typical chair back was square with a central panel slightly higher than the top rail and with the lower back rail well up from the seat. He used

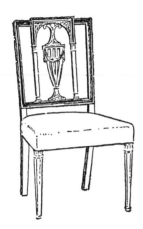

Sheraton Chair, Square Back

Sheraton Fancy Chair

more underbracing than did Hepplewhite, and in the upholstered chairs permitted part of the seat frame to show, whereas in Hepplewhite's the material was pulled well down over the wooden frame. In his work Sheraton used reeding and fluting, fan shapes, ornamental disks, the long-popular cockleshell, latticework, urns, swags, and the lyre. Like Hepplewhite, he used many beautiful woods with inlay, veneering, and painting.

By the time of his death in 1806 the French Empire style had swept Europe. Sheraton had always responded to the French style, and in his later years he attempted to design furniture in this new French Empire manner, but without much success. The American cabinetmaker, Duncan Phyfe, owed much to Thomas Sheraton.

DUNCAN PHYFE, 1768–1854

Duncan Phyfe, of New York City, was no designer but he was a good cabinetmaker. He became the fashionable furniture maker for the prosperous New Yorkers of the early nineteenth century, and this popularity led gradually to the debasement of his work because of his willingness or need to cater to the demands of a clientele eager for every innovation in decorating and architectural designs, in dress, in costumes, and in man-

Duncan Phyfe Armchair
Showing Sheraton Influence

Duncan Phyfe Chair
Showing Sheraton Influence

ners, whether good or bad, and, as the century advanced, popular taste in all these became largely bad.

Phyfe was born in Scotland in 1768 but as a child came to America where his father opened a cabinetmaker's shop in Albany, New York. In this shop Phyfe learned his trade. About 1795 he opened his own place in New York City on Partition Street (now part of Fulton), and before his retirement in 1847 he had as many as one hundred cabinetmakers working for him.

By the end of the eighteenth century fashion in England was dictated by the French capital; in fact during the years of the French Directory, 1799–1804, London was perhaps more Parisian than Paris itself. During this period in France we find a turning away from luxury, whereas in England the prosperous continued to live surrounded by every luxury and comfort. In France the furniture of these few years became a simplified version of Louis XVI, decorated, it is true, with symbols of the French Revolution. Then with the crowning of Napoleon as Emperor, in 1804, furniture tended to become heavy and solid—architectural—and ornamented with flat gilt or bronze plaques. In this French Empire period the deep primary colors were the favorite, and upholstery materials were chosen with large imperial patterns, with crowns and stars. Furniture generally was stiff and uncomfortable.

Duncan Phyfe
Lyre-back Chair

Duncan Phyfe Armchair
Showing Directoire Influence

As the styles changed from Louis XVI to Directoire to French Empire in France, we find their quick adoption by the court and prosperous citizenry of England.

Although in America sympathy turned to France during her Revolution, and although during our own Revolution and the years that immediately followed our irritation increased with England, we still had much respect for English fashion. So it is not entirely certain whether in America we received our inspiration for these new furniture fashions directly from France or by way of England.

Phyfe did his best work during the years 1795 to 1810. At this time he leaned heavily on the designs of Sheraton and of the Directoire. During the years 1805–20 a Frenchman by the name of Charles Honoré Lannuier was working in New York making furniture in the new Directoire and French Empire styles—probably influenced directly by France. Without doubt some of Lannuier's work has been attributed to Phyfe. Then, too, there were many other cabinetmakers at this same time producing good furniture in these same designs.

When Phyfe began his career as an independent cabinetmaker in New York City, many published books of designs were available from which he could choose those appealing to his own tastes and to those of his wealthy clients. He seems to have selected largely from those of Sheraton. Later he came under the influence of the more classic Directoire and then of the more architectural French Empire, of which he became the leading

Duncan Phyfe Chair
Showing Empire Influence

representative in America. Then as the years advanced he was obliged to make furniture demanded by his clients, until by the time he retired, in 1847, the products of his shop were massive, heavy, and in the type known as American Empire.

In the beginning of his career Phyfe had worked in the reddish mahogany, but after 1830 we find a great deal of his furniture made of rosewood. About 1820 furniture began to receive the high mirrorlike polish known as French, and we often find the reddish stained mahogany inlaid with exotic woods such as amboyna, a highly burled and mottled East Indian wood, or ebony, and decorated with bronze mountings.

The lyre, which had been used for a long time as a decorating motif, was a favorite of Phyfe for chair backs and table bases. He also used flutings and fine reedings. Carved motifs included leaves, plumes, cornucopias, drapery swags, wheat ears, thunderbolts, trumpets, and rosettes.

It is of some interest to know that shortly after 1800 Duncan Phyfe owned one of the interesting houses in Southbury, Connecticut, which is just south of Woodbury and at one time a part of Woodbury. The deed was recorded in his name, but other than that and many rumors little is known of the incident. One hears that he carved a mantel for this house or a newel post for another. Again it is said he never lived in the house and that it was occupied by a relative. Someday, perhaps, someone will have the time to track down all the incidents relating to this episode.

SAMUEL MCINTIRE, 1757–1811

Another American cabinetmaker, who was also architect, builder, and decorator, was Samuel McIntire of Salem, Massachusetts. Like Robert Adam he designed and built houses, decorated the interiors, and himself carved furniture as well as mantels, cornices, consoles, and other interior trim. In architecture he was influenced by the classicism of the Adam brothers and in Salem alone built some twenty beautiful houses in this style. His furniture shows the influence of Sheraton.

LAMBERT HITCHCOCK AND OTHERS

Connecticut witnessed the beginnings of many industries. One of the earliest of potters, Hervey Brooks, had his kiln in Goshen, and there Captain John Norton learned his trade from whence he went to Bennington, Vermont, to found the Bennington Pottery. The Connecticut shelf clock was shipped all over America and to many parts of the world. Shelf clocks are still made in towns named after the men who made them, Thomaston and Terryville.

As in the case of the Connecticut shelf clock, the mass production of chairs began in a little Connecticut town. Lambert Hitchcock settled in the town of Barkhamsted in 1818 and established a cabinet shop. In the beginning he made chair parts which were shipped in quantity to Charleston, South Carolina, and other parts of the South. By 1821 the settlement around the factory had grown to such a size that it was given a name of its own—Hitchcocksville. Today it is known as Riverton. After a number of years of manufacturing chair parts Hitchcock decided to make a finished chair in quantity to be sold at a reasonable price. He made chairs in several styles: the turtleback, the pillow back with a cutout back

Hitchcock Chair

slat, with a curved back with spindles, and with a crested back. They were marked on the back with a stencil "L. Hitchcock, Hitchcocksville, Warranted." At first the chairs were grained to resemble rosewood, the red of the first coat of paint showing through the black. The stenciled designs most popular were the basket of fruit, the horn of plenty, a fountain with birds, and conventionalized fruit and leaf. Later a lemon-yellow was sometimes used as the background color. Seats were first of rush, then cane, then plank. Today the factory has been reopened, and chairs are being reproduced according to the old methods and are sold at a price in excess of good originals.

With the development of machinery for turning we find almost mass production of the so-called spool furniture, sometimes called Jenny Lind, from about 1815 to the close of the Civil War. Then came the Gothic

Revival, and as early as 1830 this influence was seen in the furniture styles. After the Civil War the manufacturers of furniture attempted to keep pace with all the changing fads and fashions, many of them unimportant and often very ugly. They made many pieces of black walnut

Victorian Chair

and upholstered with horsehair. Marble for bureau and table tops was popular.

John H. Belter made a great deal of furniture in rosewood and walnut at his New York City shop after 1840. The framework of this furniture was elaborately carved and curved, and it was usually upholstered in rich brocades and damasks. Belter was a good craftsman, and today much of this furniture is greatly coveted for Victorian interiors.

Palladian Room, Gunston Hall, Lorton, Virginia; 1755-58. Home of George Mason, author of the Virginia Declaration of Rights. Carving designed and partly executed by William Buckland, brought from England under indenture to complete the house. Woodwork, original buff color. Walls above chair rail covered with crimson silk damask. Many of the chairs upholstered in the same material. Painting over mantel is of Mrs. Mason, a copy by Boudet of a lost painting by John Hesselius. Porcelain, including urns, Oriental export. Courtesy Board of Regents of Gunston Hall

II

Backgrounds

THE FOUR ARCHITECTURAL AND DECORATING PERIODS

EARLY AMERICAN, COLONIAL, FEDERAL, AND VICTORIAN

[ABOVE] Victorian interior in the period. Courtesy Mrs. Arthur Taylor Gillette
[BELOW] Victorian interior today. Harold de Graff, Berlin, Connecticut, decorator

EARLY AMERICAN—TO 1720

HOUSES

I F YOU already own a house or even if you live in a city apartment, your decorating problem is one of adaptation. In a new house or in an apartment, as well as in a house of the period, it is possible to create a home in any of the decorating periods. It is perhaps a bit more difficult, but with your house or apartment as a background, with careful study and considered selection, you evolve your decorating scheme.

One friend of mine who lives on the top floor of an old apartment house in the Gramercy Park section of New York City has achieved a home that begins as late Early American in most of the rooms with early Colonial in the dining and drawing rooms. The moment you enter this apartment—after climbing three flights of stairs—you have the feeling of being in a lovely home in a quiet, peaceful New England village.

If you do not own a house and are considering the all-important question of whether to buy one already built or whether to build, sit down by yourself and think the matter through very carefully. Shall the new home be an old house? Shall it be a recently built house? Would it be better, perhaps, to build, and if so, what style house is best suited to your tastes and needs?

If you decide you want an old house, particularly one built before 1820, ask yourself further questions. Do you really love and understand an old house or do you think you want one because it would be "quaint," perchance, or because many of your friends are living in charming old houses? Or do you imagine it would cost less to restore an old place? It never does.

Let us consider first an old house. Have you ever gone into such a one, half dilapidated, poorly lighted because of the dirt on its small windows, musty from being long closed, with tiny entries, low ceilings, steps up to one room and down to another, cobwebs in the attic, and many old boxes, barrels, bottles, and crocks in the cellar? As you wandered through this house, have you sensed a gentle welcome from it that made you want to live there no matter what the cost? Did you feel it asking you to make it into a home again? Were you willing to sacrifice comfort, even financial peace of mind, to have this house? If you can honestly say yes to all these questions, then I believe you should buy it, knowing full well there will be many times when you will doubt your own wisdom in doing so. There will also be times when you will be so tired from working in the old house, doing your share in making it into a home, that you will wonder if it is worth it. But only as you put of yourself into this work will the old house respond with a rich reward of satisfaction and happiness.

As you become acquainted with the construction, you will recognize its periods of growth; here a lean-to, there a widening of the end to include the old chimney, perhaps a raising of the roof. You may discover the old fireplace behind two more recent ones, built in to make the old one smaller and then again smaller; perhaps all hidden behind a wooden or plaster wall installed when stoves became popular. You will study the huge chimney root in the cellar, and the old pegged framework in the attic. You will search for secret panels, for loose boards in the attic floor that may hide treasure, and you will surely find some things you will long cherish. You will notice the doors, some batten, some paneled, some-times both in the same room. You will search the tiny windowpanes for scratched names of those who lived there long ago. You will adore every handmade latch and hinge—hardly two alike in the whole house. You will admire the old floor boards, uneven, some loose and with wide cracks from which you will carefully and painstakingly dig the accumulated dust. And always will you imagine stories of those who lived here. You will think warmly of those who loved, of those who were born, and of those who died in these rooms. And the more you study and examine this old house, the more it becomes yours.

Restoring an old house does not mean building it over completely to meet modern requirements. The only excuse for tearing out the interior and rebuilding it is when the framework alone is worth saving. Even then you should study other buildings of the same period and rebuild in a traditional manner. I do not believe it is possible for anyone to buy an old house, turn it over to a local carpenter or even a trained architect, and get the same happy result attained by restoring it gradually while living in it. The slower you work, perhaps the better. In most cases the help of a carpenter and often of a trained architect will be needed, but they should work with the homeowner. Often your first ideas change radically as you progress in this work of restoration, especially if you are living in the house during this time, studying its construction, growing to know it better, and learning to love its many eccentricities and inconveniences. I have learned that the less you do to the structural part of an old house the better. Often the greatest problem aside from replacing sills—ground-sill or "grundsell" to our ancestors—shingles, clapboards, and making other repairs is the undoing of "improvements" made by others. If you can find a house that has not been subjected to the unintelligent enthusiasm of someone, your difficulties will be much less.

If you finally decide to buy the old house it will absorb most of your waking thoughts and time, take a great deal if not all of your money, and cause every bone and muscle to ache as you work in helping to restore it, but when you come home from even a short time away there will be a warm welcome, almost human, awaiting you. You will begin to know that you really own this house. As you lie in bed on a cold winter night, awakened by the groaning and the thumping of the old house through its entire foundation from the frost, you shudder with it, and hope morning will soon come when the sun's warmth will give it comfort and surcease from its wearisome travail. Or as you awake some early morning of a sunny day your eyes will caress the uneven boards of the chimney-wall paneling, the crookedness of the old ceiling with its summer beam, and the distortion of the houses and trees across the street through the wavy lights of the old window. And you are happy with the thought that the old house knows you have helped it to live again, that you have given it a family to shelter, and that it is grateful you are not one who would have taken up the old floor boards and replaced them with hardwood flooring, who would have had large picture windows instead of the little irregular ones, who would have evened up the crooked doorframes, and in doing all these things would have robbed it of much of its character and made it into a house like many others.

If you do not feel you can love and work over this old house, let me urge you not to buy it. There are so few old houses left, and they should belong to those who really love and understand them as a heritage that can never be replaced once destroyed. I can assure you your problems will be much simpler if you decide to build. You can select the type of house that appeals to you—Early American, Colonial, Federal, Victorian, or Modern. You can have it arranged as conveniently as you like, with all the closets, baths, picture windows, and the efficient kitchen most moderns demand. You will have the satisfaction of knowing you have the best today's science and industry can offer. And you can still achieve the decorating period that appeals to your tastes.

It seems beyond doubt that the oldest standing house in the United States is in St. Augustine, Florida—that building now occupied as a Museum by the St. Augustine Institute of Science and Historical Society. The society cannot give the exact date of the building but believes it was built as early as 1571. It is probable that this "oldest house" was built for the Franciscans who came with Menendez and that it was used as a private dwelling after the monks moved into a larger building. This oldest house is a timber house with heavy beamed ceiling. Stone walls were added at some later date, but where these have cracked, the heavy timbers are visible.

The Palace of the Governors in Santa Fe is without doubt the second oldest building in the United States. This was built some time between 1598 and 1609. When first constructed it was about one hundred twenty feet long and enclosed by an adobe wall four hundred feet long with a tower at either end. In one tower was the chapel; in the other storage space for ammunition. The building was of adobe, the roof supported by huge pine beams, and the floors were of dirt. The entire palace was rebuilt in

1744, but some of the original timbers supporting the roof are still in use today.

Until recently this was the residence of the governor. In this building Governor General Lew Wallace lived, and here he wrote his *Ben-Hur*. Here, too, his wife wrote *The Land of the Pueblos*. Today the palace is a museum and is filled with interesting relics. As you wander through the shadowed rooms you sense the mysterious and romantic events that occurred here—events peopled by Spanish grandees and their ladies, by bloodshed and treachery, and later by General and Mrs. Lew Wallace and the people of their dreams.

No trace remains of the crude shelters built by the earliest settlers in New England. Leyden Street (originally called First Street) in Plymouth, Massachusetts, contains no portion of any hut which comprised the first settlement. A group of Plymouth citizens has recently begun plans for the construction of a reproduction of the town's first settlement along Leyden Street, as it was in 1623 when there were twelve houses, a fort, the common storehouse, and the governor's house.

You can visit and study a replica of the early settlement in Salem, Massachusetts, as it was in 1630. In 1930 Salem, celebrating its three hundredth anniversary, reconstructed a village of the first sod-roofed dugouts and the little thatched pine cottages which were the shelters of the first settlers. This pioneer village represents the settlement when Governor Winthrop arrived with the charter from Charles I. It covers a plot of three acres and consists of the "Governor's Fayre House," thatched and weatherboarded houses, wigwams, and dugouts—twelve buildings in all along a village street with pillory and stock. The governor's house is the largest and is of the central chimney type with huge fireplaces. This village is open from early June to late October, and is well worth visiting. It gives an idea of how simple and crude these early shelters were. And yet there is a homeliness and warmth about them, for they were a refuge from the rigors of a bleak New England winter and a protection against unfriendly man and beast.

From the very beginning of the Plymouth settlement there had been trading with the Indians, at first by barter and then with wampum as a means of exchange. We learn from the writings of Captain John Smith and from Bradford's *History of Plimoth Plantation 1606–1646* that as early as 1623 ships bringing colonists from England returned home laden with "clapbord" and furs of various kinds.

In 1626 the Dutch bought the Island of Manhattan for sixty guilders and the settlement known as New Amsterdam followed. In 1627 the Plymouth Plantation received a letter from Isaack de Rasieres, governor of Manhattan, suggesting that there be trading between the two settlements. In agreement with this suggestion, the Plymouth men built a small

Settler's Hut, 1620

trading post at a place called Aptucxet, near the mouth of the Manamet River where the town of Bourne now stands. This was about twenty miles by land from Plymouth, but much of this distance could be traversed by boats along the creeks. In 1852 the foundations, which were all that remained of this trading post, were excavated and found to be of small flat stones laid in a cement made with oyster shells. In 1926 further excavations by Mr. P. H. Lombard, the late president of the Bourne Historical Society, disclosed an L-shaped building measuring 46 feet by 27 feet 6 inches with two small cellars about six feet below ground. Between the two cellars there was a huge chimney stack containing two fireplaces back to back. In 1930 the Bourne Historical Society, in co-operation with the General Society of Mayflower Descendants, carefully reconstructed the trading post on this old foundation. Long and patient study has made this restoration an accurate replica of the original building, and anyone interested in the construction methods of the early settlers will find it worth examining.

In 1628 a second trading post was established by the men of Plymouth at Kennebec, the site of Augusta, the capital of Maine, and in 1633 we have the beginnings of settlements in Connecticut, Rhode Island, and then New Hampshire. There are no seventeenth-century houses in Vermont. The oldest standing house is the frame dwelling built by Parson Jedediah Dewey in the new settlement of Bennington in 1763.

All along the coast from Maine through Connecticut and at many inland points, particularly along the rivers, you will find these houses of the seventeenth century with which we are now concerned, varying from section to section and from colony to colony. These houses were not a development of the first crude shelters into less crude dwellings, for this was not an evolutionary process. Following the first pioneers came boatloads of settlers with many good craftsmen among their number and soon they were building permanent dwellings. The first shelters were hastily constructed with but one thought in mind—protection. As the permanent dwellings were built, however, the settlers constructed traditional wooden buildings similar to those in which they had lived at home.

In general these New England houses were like those in the mother country but there were variations in details because of the variations in building styles and methods in the different sections of England from which the colonists had come, and also because of the differences in materials available and in use in the various sections where the houses were erected.

It is apparent from records, inventories, wills, and museums that from the middle of the seventeenth century the colonists were able to have whatever of comfort and refinement they desired—that is whatever was available to people of their own class at home in the mother country. It is probable that until the arbitrary date of 1680, which we have chosen as the beginning of our Early American decorating period, the houses in the colonies were built largely from memory, but shortly after that date manuals of architecture and building which were being published in England and other countries of Europe found their way slowly to this country. As the colonists grew more prosperous, houses became larger. With an increased number of rooms, life became more comfortable and there was a greater degree of individual privacy.

In the *Collections* of the Massachusetts Historical Society (1865, Vol. vii, pp. 118–20) you will find a description of the instructions written by Deputy Governor Samuel Symonds of Ipswich in 1638, evidently for the one who was to build him a new house:

I am indifferent whether it be 30 foote or 35 foote longe; 16 or 18 foote broade. I would have wood chimnyes at each end, the frames of the chimnyes to be stronger than ordinary, to beare good heavy load of clay for security against fire. You may let the chimneyes by all the breadth of the howse if you thinke good; the 2 lower dores to be in the middle of the house, one opposite the other. Be sure that all the dorewaies in every place be soe high that any man may goe upright under. The staiers I think had best be placed close by the dore. It makes noe great matter though there be no particion upon the first flore; if there be, make one biger than the other. For windowes let them not be over large in any roome, & as few as conveniently may be; let all have current shutting draw-windowes, having respect both to present & future use. I thinke to make it a girt howse will make it more chargeable than needs; however the side bearers for the second story, being to be loaden with corne &c. must not be pinned on, but rather eyther lett in to the studds or borne up with false studds and so tenented in at the ends. I leave it to you & the carpenters. In this story over the first, I would have a particion, whether in the middest or over the particion under, I leave it. In the garrett noe particion, but let there be one or two lucome windowes, if two, both on one side. I desire to have the sparrs reach downe pretty deep at the eves to preserve the walls the better from the wether. I would have it sellered all over and soe the frame of the howse accordingly from the bottom. I would have the howse strong in timber, though plaine and well brased. I would have it covered with very good oake-hart inch board, for the present, to be tacked on onely for the present as you tould me. . . . I think it best to have the walls without to be all clapborded besides the clay walls.

Not all early houses were as large as this of Mr. Symonds with its two stories besides attic and cellar and with two rooms on a floor. Those of the simpler colonists usually consisted of a one-room house with "porch" (entry) and chimney stack at one end. If there was a second story, the staircase, a steep arrangement with circular steps at the turns, was usually

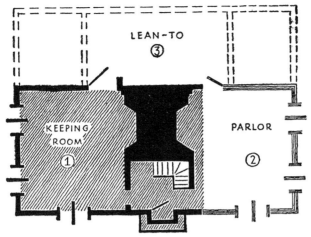

Diagram showing development of floor plan as house was enlarged

When the one-unit house was enlarged (1), a second room or unit was added on the opposite side of the chimney stack and porch (today's entry) (2)

When more room was needed, a lean-to was added (so-called salt-box house) (3)

When the back of the house was raised to the same height as the front, it became the central chimney house

in the "porch." Soon these "dancing" steps were replaced by square landings.

If the one-unit house was enlarged, a second room or unit was added on the opposite side of the chimney stack and porch. When more room was needed, a lean-to or ell was added to the structure. This lean-to was usually the scullery, and at the back of the house, very low, with the steep main roof carried over it at a slightly easier pitch. This lean-to soon became a characteristic feature of the period, and as new houses were built it became an integral part of the house with a continuous roof line from the ridge down. Thus evolved the so-called salt-box type of house. Then the carpenters abandoned the lean-to when more space was needed, and raised the back of the house to the same height as the front, making a full two-story house—the well-known central chimney type so beloved today.

The most important room was the place of all work, the "hall," at one side of the porch. This was a direct descendant of the "great hall" of the Middle Ages. As the family grew and prospered, the second room added on the opposite side of the porch was called the "parlor." A shed,

Salt-box House

often a lean-to, was especially constructed for the very important looms.

The sleeping rooms on the second floor were always called "chambers" and corresponded to the room below—"hall chamber," "parlor chamber," et cetera. The only sleeping room referred to as a "bedroom" was that on the first floor, usually connecting with the "hall." In any event, it was for the master and mistress of the family and was usually the room with the warmest exposure.

Brick houses were scarce in the seventeenth century. They were more common in the southern colonies, and one of the best was Bacon's Castle in Surrey County, Virginia, built in 1657.

The roofs of our earliest houses were very steep, sixty degrees in some instances, undoubtedly because they were intended for thatch. Later, with the use of shingles, they became flatter. Thatch was used extensively for roof covering during the first fifty years, that is up to about 1670. It had two great disadvantages: the deterioration owing to the bleak winter weather and the danger from fire. Shortly after the middle of the century shingles were used on all the better buildings. About 1650 slate came into use, especially upon the finer brick houses of Pennsylvania and New York State. There is some evidence that tiles were used in some of the colonies, especially in Virginia. Sometime about 1700 the gambrel roof made its appearance and became quite popular. This popularity was perhaps owing to the fact that it gave better headroom in the attic.

Central Chimney House

The very earliest chimneys were of small logs laid "cob-fashion" and plastered inside and out with clay. Others were built of four upright posts between which wattle or laths were fastened and plastered on both the inner and outer faces with clay well mixed with hay. This was a chimney type much used in England at the time. So long as the clay was moist and filled the joints well there was little danger from fire, but as the heat gradually dried the clay, pieces dropped out, leaving spaces for sparks and flames and then the disastrous fire. As late as 1706 a "chimney viewer" was elected in Hartford, Connecticut. This does not mean that clay chimneys were common as late as that date. By 1650 chimney stacks were built of stone wherever possible. Brickwork developed slowly as the manufacture of bricks spread over New England. You are often told that the bricks in this or that old house were brought from England or

Holland, but brickmakers were among the first arrivals in the Massachu-setts Bay Colony and bricks were made from a very early date. Often stone would be used up to the second floor, sometimes to the attic floor, and then the chimney finished off with brick.

One of the interesting features of some of the early houses, particularly in the Connecticut and New Haven settlements, as well as in and around Salem, Massachusetts, was the overhang. Two types were used. The earlier was the framed overhang which was like that used in the old country. In spite of some tales to the contrary, these overhangs had noth-ing whatever to do with protection against Indians. In none will you discover any loopholes for bullets, hot water, or molten lead. In this type of overhang the frame of the building was constructed so that the second story extended several inches beyond the lower. Under the corner posts are found many interesting turned and carved drops, pendants, or pen-dills. At the end of the seventeenth century the framed overhang was replaced by the hewn overhang in which flared and shouldered posts and wide girts were used to make the upper story overhang the lower up to six inches. This type is not known to have been used in England. In some of the colonies this hewn overhang was popular well into the first years of the Colonial period.

Many examples of the framed and hewn overhang houses are still in existence. On Main Street, Farmington, Connecticut, there is an interest-ing old house showing the framed overhang with fine pendills, and in Guilford, Connecticut, there is an interesting old house showing the hewn overhang. The John Ward house, now in the garden of the Essex Institute in Salem, Massachusetts, was built in 1684 and is of the overhang type. This house formerly stood on St. Peters Street, but when the land upon which it stood was needed to enlarge the jail, the house was moved to its present location. The original house was the usual one-unit type, the stairway winding up around the chimney. As more space was needed, a second fireplace was built, using the same chimney stack, and a second unit and attic added. There was no cellar, and the floor was of earth. The windows are of the casement type with small diamond-shaped panes. This house is open to the public and is most interesting. One room is fitted up as an early nineteenth-century apothecary shop. Other houses in Salem of the overhang type are the Witch House, built in 1692, and The House of Seven Gables, built in 1668 and restored in 1910. This house has a secret staircase.

Early houses were usually clapboarded, the clapboards nailed directly to the studs. These early clapboards were not the plain variety used today but were "beaded" along the lower edge. They were laid with an exposure of about three and one half inches at their greatest exposure width. Beginning at ground level, the first few rows were laid at about two inches to the weather, thus protecting the floor level against cold and damp. Then the exposure width was graduated until the maximum was

John Ward House
Salem, Mass., Showing Overhang

reached. Neither were the clapboards mitered at the corners, as is the general custom today. In the early houses you find a finishing board at the corners against which the clapboarding is cut. "Birchlands" in Woodbury, Connecticut, shows the beaded clapboards, the varying widths of exposure, and the finishing boards at the corners.

Windows were small for protection as well as to conserve heat. At first they were of the casement type with oiled paper or isinglass filling the rectangular or diamond-shaped panes, separated by either wooden or lead sash bars. Many windows in the simpler homes had nothing in the panes but were furnished with wooden blinds. Soon, however, glass took the place of these early makeshifts. Later there were inside shutters to be closed at night or when away. When closed, the paneling of these usually fitted into the room paneling to form an interesting unit. Often they slid back under the wall paneling when not in use. Not until after 1700 did the double-hung sash with heavy muntins come into use.

Judging by the earliest door now preserved, that from the Sheldon House at Deerfield, Massachusetts, the Early American exterior door was constructed of wide boards in two thicknesses, vertical on the outside, horizontal on the inside, and studded with heavy handmade iron nails.

There is no documentary evidence to show that any old house standing in New England today was built before 1650, but many a wonderful old place is credited with having been built, in part at least, years before that date. Martin S. Briggs, F.R.I.B.A, has compiled a list of surviving timber houses in New England built before 1685. Many of these are on the list in the Appendix open to the public, and a careful study of them will give an excellent basis for the development of your own home, whether you are planning to build, to restore an old house, or simply to redecorate an interior in the Early American tradition. In the Appendix you will also find a list of houses all over New England open to the public: houses of this early period and of our later architectural and decorating periods as well.

The main features of these seventeenth-century houses of special interest to us in our decorating study will be found in the interiors: the low-beamed ceilings, the small-paned windows, the fine old fireplaces, the sheathed and paneled walls, the narrow winding staircases hugging the chimney stack, the wide plank floors, and all the other charming and heart-warming characteristics of the Early American house. These are the centers of interest to be kept unspoiled, to be played up, to love and protect. Each period has its own features to identify it, although, as I have said before, there is always a carrying over from one period to another, and always a time lag between sections of the country.

INTERIORS

The structural beams and posts of the houses of the Early American period always protruded on the inside, and this became a characteristic part of the room decoration. It was the general custom to cover the beams and posts with boards with ornamental moldings of varying shapes. If not treated in this way, they were planed smooth with the edges chamfered. Sometimes there was a simple cornice of molded board with dentil-like notches at the edge. These notches were occasionally painted alternately black and red. Only in sheds and barns were the structural members left with the adze marks showing. Lime for mortar was not found in quantity until 1680. Even then, however, it was very expensive, and until we enter our third period, the Federal—after the Revolution—we find it usual to have the walls sheathed in wood, or in the better homes the exterior walls plastered with the partition walls of wood planking used either horizontally or vertically, or paneling. In those houses using planking the planks were sometimes more than three feet wide and were used in varying widths. To take care of shrinkage, a tongue was cut along the edge of each plank to fit into a groove on the adjoining plank. In most houses of this Early American period, then, we find in the earliest the walls sheathed in wood, and in the better houses three plastered walls, sometimes with dado, and one wooden wall, the chimney wall.

The space around the fireplaces was usually turned into closets, cupboards, and sometimes a secret passage. Often a small hiding place from Indians was constructed behind the fireplace. Later, during the Revolution, it came in handy for Tory sympathizers when they found it necessary to conceal themselves from searching Vigilantes. This secret place was entered through a movable panel or sometimes through a space at the bottom of the chimney wall cupboard, the lower shelf and the back panel being easily removed.

The rooms were low ceilinged, seldom more than seven feet in height. Stone was sometimes used for flooring the first story, but oak, chestnut, and pine planks of varying widths were most common throughout the entire house. These boards had a natural finish and were pinned to the joists below. Interior doors were of wide vertical boards with horizontal braces at top and bottom on the reverse. Hardware was black wrought iron in a great variety of design.

Until about 1700 whitewash was usual for the plastered walls. When a color was used, Spanish brown—a dark bricky color—seems to have been common during the early period, although azure blue, a grayed blue, royal yellow, olive-green, and many other colors were used. In this first period wallpaper was rarely used.

In this Early American period and well through the Colonial the chimney was the heart of the home as the fireplace was the center of home living. The kitchen and living-room fires were kept burning from the first cool days of fall until the heat of summer made them unnecessary. Even in warm weather, however, the kitchen fire was rarely allowed to go out, since there was no other means of cooking, and matches did not become common until 1830.

Fire, man's greatest friend during the cold weather, was his greatest fear, and a house was never left alone with a fire burning. The master's bedroom was usually off the kitchen, so any fire during the night would be quickly noted. Bedroom fires were carefully banked and guarded subconsciously by sleeping members of the family or guests.

In the early fall and all through the long winter an immense backlog, sometimes as much as eighteen inches in diameter, was drawn to the hearthstone, often by a horse driven into the kitchen. Against this the smaller pieces of wood were piled. In front a "forestick," always of green wood, kept guard lest any burning log slip forward. A supply of "swingling tow," that part of the flax stalk after the flax for spinning and any usable tow has been removed, was always on hand to help in lighting the fires. This was very dry and very inflammable. When the fire was ready laid, the king's arm (a type of flintlock) was taken down from its place on the wall. Some powder was placed in the flashpan and this was held under the tow. The flintlock was then snapped, and this set the powder and tow alight. At night the burning coals and embers would be piled against the huge backlog, which often lasted an entire week, and the fire carefully banked, leaving only a tiny air space so it would not go out. In the morning, when the ashes were raked away, there would be a bed of hot coals for cooking breakfast.

Some of the old chimney roots measure as much as fourteen feet square. That in our house in Woodbury, Connecticut, is at least twenty by twelve feet. The fireplace in the kitchen was always the largest in the house, often being twelve feet long. As part of the kitchen fireplace was the great oven. Before bricks came into general use, this was built of stone. Its iron door was about three feet from the floor and beneath it was a large open space for storing the big kettles or at times the oven wood. Another feature of the early chimneys was the smoke chamber. This was several feet wide and started a few feet above the hearth in order to catch the smoke for curing the hams and other meat. Sometimes this smoke chamber was in the attic, sometimes in the cellar. More pretentious dwellings had separate smokehouses.

Hearths were sometimes built of brick or cobbles but generally of flat stone, and varied in width from a foot and a half to two yards. Seldom were they entirely enclosed by the chimney walls. And around this ample fireplace and hearth we find the various members of our Early American family cooking, knitting, weaving, spinning, whittling, courting, entertaining, and carrying on all the activities of a busy household. Here the aged warmed their old bones and the newborn slept in wooden cradles. Here were warmth and cheer for family, neighbor, and stranger. Here indeed was the center of family life.

FURNISHINGS AND ACCESSORIES

Our early settlers were men and women of stern conscience and well equipped mentally to endure the hardships in a pioneer country. Those who lacked physical endurance died quickly, and in the first years of the settlements the number unable to endure the sufferings of winter and the many other privations was appalling. What we today would consider absolute necessities were then unheard-of luxuries. And yet those early homes were filled with love and cheer. The sturdy oak furniture brought from England and the simple pieces made from native woods by the Colonial carpenters fitted well against the whitewashed walls or melted into the darkness of the wooden sheathing mellowed by the wood smoke from the busy fireplace. The gleam from glowing fire or stray sunbeams through the small-paned windows picked up the glint of shining pewter and brass. Brightly colored cushions on chairs and stools gave patches of gayness.

In large households, and in those days most contained members of several families, there were always new babies to love, children of various ages to comfort and care for, and the aged to cherish a little longer. Bachelors could not enjoy a home of their own but were assigned to some family by the magistrates. Spinsters of twenty-five were called "anciente maides," while those older were "thornbacks."

Seldom did a door have a bolt or bar except as necessary for protection against unfriendly Indians. Stranger or friend was welcome at any time and was greeted at the door with "you are welcome." All classes had "manners." Guests arrived expected or unexpected in those days before there was postal service or telephones, knowing there would always be someone at home to receive them. Many families had indentured servants, and before too long even slaves from the West Indies, who did the heavier chores, leaving the mistress free to attend to the many other duties. There was constant weaving, knitting, sewing, or cooking to be done.

The furnishings of these homes were simple and sturdy and suitable for this new life. The chest was probably the most important because the most necessary piece of furniture. This can readily be understood when we realize that it served the need, later filled by trunks, for transporting clothes and bedding; it was easily stored on the tiny ships and was indispensable in the new home. Next in importance were cupboards, tables, settles, stools, and long or short benches called "forms."

In England at this time chairs were used only by the head of the family or very important guests. We know that Governor Carver brought over his large and heavy chair on the *Mayflower* and that this was much copied by the local carpenters. Banister-back, several kinds of slat-back, and Windsor chairs soon made their appearance.

The cupboard was probably the most imposing piece of furniture in the more pretentious Early American home. It was of oak, covered with the typical carvings of England or Holland of this period and came in several types—the press, the court, and the livery cupboard. These held the pewter and silver, the table linen, and sometimes food. Since they were very expensive and not available to many, we find their places filled by various kinds of built-in cupboards and dressers in the less pretentious homes.

At this time the bed was not an important piece of furniture. It usually consisted of a simple wooden frame. There were trundle beds, wooden cradles, even the cricket bedstead, the forerunner of the modern cot, the very necessary brass warming pan, the all-important chest, stools, an occasional chair, a simple loomed rug, and the bed furnishings to supply

Oak Cupboard

the requirements of the bedroom when there was a separate room for sleeping. Mirrors and pictures were almost non-existent. Candles and fireplaces gave the only light at night.

Mealtime was the time of greatest activity in the home. The women of the household and the servants or slaves busied themselves with preparation around the big kitchen fireplace. The fire glowed in its effort to give needed help. Meats were baked or pot-roasted in the great oven. Sometimes they were broiled before the fire, hanging from several kinds of homemade spits, a pan set on the hearth beneath to catch the dripping. If there were to be biscuits or cake, the iron bake pan could be pushed into the coals. A small iron kettle with handle and legs, called a skillet, was used for gravies or sauces. A foot-high brass or iron trivet set near the fire kept things hot. An iron frying pan, not unlike the pans used by today's cooks but with a handle three feet long, and the sausage baker standing upright before the blazing coals served their different purposes.

There was much coarse earthenware, woodenware, and hollow ironware. There were bulbous pots with covers and kettles with sloping sides and no covers. There were pie plates of coarse earthenware. When filled with the liquid pie mixture, they were placed far back in the hot oven with difficulty, so the pastry shell was half filled, pushed into the oven, and then filled from a big wooden spoon with a very long handle. In the oven the bread was baked, meat roasted, the beans and Indian pudding slowly cooked for many hours, and at the proper time the stone jars of preserved fruits were cooked. There were innumerable iron spoons, forks, toasting racks, peels, and wooden articles of all kinds.

Never did any dining room seem more inviting with its warm firelight glow, the busy activity of the mistress, older children, and servants preparing dinner, the delectable odors of baking and roasting food, than did the Early American "hall" to the men of the family as they came in from chopping wood or other outdoor work, from the mill or store, on a frosty winter day—except, perhaps, after an arduous trip on horseback to town. Then it seemed almost too good to be true.

As the steaming food in pewter basins and platters or on wooden trenchers was placed on the table, the members of our Early American family found their accustomed places but stood until "grace before meat" had been said. Children too small for the chairs or benches sat on the laps of the grownups or stood at their places during the meal. They waited eagerly but well manneredly for their shining pewter porringers which were being filled for them by the mother or serving-woman. Each child had his own pewter or silver spoon. After the children had been helped there was much passing and repassing of the large pewter and wooden serving dishes with their steaming contents, until each hungry member of the family had heaped high his own pewter plate. Forks had not been in use too long, but the family had them as it had "linen" (home-woven) and "holland" (imported) tablecloths and napkins.

The main meal was at midday. The first course was often a pudding made of corn meal and boiled for many hours. Then came vegetables and whatever there might be of meat or fish. As yet potatoes were far from plentiful. This was followed by pies or puddings, or baked apples that had stayed in the big oven all night to cook slowly as it cooled after the day's baking. For the hot breads there was sweet butter, made in the early summer and sprinkled with sugar between the layers as it was laid down. On the farms cheese was a popular food. Without ice, milk could be kept but a short time, so during hot weather particularly all excess milk was made into cheese. For drink there was cider to fill the pewter pint pots; perhaps even home-brewed beer. Tea was still a luxury, costing several dollars a pound, and saved for special occasions when the choice handleless cups and saucers were used to honor the welcome guests. Coffee and chocolate were found only in the coast towns.

When the meal was over, the servants, if there were any, did the clearing up while the mistress found ample to do with knitting, weaving, the care of the children, and the making and mending of clothing. After the evening meal all gathered round the fire for evening prayers, and then, with the children tucked away in their trundle beds, quiet descended upon the Early American home. The candles flickered dimly in the brighter glow of the fire, the grownups relaxed, but always with some piece of work in hand, as they discussed the day's happenings. If there were several men, there might be a game of checkers or chess, or one might read aloud from the Good Book as the others busied themselves with some quiet handwork. Then after mugs of steaming hotness the fires were banked, the candles snuffed, and another day had gone.

COLONIAL—1720-1790

CUSTOMS AND COSTUMES

MANY writers and lecturers speak of the eighteenth century in the colonies as though it were a century of sameness, whereas it encompassed a gradual change from the crudeness and simplicity of Early American through the magnificence of Chippendale to the extreme classicism of the Adam brothers and the elegance of Hepplewhite and Sheraton. True, as I have said before, there was a time lag in various parts of the country, a time lag dependent upon distance from the seaports and lack of other means of easy communication. What most writers and lecturers do mean by the eighteenth century, however, is what we shall call the Colonial period, for which we have set the date boundaries of 1720 to directly after the Revolution—about 1790.

Several factors influenced the gradual change from Early American to Colonial. The colonists were entering a period when mere survival was not their greatest effort. They had more time to think of beauty in their surroundings. And the colonies were still England in a new country in constant communication with the mother country, whether it was the Royal Colony of Williamsburg in Virginia with its regal Governor's Palace and its miniature "court," or the more simple town of Portsmouth in New Hampshire, with its royal governor and the Great House on Little Harbor. When the King died in England, the bells tolled his death in New England and the people grieved; and then they were taxed for the new King's maintenance.

During this period Portsmouth, New Hampshire (which we are using for the detailed description of a town during the Colonial period), was a typical New England town—perhaps a little more prosperous than some; perhaps a little more sophisticated because of its location on a busy harbor. Many of its people were stanch friends of royalty. The social life of the town centered around the royal governor even though his court was not of an equal magnificence with that of Williamsburg to the south. Often the colonists felt a nostalgic longing for the old homes in England, for their relatives and friends there, and the social life revolving around the governor and his lady helped assuage this homesickness.

Although Portsmouth had been called Piscataqua for the river along which it was built and another section Strawberry Bank for the strawberries that grew there in sweet abundance, and the part facing the water where the governor's Great House stood Little Harbor, the surrounding forests were the King's Woods, the church where the fashionable worshiped was Queen's Chapel, and the main highway was Queen Street.

The first half of the eighteenth century was a time of much prosperity in such Colonial seaports as Portsmouth, and the merchants and *beaux galants* and their wives and children dressed in the styles prevailing in England and France. For daily wear the men wore coats of cloth with breeches and buckled shoes, powdered wigs, and cocked hats. For social functions they had suits of fine colored cloth or velvet with beautifully brocaded waistcoats, broad cuffs, and fine lace ruffles and neckties. About the middle of the century plum-colored cloth became very fashionable for men's suits and the gentlemen wore pigtails. About this same time the stylish square-toed shoes were discarded by both men and women in favor of those with pointed toes. Instead of a sword, the man about town now carried a long stick—the ancestor of the cane—and affected a mincing walk.

The snuffbox was an absolute necessity for the young man of fashion. In fact, everyone took snuff, the fashionable and the unfashionable, only the fashionable went to school to learn how to use it with style. The others got along as best they could with soiled hands and stained clothing. Many of the "nutmeg graters" collected today are really snuff grinders because snuff came pressed in a little hard cake. Collecting snuffboxes became the greatest hobby of the day. They were made of gold and silver, of jade and lapis lazuli, of papier-mâché. They were set with diamonds and rubies. They came from France, from England, and from China. Some had little spoons made of gold or other material to help the ladies keep dainty while enjoying the sweet stuff. Not only in New England was it fashionable to use snuff and to collect the little bejeweled boxes and bottles. Pompadour, Josephine, and other ladies of the French court, the ladies of England and their gentlemen, and the fashionable ladies and gentlemen of all the Colonial towns had their beautiful snuff-boxes—sometimes hundreds of them. Today many of these bring fabulous prices. One sold some few years ago for $36,000!

Gorgeous as was the male of the species in this fashionable period, he was surpassed in all respects by the ladies of such seacoast towns as Portsmouth and Salem, and of course Boston. Ships from the Indies and China brought beautiful materials for costumes, and constant communication between England, France, and the colonies enabled them to keep up with the latest fashions. Jointed dolls were dressed in the newest styles by the London and Paris couturiers and sent to the colonies by monthly packet in much the same manner as the French fashion magazines of today. Upon their arrival the dolls were displayed in shops and store windows, were studied, admired, and avidly copied by ladies of fashion. Many of these dolls have since found their home in today's doll collections.

Coiffures and caps—"tower and commode"—were extravagantly high, sometimes as much as two feet. Skirt hoops varied during the period. At first they were very full on all sides, then they flattened out in front and back and bulged at the sides. Pounds of whalebone were worn by every lady—this made whaling one of the profitable industries. Stays at that time were not made of two-way-stretch elastic. They were a formidable and rigid part of the costume.

Preserved for our perusal is a memorandum in Washington's own handwriting, dated 1759, ordering from Europe for his wife

A cap, handkerchief and ruffles of Brussels or Point lace to cost 20 pounds
Two fine flowered aprons
One pair women's white silk hose

Four pairs thread hose
Six pairs women's fine cotton hose
One pair black satin shoes
One pair white satin shoes of smallest 5's
Four pairs calamance shoes
One fashionable hat or bonnet
Six pairs women's best kid gloves
Eight pairs women's best mitts
One black mask
One dozen most fashionable pocket handkerchiefs
One piece of narrow white satin ribbon with pearl edge
Four pieces of binding tape
Six thousand miniken pins
One thousand hair pins.

A black mask was often worn in the winter to protect the face from the cold and one of green silk as a protection from the summer's hot sun when riding horseback. Arms, faces, and necks were carefully swathed against tanning, which was not in good taste for ladies.

Accessories of all kinds were in abundance—lace tippets; diamond and paste buckles; diamond necklaces and earrings; hoods and bonnets; aprons—long, then short, then long again as the century advanced; the gypsy straw hat of 1745; the French curls of the same period which are described as "looking like eggs strung in order on a wire and tied around the head"; silver hair pegs; sleeve buttons of gold and silver; silver cloak clasps; silk and linen handkerchiefs; much beautiful lace and embroidery; and of course the pomander balls of sweet scent; the etui which hung from the waist and held scissors, thimble, and other necessaries—the great-grandchild of the chatelaine of medieval days; and the ever-present snuffbox and fan.

According to Frances M. Caulkins in her *History of Norwich, Connecticut*, published in 1866 and referring to this Colonial period:

Women of mature age wore close linen caps. Parasols and umbrellas were unknown or of rare occurrence, but a fan nearly a foot and a half in length, and spreading like the train of a peacock, was often carried to keep off the sun as well as to catch the air. At one period feathers were much worn upon the head, surmounting a high turban of gauze or muslin raised on wire and adorned also with ribbon.

A lady in full dress for great occasions displayed a rich brocade with open skirt and trained petticoat trimmed with lace; an emboidered stomacher and full ruffles at the elbow. Hood and scarf were of silk. No sumptuary laws restrained the feminine taste for rich attire at this period. When the ladies walked out, they threw the end of the train over the right arm. The foot was dressed in a silk stocking, a sharp-toed slipper, often made of embroidered satin and with a high heel.

And children were little replicas of their fathers and mothers so far as costume went.

All this, of course, does not apply to the laboring man or woman, to the inland villagers, to the servants whose outfits were provided by the employer. These wore the simple clothes usual to their groups everywhere.

In this period of beautiful costumes and gaiety it was the fashion for almost everyone of importance to have his portrait painted. Fortunately many of these portraits have been preserved in our museums or private collections and enable us to see these men and women of an earlier age and to study their clothing.

Shortly after 1750 in and around Boston, Massachusetts, and Portsmouth, New Hampshire—a small section of New England which we are taking as typical for our detailed description of this period—two artists were in demand for this portrait painting—John Singleton Copley and Joseph Blackburn. Copley is better known today but Blackburn painted some eighty good portraits of the aristocrats of both Boston and Portsmouth.

Copley was born in 1738, the son of Irish immigrants. His father died shortly after his birth and his mother eked out a precarious livelihood in Boston selling tobacco and probably snuff. When John was eleven she married Peter Pelham, an English portrait painter, drawing master, dancing teacher, and owner of a small store where he sold the then popular mezzotints and other pictures. It is probable that he recognized a talent for painting in the young Copley and became his first teacher. Pelham was a friend of John Smibert, a leader of the fashionable art set in Newport and Boston. Smibert also taught painting and sold art supplies, and it is said that he numbered Charles Wilson Peale, John Trumbull, and Washington Allston among his pupils.

Because of the friendship between Copley's stepfather, Peter Pelham, and Smibert, young John early came under the guidance of this excellent teacher, and by the time he was sixteen or seventeen he was painting portraits of well-known people around Boston in both oil and pastels as well as miniatures. In fact, he soon became the fashion. When he was thirty-one years old he married the daughter of Richard Clarke, a wealthy merchant and Tory sympathizer who later lost some 15,000 pounds of English merchandise during the Boston Tea Party—dumped by the irate colonists. Copley's sympathies were evidently with his father-in-law in his leanings toward England, for shortly after the famous tea party he and his family moved to England, where he spent the remainder of his life. However, between 1754, the date of his first portraits, and 1774, when he left America, he had painted many fine likenesses.

Joseph Blackburn was a man of mystery from first to last, but this did not lessen his attraction for the ladies, you may be sure, especially since he was not unattractive. He had arrived in Connecticut about 1753, presumably from Bermuda. He was unquestionably an Englishman of good birth with good English training in the fundamentals of art. He soon reached Boston and painted there and in Portsmouth for about ten years. Then in 1763 he completely vanished.

Having one's portrait painted was not all pleasure for the sitter nor all hardship for the artist. Sittings generally lasted about six hours, and the number required for a portrait averaged between twenty and twenty-five. When the sitting was over, however, relaxation was pleasant over the teacups or madeira, especially if the sitter was a beautiful young lady and the artist a mysterious handsome Englishman.

One English visitor wrote at this time:

Both the ladies and gentlemen dress and appear as gay in common as courtiers in England on a coronation or birthday. And the ladies here visit, drink tea, and indulge in every piece of gentility to the height of the mode and neglect the affairs of their families with as good grace as the finest ladies in London.

For a portrait demanding so many hours of time on the part of the artist, Copley—and probably Blackburn too—received approximately $35 to $100. Copley writes in one instance that he received little more for his portraits than for the frames he supplied for them.

The middle of the eighteenth century was one of high adventure for the colonists because of the privateering during the French War of 1756–63. Much captured loot was brought back to the colonies and sold at auctions, which were just as popular then as today. Then you could bid in—especially if you got there early—beautiful Aubusson rugs, fine French furniture, French tapestries, and Sèvres, and if any of you have among your inherited possessions some of these French treasures, they might tell you an exciting tale.

As the century advanced toward the three-quarter mark, however, the feeling of love for England began to wane except in the hearts of the Royalist Tories, and soon we find a strong sentiment against everything English. Men and women refused to wear English imports. Dress became simple and even somber. Woolen cloth and linen of home manufacture became more fashionable than imported silk. The whir of the spinning wheel was heard everywhere as mistress and servant attempted to supply the needs of the family. Homespun parties were popular, and at these the gentlemen and the ladies wore nothing that had been imported, and only food that had been grown or raised in the colonies was served, and no one drank tea—that is, except the Tories.

Don't let anyone tell you there is anything stodgy about tradition, for it is the main stream of all the best of the past. Believing in tradition does not mean we do not accept the best of the present. We do, and in turn this becomes part of the tradition our generation passes on. From the caveman on those of each age have been eager for the new, have adapted and selected from what the times had to offer, and what was of worth endured and became part of that which was carried on as a heritage. True there were periods in history when no progress was apparent, when there seemed to be only regression, but at least the tradition persisted.

No one can ever suggest that the American colonists did not eagerly desire the new. They awaited every packet boat from England and France and every little ship from the Indies and China to see what might be brought in. And as they added these new products to what they already possessed, they added interest to their homes. Not every new style endured. As I have said elsewhere, our Early American of today is not the Early American of 1680 to 1720. Our American Modern of today will not be the same one hundred years from now if at that time it takes its place as a decorating period. We add to our heritage unconsciously as well as consciously as we pass through life. That is normal and natural. Everything of the past does not have beauty and charm and utility. If utility is available with beauty and charm, why have it without? Sometimes we do not want utility at all in an accessory or even in a piece of furniture—just charm and beauty. So don't accept everything from the past as desirable simply because it is old, and don't reject everything of the present simply because it is new. It is the keying and blending together of both old and new that make for successful homes. The traditional gives dignity, stability, and continuity; the new should give interest and convenience. All that seems important and enduring today will never become part of the main stream to be passed on to future generations. All of the present never does.

The beautiful things of the past had one quality, however, that the mass of things produced today does not. Every piece of furniture, every example of beautiful needlework, in fact almost everything was the work of an individual man or woman. It was made with care and patience. It had a quality no machine-made product ever can have. Quantities of the same article satiate and fatigue. Today there is a turning back to this individual work by craftsmen that is most hopeful.

And then these beautiful things that have endured, the ones we admire and covet, had care. The patina of old furniture is not the result of just time alone. The beautiful highboys and chests and tables were rubbed with beeswax and polished until they shone like mirrors. The silver and brass were kept bright as sunshine. In the important households slaves and servants did this constant work. In the simple homes the housewife herself cared for her few treasures and the pewter was boiled in the dish kettle over the fire and polished after every meal. The furniture and brasses at Williamsburg are proof of this kind of constant care. Have you ever seen a dull candlestick or drawer pull there?

HOUSES

Did you ever notice the relation between customs, costumes, houses, and accessories? When the formality and elegance of costumes increase, the houses and their furnishings become more formal. When a large number of people turn to the utmost informality in dress, as today, then their houses become streamlined. And so in the early part of the eighteenth century a change in Colonial architecture took place corresponding to the change in customs and costumes. Who can say which was the cause and which the result? This change occurred first in the seaport towns but slowly advanced into the interior of the country, although the house types of the earlier settlers still persisted well throughout the entire century. Following the trend in England, architecture in the colonies became academic. No longer was it necessary to build a house with the chief emphasis on its functional possibilities, so functional elements gave way to the ideas of Inigo Jones of England, who, in turn, was greatly influenced by Andrea Palladio of Italy.

Let us go back a bit in architectural history. Early in the fifteenth century there was a turning back from the Romanesque and Gothic architecture that had dominated Europe for the past thousand years to the Greek ideal—to the classical. This was the beginning of what is known as the Renaissance, or rebirth. In Italy in the early seventeenth century we find Andrea Palladio of Venice, among others, designing splendid buildings in this classical style, with a few ideas of his own added. The Renaissance architecture spread to France and other parts of continental Europe. Early in this same century Inigo Jones made a trip to Italy to study landscape painting, but fell under the spell of Palladio and his splendid Venice. Returning home, he introduced these new ideas into his architectural designs and became known as the father of English Renaissance. Following him came Sir Christopher Wren, the designer of

St. Paul's in London (and the designer of William and Mary College in royal Williamsburg). Wren's interpretation of Palladio's classicism was a more robust and rococo one than was Jones's since he had come under the influence of French ideas.

In 1714 George I came to the throne of England, and he was followed by the other three Georges, so that England was ruled by a King named George successively from 1714 to 1830. Hence this style brought to England and adapted by Inigo Jones, elaborated by Sir Christopher Wren, and carried on by his pupils, is called Georgian. In reality it is English Renaissance.

Although Palladio's book on architecture was published about the middle of the seventeenth century and although Jones had been working away in England during this same period, their influence did not extend to the colonies until the beginning of the eighteenth century. One reason for this was that the many books on architecture published during the seventeenth century were of little use to the ordinary Colonial builder, since many of them were in a foreign language he could not read, and because the designs shown were suitable for elaborate continental manor houses and not for homes in the colonies. In 1715, however, a complete edition of Palladio was printed, and the designs of Jones were published in 1727. Probably of greatest help to builders in the colonies—the average builder—was the publication in 1747 of Halfpenny's *Modern Builder's Assistant*, since this was the first book to present general designs.

During the early eighteenth century there was constant communication between England and the colonies although there was no longer such an inpouring of settlers as there had been in the previous seventy-five years. However, more and more did Colonial merchants and other travelers visit England, and many of the wealthy families sent their sons to Europe to school. Then, too, there was a rather rapid succession of royal governors, and important people often accompanied them to the colonies. All these demanded more comfortable and more pretentious houses than the colonies had to offer, and so, following the trend in England, houses of the early Georgian type popular there were constructed for them in America. The prosperous merchants and other colonists viewed these new structures with desire and quickly accepted them as the latest building fashion.

Even so, this change in architectural design occurred chiefly in the houses of the wealthy rather than in those of the simple people. Then, too, the earliest changes in New England with which we are chiefly concerned were in such coast towns as Salem and Boston and Portsmouth. In the South the change occurred in the important houses even more quickly than in the North, and there brick and stone, which are so highly suitable for the dignified Georgian mansion, became popular much more quickly than in the North, where the wooden house long retained its

Longfellow House, Cambridge, Massachusetts

prestige because of the common belief, perhaps well founded in those days without central heating, that stone and brick houses were damp.

In 1799 Elias Hasket Derby, a big shipowner of Salem, had a brick house built in the vicinity of Town House Square at a cost of $80,000— the most magnificent house in all Salem. It is said that Mrs. Derby believed this house to be damp. Be that as it may, it was occupied but a few months when Mr. Derby died, and, since no buyer could be found for it, it was torn down. By 1801, which rightfully comes in our next period, Chestnut Street had become the fashionable street in Salem, and there Samuel McIntire was building his remarkable houses which make it even today one of the most beautiful streets, architecturally, in America.

The general use of books as an aid in building a house tended to make the building style during this period more of a general type, especially in the important houses. The simpler homes were more dependent upon local materials and traditions, so here we get representative types differing from locality to locality, such as the Connecticut house and the Pennsylvania Dutch, whereas the important house in Massachusetts is not too unlike the important house in Pennsylvania or Virginia.

It is doubtful whether the finest example of the Georgian house as developed by the middle of the century ever has been or ever will be surpassed. It reached its most glorious climax in the South in such buildings in Virginia as the Governor's Palace in Williamsburg; Jefferson's beautiful home, Monticello, in Charlottesville; and Westover. However, in the North we had such outstanding examples as the John Vassall (Longfellow) house built in Cambridge, Massachusetts, in 1759; the Roger Morris (Jumel) house built in New York City in 1765; the McPhedris (Warner) house built in Portsmouth, New Hampshire, before 1728; and the Hancock house built in Boston between 1737 and 1740.

In what manner did this new type of house differ from the central chimney house of the Early American period? Probably the chief factor was in its formality. Specifically, the chimney was one of the main differences. It was taken from the center of the house and at first placed in the middle of the dividing wall between the two rooms on either side of the central hall and then at the ends of the house; sometimes with a chimney at either end, sometimes with a chimney at each of the four corners. This change permitted a spacious transverse hall with the staircase generally at the back. The house itself usually had its length toward the street with a central door and two windows on either side on the first floor and five windows on the second floor directly over those below. Within the house were two rooms on each side of the hall symmetrically arranged. This made a more formal house, a more convenient house, one in which all rooms could be entered from the hall without going through another room. These new houses filled the requirements of a prosperous people for more comfort, more privacy, and more convenience—a people no longer satisfied to have their living room and kitchen one or a bed in the parlor.

Although most houses continued to be of two stories during this period, houses of three stories became increasingly numerous in the towns, especially those near the coast. Ceilings became higher and averaged between ten and twelve feet on the first floor and only slightly less on the second, the height depending largely upon the wealth and pretentiousnss of the one for whom the house was being built. Jefferson's house, Monticello, has some ceilings eighteen feet high.

If these had been the only changes, the façade of the new-type house would not have appeared too different to the casual observer from the old central chimney house. He would have noticed the new location of the chimneys and the added third story. However, there were other important differences. The house became a more formal, symmetrical house mass. Outbuildings took their place in an orderly arrangement in relation to the central house, this arrangement differing in the various colonies.

The main entrance to a dwelling place has been its important feature for untold generations, and from the earliest days of the colonies our ancestors gave it considered attention. During this Colonial period, however, the door and its enframement became an even more important and elaborate detail. In fact, both doors and windows received much more attention than in the Early American house and were embellished with segmented or scroll pediments. Lights appeared in the upper panels of doors around 1760, but side lights and fanlights were not used until after the Revolution. Small windows appeared on either side of the door, but these were not within the door enframement itself. In general, all doors and windows were carefully and regularly spaced and were uniform in size.

The Palladian window made its first appearance in the colonies shortly before the middle of the century. This was a favorite of Wren and consisted of a central window with a rounded top with a rectangular window on either side, each with an entablature and pilasters. This window group usually occupied the important location over the main entrance. Windows themselves changed with regard to the number of lights. Whereas fifteen to twenty-four panes continued to be used in the earlier and simpler houses, twelve is the usual number in the later and more important houses. Dormers were widely used in the Colonial house. In fact a Georgian house without dormers does not look quite right. If dormers were omitted, it was usually because the garret was too narrow for rooms or the rooms were lighted by gable windows. The most common dormers had a square-headed window with a triangular gable or pediment, but toward the end of the period this type became less popular than one with a semicircular head with a triangular pediment.

Kimball states that it was not uncommon for the Colonial house to have outside window shutters as the century advanced, although it was equally common for a house to be found without them. Kelly says that blinds and shutters are a late feature, not coming into use until the end of the eighteenth century. At any rate the Hancock house built in Boston in 1737, the John Vassall house built in Cambridge in 1759, the Royall house built in Medford, Massachusetts, about 1733, all show shutters of the louvre type although these may have been added at a later date. Photographs of the William Penn house built in Pennsylvania in 1683 show paneled wooden shutters. Both authorities agree, however, that the paneled variety was used in the middle colonies, whereas in New England those with fixed louvres were the type adopted. Shutters with movable slats came later.

The roof of this new type of house sloped more gently than did its predecessors. Many of the important houses had a hip roof with a level cornice line on all sides. At first the new, more gently sloping roof rose to a ridge, and this continued common in the narrow house. In the wider house, however, that approaching the square mass of the next period, the roof was cut off at the top to form a deck, and this deck was often surrounded by a balustrade. Sometimes there was an eaves balustrade, as on the Pickman House built in Salem, Massachusetts, in 1764. On the gambrel-type roof, which continued on into the Colonial period as a survival of the old steep roof, balustrades were also used. The earliest type of this is the McPhedris house built in Portsmouth, New Hampshire, between 1722 and 1728. On this house the balustrade is along the curbs dividing the upper and lower slopes of the roof and extends from chimney to chimney. The Hancock house in Boston has a similar balustrade.

A few of the Colonial mansions, such as the Jeremiah Lee house built in Marblehead, Massachusetts, in 1768, added a cupola although cupolas were much more common in our next period. The cornice also received attention and in some instances became elaborate with modillions (brackets), dentils (little wooden blocks), and other embellishments of classic architecture.

The house itself was made more splendid by the use of the "orders." Do you know what these "orders" are? Classic architecture as it origi-

Top Row: Three Greek Orders: Doric, Ionic, Corinthian
Lower Row: Two Roman: Composite, Tuscan

nated with the Greeks makes use of three orders, each composed of a column with a base, a shaft, and a capital. The part resting upon the column is called the entablature. This, in turn, is composed of an architrave, a frieze, and a cornice. The three orders are identified by their capitals. The Ionic is probably the most beautiful. It has a pair of spirals called volutes. The Corinthian is certainly the most magnificent, its capital covered with acanthus leaves. The Doric is the simplest, having only a block with a bed mold beneath. To these three orders the Romans added two more, the Tuscan and the Composite. The Tuscan is simpler than the Doric. In reality it is the Doric made stronger by shortening its column and simpler by increasing the size, and thus reducing the number, of its moldings. The Composite, in its simplest definition, combines the volutes of the Ionic with the leaves of the Corinthian.

These orders were used to embellish both the exteriors and the interiors of the Colonial homes, particularly the main entrances and later the projecting pavilions. The John Vassall (Longfellow) house in Cambridge, Massachusetts, shows the exterior use of these orders better than a written description can. Columns rising the entire height of a two-story portico did not occur until after the Revolution. During the Colonial period, however, builders made much use of the portico with columns one story high, standing free, as on the Jeremiah Lee house in Marblehead.

Every rule, of course, has its exception, and the Roger Morris (Jumel) house built in New York City in 1765 was apparently designed and built by men far in advance of their contemporaries in architectural knowledge. This house has an authenticated two-story portico and a rear wing octagonal in shape with unequal sides, without doubt part of the original structure. Both these features were rare in the colonies before the Revolution.

INTERIORS AND FURNISHINGS

In the houses of the Colonial period the most common interior arrangement was a transverse stair hall with four rooms to a floor. Some houses, such as the Governor's Palace at Williamsburg, Virginia, had this transverse hall separated into two rooms, the front used as a reception hall. In other houses of this period the hall was expanded to one side to accommodate the stairs, and after 1760 a broad transverse hall with the stairs in a separate compartment was the popular arrangement.

Within the house there was the formal academic treatment of doorways, windows, fireplaces, cornices, and stairways demanded by the new formality of the exteriors. The rooms were either rectangular or approaching a square room. Not until after the Revolution were there circular or elliptical rooms.

When the stairs were in the large transverse hall, they afforded the builders an opportunity to develop them as the keynote of the entire interior. An open string of stairs with the tread ends showing was now used, and these tread ends permitted elaborate details. Plain balusters were no longer fashionable. Both turned and spiral were common, sometimes three different designs in the same staircase, with three balusters to a step. Handrails were beautifully molded of walnut or mahogany, and the newel post became an important decorative feature. On the wall opposite the handrail, a sloping wainscoted dado was often used in the fine staircases of this period.

In any principal room the simplest wall treatment consisted of a baseboard, chair rail, cornice, and molded trim about windows and doors. After 1725 builders' handbooks showed elaborate details for all these features as well as for chimney pieces and stairs, and soon these designs were copied so faithfully that it is not difficult to discern which book a builder was using. After 1750 the paneled room is found less often although some late paneled rooms may be seen, such as the mahogany room in the Jeremiah Lee house in Marblehead, Massachusetts. This is most elaborate, with richly carved festoons and other rococo details. As the fashion for wallpapers and other wall coverings increased, the use of paneling decreased, although the dado continued popular. In rooms with paneling it was customary, until about 1765, to use the type found in the earlier houses, that with a beveled raised panel, its center flush with the surrounding rails and stiles and with a quarter round molding. Then about 1765 it became the fashion to use larger and fewer panels.

"Birchlands," Woodbury, Connecticut, a central chimney house, shows a most interesting development of paneling. The big reception room, which is the oldest part of the house; the library, which at one time was the kitchen; and the south master bedroom, all show sheathing—horizontal in the first two rooms, vertical in the bedroom. The dining room and the north master bedroom show paneling of the chimney wall with the beveled raised panels described above. There is also a paneled dado in the dining room with panels of varying sizes, probably dependent upon wood avail-

able for use. In the north bedroom there is a double closet over the fireplace and a closet at the side, both with paneled doors. In the drawing
room the paneling of the chimney wall is more sophisticated, probably
because this room was the last to be finished, with larger panels and with
interesting pilasters at either corner of the fireplace with five grooves. This
room also has a cornice. Like so many houses, "Birchlands" was added to
and enlarged at various times, the first one-room structure having been
built in the very late seventeenth century and the other sections added and
completed during the next fifty years.

As the eighteenth century advanced doorways, window casings, and
cornices became more elaborate. Arched doorways were occasionally
used, and from about 1725 to 1760 cupboards with arched doors flanking
the fireplace became common. Sometimes there were open semicircular
niches instead of these cupboards. Generally the square-headed door was
used until about 1760, when it became customary to treat important
doors with a frieze and cornice at least, usually with a broken triangular
pediment. Even at this time, however, the window casings were seldom
embellished with more than an architrave. In some sections interior
paneled shutters were used, the paneling in conformity with that in the
rest of the room and folding into the window jambs when not in use. In
the more pretentious houses the "orders" were used freely within the
house itself, although in less important dwellings they were limited to the
fireplace unit.

The fireplace has been left until last, but it was still the most important feature of any principal room. At this time it became smaller in
size, seldom wider than four feet, and usually wider than high. For a long
time it remained without a mantel shelf, depending solely for embellishment upon the bolection molding that framed it. By 1750, however, it
was customary for the fireplace opening to have a special overmantel.
This was of two kinds. If the fireplace was flush with the wall, this overmantel was often a single large panel topped by an architrave. If it was
built with a chimney breast extending out into the room and up to the
ceiling, it usually had pilasters on either side and other architectural embellishments. The fireplace openings often had marble facings, and by the

middle of the century mantelpieces made entirely of marble were being imported.

Floors were more carefully laid than in the Early American house. Boards were selected with more attention for this purpose and were narrower, while in some of the finest homes there were floors of marquetry.

In addition to the increasing use of wallpapers, damask, chintz, and other fabrics for wall coverings, the painting of walls and woodwork came into fashion. In some houses the plastered walls were left unpainted, with colored woodwork. The Governor's Palace at Williamsburg, as well as other buildings there that have been authentically restored, and rooms in the American Wing at the Metropolitan Museum of Art in New York City all show very conclusively that white was not the popular color in Colonial days for woodwork and walls. The colors used are rich, of great variety, and there are many of the dark tones so popular today for backgrounds. Apparently wood paneling and trim were left unpainted only when they were of exceptionally fine quality.

I wonder if this is not the place to make a suggestion to those who are beginning to study architectural and decorating periods for pleasure or to enable them to work out their own decorating schemes with more understanding; to those who are learning to recognize the various steps in the development of building and decorating in our country, the corelationship between houses and their decoration, their furnishings and accessories. The reading and studying of books will give a basis of knowledge, and a very helpful and necessary basis, but no reading or studying will ever give the understanding gained from seeing properly decorated and arranged interiors. For this seeing I recommend that you first study those houses that have been restored and decorated by experts. There are several at Williamsburg. There are the many rooms in the American Wing at the Metropolitan Museum of Art in New York City. There are houses all over the country, open to the public for a small fee, that have been restored and furnished within the tenets of the period in which they were built. In the Appendix there is a list of houses in all the New England states. In this list is given the date the house was built and notes as to whether it is furnished in the period and what it contains. From this list you may select houses of whatever period you wish to study, whether it be Early American or Victorian.

Everyone enjoys the tours of old houses so popular today, especially in New England. They give a wonderful opportunity to study privately owned homes of the various periods, and of seeing how others handle their decorating and furnishing problems. Often, however, these tours are confusing to the beginner, because so few of the houses are decorated and furnished in accordance with the simplest rules regarding the period in which they were constructed and which they claim to represent. I doubt if anyone is more lenient than I am regarding adaptation within a general keying. I detest regimentation even in period decorating. But I do inwardly rebel when I see a small Early American house with ceilings lower than seven feet, with tiny-paned windows, and small irregular rooms furnished with massive American Empire. Neither is it more pleasing to see a room decorated with beautiful Colonial wallpaper, damask hangings, Chippendale or Sheraton furniture—even if they are reproductions—with a ceiling supported by rough-hewn beams brought in from the barn by some enthusiastic novice. It is even more disconcerting when these beams are painted. I certainly believe that if a homemaker wants a Victorian cozy corner of the brash Gay Nineties or rough-hewn beams and corner posts of the crudest Early American sheds or barns in her formal Colonial drawing room, she should have them, but I maintain that these houses should not be shown to hundreds of people as outstanding examples of the periods they purport to represent when they represent only the individual decorator's desire for a certain something—"quaintness," perhaps.

As your knowledge increases, you learn to discriminate. In the beginning study authentic exteriors and interiors and then you will discover new interest in all decorating—you will know what has been done well and what has been done poorly.

In perspective, then, the most important differences within the homes of the Colonial period and those of the Early American were formal beauty of furniture and accessories and formal arrangement of rooms to give more convenience and privacy. It is doubtful whether any but the hardiest of us could live with any degree of comfort or happiness in one of the Early American homes of the period, at least for any length of time. But most of us, I think, could do so in one of the well-designed and beautifully furnished and decorated homes of the period between 1720 and the Revolution. True we would miss electricity, central heating, and modern plumbing. But unless we had broken completely with the traditional in our decorating schemes and were happy only with utility as the apex of achievement within our homes, these houses of the Colonial period (call them Georgian or eighteenth century, if you will) would please us. Today we can follow the decorating and furnishing as they were done in the Colonial or Federal period much more closely than is possible in the simple and somewhat uncomfortable Early American period and in the overdecorated Victorian period.

In the Colonial period the furniture was chiefly of the Queen Anne type until the middle of the century. This style had just begun to seep into the colonies when the Queen died in 1714, but it continued popular until it was slowly superseded by the Chippendale type. The Colonial cabinetmaker and his customers liked the Queen Anne furniture, and it remained in vogue here long after it had gone out of fashion in England, much longer than could be accounted for by the usual lapse of time in style fashions between the two countries. In many of the homes of this period there would also be some of the less comfortable oak furniture of the William and Mary style which had preceded the Queen Anne as a survival from that era.

At this time the merchants and shipowners were a prosperous generation demanding convenience and comfort in their surroundings. They also demanded beauty, and their furniture was no longer chosen because it was a necessity. It was selected for beauty of design and workmanship and it still followed closely the furniture being produced and used in England, with the usual lapse of thirty or more years in time from its appearance in England to its advent in the colonies. It also remained popular in the colonies for an equal length of time after it had been superseded by another style in England.

At the beginning of this period some walnut was used for the finest cabinetwork, but for most of the furniture the cabinetmakers used maple, cherry, and pine. Then Cuban mahogany was brought in from the West Indies, along with slaves, and the beauty of this wood for the making of furniture was quickly recognized by the craftsmen. In fact, mahogany was used in the colonies at least ten years earlier than it was used in England.

The Chippendale type of furniture was the last important style of the Colonial period. Although Adam, Hepplewhite, and Sheraton were working in England, their influence did not have any great effect upon Colonial designs until after the Revolution.

In the important homes of the Colonial period, then, and to a lesser degree in the simpler homes, there was a formal, well-organized interior house. The doors, windows, chimney walls and fireplaces, the dados, paneling, and cornices were all treated in an academic manner. The walls were papered with scenic, Chinese, or other wallpaper, or hung with damask, chintz, or other suitable material; or there were walls of unpainted plaster with painted woodwork or with plaster and woodwork both painted. There was less white woodwork than colored, and among the favorite colors were gray-blue, greens of many shades, mustard, cream, brown, olive-green, and sometimes a deep brownish red. There were draperies of damask, brocatelle, chintz, and velvet. Venetian blinds were used but always painted the color of the woodwork. Floors were in keeping with this new elegance. For floor coverings there were Oriental and Aubusson rugs, and in the simpler homes as well as in the bedrooms of almost any house there were hooked or loomed rag rugs. In the homes of the most prosperous there was the beautiful rococo mahogany furniture in the new Chippendale style with elaborate carvings and wonderful brasses.

There were highboys; lowboys for dressing tables often as companion pieces to the highboys; sofas upholstered in velvet, damask, or needlepoint; day beds and couches either upholstered or with loose cushions; footstools; chests of drawers; desks; tables of all kinds, including the new fashionable tea tables, the Pembroke tables often used for breakfast, the drop-leaf dining-room tables, night stands and candle stands; tall clocks to replace somewhat the small portable ones previously available; fire screens; the Chippendale type wall brackets; mirrors and more mirrors; tall-posted beds with elaborate draperies; quantities of silver on the long side tables—no sideboards as yet—beautiful china and ornaments from France, England, and China; imported crystal; innumerable brass, silver, and crystal chandeliers, side lights, and candelabra; and on the walls paintings, portraits, color prints, and mezzotints. The Colonial house glowed with brightness and color.

Silver was usually domestic unless brought from home by the colonist, since from the earliest days there were outstanding silversmiths in the colonies—Coney, Hull, Revere, Dummer, and Hurd, to mention but a few. The Colonial house and its furnishings formed a fitting background for the costumes of the day.

Can you picture anything more graciously beautiful than one of these classically perfect rooms on the night of a banquet—the long table with its snow-white cloth, the shining silver-and-crystal candelabra holding a myriad lighted candles, the silver, the china, and the crystal? And around this lighted and gleaming board the men and women in their gorgeous costumes, elaborately coiffed, and sparkling with jewels. Perhaps it would be equaled only by the beauty of the ballroom in the shimmering light of hundreds of candles in chandeliers and side lights, their lusters agleam, as these beautifully costumed men and women wove to and fro in the cadenced measures of the stately minuet to the wailing of a violin and the thin tinkle of the harpsichord.

Don't make the mistake, however, of thinking of these men and women of the late eighteenth century as merely gay, well-dressed manikins. They played hard but they also worked hard. Like it or not, these were the days of smuggling, of slave-running, and of that form of piracy called privateering, and the foundation of many a huge fortune that lies back of the industrial development in New England was begun in this way as well as in legitimate trade. Youths of eighteen often mastered a ship on the long and perilous trip around the Cape of Good Hope to Cathay and did a good job of it. Midshipmen in the small armed vessels were often no more than twelve years old, and Jennings in his fascinating story *The Salem Frigate* tells of the heroism of these youngsters in battle.

England's only interest in the colonies was economic. To her they meant trade, raw materials, and income from taxation. The royal governors seldom had any interest in the welfare of the colonists. And yet these colonists were not a subject people and resented being treated as such— taxation without representation was the very basis of the Revolution. Habits of thought change slowly, and it was not easy for these men and women to rebel against the mother country. Many did not. Some remained neutral, neither helping nor hindering in the struggle that came so quickly as the century reached the three-quarter mark. When it did come, however, many showed the spirit that was within. Gone were the frivolous parties—except among the Tories, and many of them found it best to trek to Canada unless they lived in a town occupied by the British troops. Those who fought and won the war did so with little equipment, with few men against what seemed overwhelming odds, with much suffering and disease. And the women fought on at home, caring alone for their children, making ammunition, supplying clothing for the Army, and at times even fighting. Liberty to live as they chose, to carry on free trade, to worship as they pleased, to have a voice in their government were as necessary to them as life.

Today in Portsmouth, New Hampshire, you will find an unequaled opportunity to study houses of all periods, since there are many of each of the first three architectural and decorating periods open to the public, and then if you care to travel another sixty miles to Portland, Maine, you can see an outstanding example of Victorian in the Victorian mansion on the corner of Park and Danforth streets.

In Portsmouth the house representing in its entirety the Early American type is the Jackson house, built in 1664 by Richard Jackson. This house remained in the same family until 1926, when it was sold to the Society for the Preservation of New England Antiquities. It is a central chimney house with an interesting lean-to in the rear extending to the ground—quite unusual—and with a western lean-to and an eastern ell. This is the oldest house in Portsmouth.

The McPhedris or Warner house was built by Captain Archibald McPhedris, a Scotch merchant, between 1722 and 1728. He married

Sarah Wentworth, one of Governor John Wentworth's sixteen children. Captain McPhedris died in 1728, leaving one daughter, Mary, who married Jonathan Warner. This Mary McPhedris Warner died childless, and when Jonathan remarried, this beautiful old house passed out of the McPhedris family. There are portraits of Mary Wentworth McPhedris and Mary McPhedris Warner by Blackburn.

Other houses to visit, if possible, are the Boardman-Marvin house with its Lady of the Lake wallpaper and its McIntire mantels and doors; the Moffatt-Ladd house with its Grinling Gibbon mantel; the Lear house on Hunking Street, built in 1760, a house at which Washington called on occasion, since Tobias Lear became tutor for Martha Washington's children; the Governor John Langdon Mansion Memorial built in 1784, where Washington visited and which he described as the "handsomest house in Portsmouth" (this house has not only beautiful paneling and antiques but an old-time garden); and the Wentworth-Gardner house, built in 1760 by Madam Mark Hunking Wentworth, a perfect example of Georgian architecture with fine carving and old scenic wallpapers.

Privately owned but still the most romantic house in Portsmouth is the Governor Benning Wentworth house at Little Harbor, about two miles from the center of Portsmouth. The earliest part of this house was built about 1695, but it was added to until by 1750 it was the most important dwelling in New Hampshire. Benning Wentworth was a royal governor for twenty-five years—the longest period any royal governor served—but resigned in 1766 because the colonists resented his strong allegiance to England. He died in 1770, and Martha, his widow, married another Wentworth, Colonel Michael. In 1789 General Washington was their guest in this house. In the council chamber here Governor Wentworth presided at the council meetings during his entire administration.

But the tale of Governor Benning Wentworth, his great house, and his marriage to Martha Hilton is much more romantic as told by Longfellow in his *Tales of a Wayside Inn*. Let him tell you the story. We will omit the first half, but if the reader is interested, he may read the entire poem in the second part of the *Tales* as told by the poet. It is entitled *Lady Wentworth*.

For this was Governor Wentworth, driving down
To Little Harbor, just beyond the town,
Where his Great House stood looking out to sea,
A goodly place, where it was good to be.

It was a pleasant mansion, an abode
Near and yet hidden from the great highroad,
Sequestered among trees, a noble pile,
Baronial and colonial in its style;
Gables and dormer-windows everywhere,
And stacks of chimneys rising high in air,—
Pandaean pipes, on which all winds that blew
Made mournful music the whole winter through.
Within, unwonted splendors met the eye,
Panels, and floors of oak, and tapestry;
Carved chimney-pieces, where on brazen dogs
Reveled and roared the Christmas fires of logs;
Doors opening into darkness unawares,
Mysterious passages, and flights of stairs;
And on the walls, in heavy gilded frames,
The ancestral Wentworths with Old-Scripture names.

Such was the mansion where the great man dwelt,
A widower and childless; and he felt
The loneliness, the uncongenial gloom,
That like a presence haunted every room;
For though not given to weakness, he could feel
The pain of wounds, that ache because they heal.

The years came and the years went,—seven in all,
And passed in cloud and sunshine o'er the Hall;
The dawns their splendor through its chambers shed,
The sunsets flushed its western windows red;
The snow was on its roofs, the wind, the rain;
Its woodlands were in leaf and bare again;
Moons waxed and waned, the lilacs bloomed and died,
In the broad river ebbed and flowed the tide,
Ships went to sea, and ships came home from sea,
And the slow years sailed by and ceased to be.

And all these years had Martha Hilton served
In the Great House, not wholly unobserved:
By day, by night, the silver crescent grew,
Though hidden by clouds, her light still shining through;
A maid of all work, whether coarse or fine,
A servant who made service seem divine!
Through her each room was fair to look upon;
The mirrors glistened, and the brasses shone,
The very knocker on the outer door,
If she but passed, was brighter than before.

And now the ceaseless turning of the mill
Of time, that never for an hour stands still,
Ground out the Governor's sixtieth birthday,
And powdered his brown hair with silver-gray.
The robin, the forerunner of the spring,
The bluebird with his jocund caroling,
The restless swallows building in the eaves,
The golden buttercups, the grass, the leaves,
The lilacs tossing in the winds of May,
All welcomed this majestic holiday!
He gave a splendid banquet, served on plate,
Such as became the Governor of the State,
Who represented England and the King,
And was magnificent in everything.
He had invited all his friends and peers,—
The Pepperels, the Langdons, and the Lears,
The Sparhawks, the Penhallows, and the rest;
For why repeat the name of every guest?

But I must mention one in bands and gown,
The rector there, the Reverend Arthur Brown
Of the Established Church; with smiling face
He sat beside the Governor and said grace;
And then the feast went on, as others do,
But ended as none other I e'er knew.

When they had drunk the King, with many a cheer,
The Governor whispered in a servant's ear,

Who disappeared, and presently there stood
Within the room, in perfect womanhood,
A maiden, modest and yet self-possessed,
Youthful and beautiful, and simply dressed.
Can this be Martha Hilton? It must be!
Yes, Martha Hilton, and no other she!
Dowered with the beauty of her twenty years,
How ladylike, how queenlike she appears;
The pale, thin crescent of the days gone by
Is Dian now in all her majesty!
Yet scarce a guest perceived that she was there,
Until the Governor, rising from his chair,
Played slightly with his ruffles, then looked down,
And said unto the Reverend Arthur Brown:
"This is my birthday; it shall likewise be
My wedding-day; and you shall marry me!"

The listening guests were greatly mystified,
None more so than the rector, who replied:
"Marry you? Yes, that were a pleasant task,
Your Excellency; but to whom? I ask."
The Governor answered: "To this lady here";
And beckoned Martha Hilton to draw near.
She came and stood, all blushes, at his side.
The rector paused. The impatient Governor cried:
"This is the lady; do you hesitate?
Then I command you as Chief Magistrate."
The rector read the service loud and clear:
"Dearly beloved, we are gathered here,"
And so on to the end. At his command
On the fourth finger of her fair left hand
The Governor placed the ring; and that was all:
Martha was Lady Wentworth of the Hall!

FEDERAL—1790–1830

THE REVOLUTION was won in America. In the new Republic, however, conditions were confused and awry. The lot of the little people was not to be envied, and in 1787 there was Shays' Rebellion in Massachusetts as well as uprisings in New Hampshire.

Salem, Massachusetts, which we have selected for the detailed study of this period, was the only town in New England that had increased in wealth and importance during the Revolution. This was largely owing to the fact that she had opened her warehouses and wharves to the merchants and shipowners of Boston, free of charge, when Boston Harbor had been blockaded by the British. During the Revolution the hammering from the shipyards was heard from early morning until late at night as all Salem helped build the fighting frigates and the little trading boats— growing wealthy in the process—and making more money as these tiny ships sailed every ocean, trading, smuggling, and privateering. By 1800 Salem was the wealthiest city of its size in the whole country.

In 1807 came the deadly embargo of Jefferson, when no ship could leave port. This embargo was imposed by the federal government because the English captured the vessels and impressed their crews. Then was Salem and the other shipping towns quiet and dejected, with ships idle in the harbor, their sails furled. The offices of the shipowners and merchants were closed, the taverns along the water front without customers, and long lines of people, hungry and forlorn, waited for the meager rations handed out at the soup kitchens. Some few ships fortunate enough to be outside the home port when the embargo was imposed did not return but traded between foreign ports, picking up a cargo here and there as they could; given up as lost or captured until the happy day of their appearance in the home harbor after the lifting of the embargo in 1809. And then, all too soon came the War of 1812. This, however, was somewhat of a boon to the shipbuilding towns, and again the sound of hammering and the smell of white pine wafted over the town from the shipyards. But never was Salem again to know the prosperity of 1800.

SOCIAL LIFE IN SALEM

We know little of the common people in Salem at this time except that the welfare of every person in town, from the youngest to the oldest, was dependent upon the shipbuilding and trading. Even as these economic factors bound the people together, politics drove a deep chasm between the Federalists on one side and the Republicans on the other. One's allegiance to one party or the other did not depend upon one's social position. Heading one side were the Derbys and opposing them, as leaders of the other group, were the Crowninshields, both important shipping families.

The merchants and shipowners were the social leaders, but even the social life of the town was strictly divided by the two political parties. As a rule these men were not descended from the wealthy Colonial families and few had been educated at Harvard. For those who followed the sea the years necessary for acquiring a college education seemed time ill spent. And without doubt the experience as supercargoes and masters of ships that sailed to all parts of the world was a broader and more fitting education than would have been gained from books in any college. They learned well from this hard taskmaster, the world, and while still young in years many of them headed businesses with widespread ramifications. Not only did they have the big warehouses and spacious homes in Salem, or some other port, and their wealth-producing ships (at one time Elias Hasket Derby had eighty afloat), they often held properties in England and on the continent, they maintained warehouses and sometimes homes at Wampoa or Macao in China, and they had foreign agents all over the world.

Generally these sea captains were men of culture and learning—whether they had been to Harvard or not—thoroughly acquainted with the Bible, with Shakespeare, and the somber Milton, and not unfamiliar with the current writers of their day. These books were carried to sea on the long voyages and read and reread. Accompanying a virile robustness was a real gentleness of soul, else they would not have searched every country they visited for beautiful flowers and shrubs to bring home for their lovely box-bordered gardens. And they valued education, for New England is dotted with the schools and academies they founded. Indeed, taste was generally high in the early nineteenth century.

Life was not unpleasant for the families of these merchants and ship-owners. Slaves brought from the Indies cared for the big square Salem houses, kept the gardens trim, and drove the gentlemen to and from their countinghouses and their wives and daughters to their fashionable teas and other engagements. Whenever a boat returned from a long trip to some foreign land, there was great rejoicing and not a little rivalry among the ladies over the treasures they received. For their gardens came seeds and slips and roots from everywhere, and even today in the Salem gardens grow the sweet tea roses from China, the damask roses from Jerusalem, and other old-time flowers from Turkey, India, and England. On one boat a cage of live monkeys arrived, a present to the children from an Indian rajah, and once Jacob Crowninshield returned with an elephant, the first ever seen in America. For the ladies there were brocades and fans from France; fragile porcelains and colorful lacquers from China; resonant, sparkling glassware from Ireland and England; shawls from India; coral jewelry from Italy; and choice tea to be sipped from the handleless teacups as they gossiped before a gentle fire in a beautiful high-ceilinged drawing room with its carved fireplace mantel by McIntire, its rich silken window hangings, and fine Oriental or Aubusson rugs. Social life in Salem, however, was simple and not to be compared with the more formal society of Boston, where at this time a group of merchant princes lived in oriental splendor, with elaborate dinners and huge private balls.

The assemblies held fortnightly in Hamilton Hall for the Federalists and in Washington Hall for the Republicans were the important functions for the young people of Salem during the winter season. In the summer picnics were popular at either Baker's or Misery Island. Often the gentlemen spent a short time fishing, while the ladies, accompanied by the slaves to do the work of preparation, awaited them on the island. Supper usually consisted of a delicious chowder cooked over a driftwood fire, of clams and lobsters baked in the salty seaweed, and some of the recently available tropical fruits for dessert. Then the couples would wander off in groups along the beach, and finally the slaves would row them back to Salem by moonlight. On Sundays, unless you were really ill, you attended church. Although no law at this time made church attendance necessary, you were severely criticized for not going.

One of the really exciting events for everyone was the launching of a ship. Then all roads leading to the shipyard were crowded with men and women afoot and in carriages on their way to this popular affair. On the platform sat the owner, the committee, the guests and their ladies, all attired in their best. The band played and the cannon at the fort blasted forth. Then the launchers could be heard pounding away at the blocks that held the ship's keel in place. The owner made a speech. The pounding mauls ceased and the hull could be seen to shiver and then to slide slowly forward. As it gathered speed, no one breathed, fearful lest something might go wrong and the ship founder as she hit the water. As she righted herself, the band played, the cannon boomed, the people cheered, and another ship would soon be ready to sail the seven seas to bring more wealth to her Salem owners.

Most of the important families kept horses, and in the summer there were drives to Nahant and in the winter sleighing in the brisk, stinging, pungent air. The air of Salem was like none other, especially on a warm summer day, scented as it was with a mixture of innumerable odors. Foremost was the salty sea smell blown in from the harbor, but this was tinged with the scent of spices from the faraway Spice Islands, the white pine from the shipyards, the hemp from ropes piled on the docks, codfish drying on the racks on the beach, the elusive smell of rum or sandlewood

from boats newly arrived after long trips to distant places, of coffee, and
of fruits ripening in the sun.

At this time the houses and their furnishings were showing the effect
of the new simplicity, the fashion in Adam's London, and this found an
echo in the costumes of both men and women. The older merchants and
shipowners felt more comfortable in their knee breeches and elaborate
waistcoats with silver buckles and buttons. But the younger generation,
many of whom were as much at home in many ports of the Old World or
the Far East as in Salem, had tight-fitting trousers looped under the in-
step. With these they wore coats shorter in the waist, with long tails in
back and closely hugging the figure. No longer was powdered hair
fashionable although it was still dressed in a queue and tied with a black
ribbon. Some of the older men continued to wear a cocked hat, but the
young man sported a soft one with a low crown and straight brim. Waistcoats were cut low and shirt fronts were beruffled. Stocks were worn
around the neck the ends tied under the chin in a bow. A greatcoat with
many capes was used in cold weather. Can you picture a Beau Brummell
of the day in tight fawn trousers, bottle-green coat, beautifully ruffled
shirt front with stock, a greatcoat of red with several capes, and topping
the whole ensemble a gray beaver hat? All this elegance, however, was
much less than the magnificence of the previous period.

As the dress of the male became less elaborate, so did that of the
women. They discarded their petticoats and hooped skirts; their heavy
brocades and rustling silks. They wore delicate high-waisted Empire
gowns of soft clinging crepe de Chine, gauze, or satin. These were made
with narrow skirts that hung to the ground, trimmed with many tucks,
folds of silk, or rich embroidery. The bodices were cut down to a danger-
ous degree, both for health and modesty, and the shoulders were usually
bare. No longer did the ladies wear wigs but pinned their hair high on
the head with a comb or ribbon, with little curls escaping in bangs or
hanging back of each ear. Their hats fitted closely to the head, and they
wrapped themselves in long cloaks or beautiful shawls from the Indies.
They all had fans from China or France and pearls and jade from the
Orient. Young girls still dressed much like their mothers, and they often

had their long dresses of striped Chinese nankeen or of cambric in wonderful yellows and blues.

ARCHITECTURE

Although books of building designs from England for carpenters and builders were still important, they were used less and less in America as the professional architect increased in number and as American building books became available. At this time, however, new publications from abroad introduced the Adam style popular in England for many years, and from the beginning of the Federal period until some years after 1800 architecture, particularly in New England, was directly influenced by this new classicism. The older Colonial house type based upon an English Renaissance, or Jones-Wren interpretation of Palladian tradition, by no means disappeared. It remained as the basis of much of the building of the early years following the Revolution. In many instances the details alone of the houses built at this time proclaimed the coming of a new classicism.

If you remember, the architects, builders, and decorators of western Europe and England had been greatly inspired by the excavations at Herculaneum and Pompeii in the middle of the eighteenth century. Robert Adam on his trip to France and Italy about that time had seen these ruins and all his subsequent work showed how greatly he had been impressed by them. Upon his return to England he was appointed architect to the King, and with his brothers he organized a company called "The Adelphi," a Greek word meaning brothers. The brothers then built a crescent block of buildings in Portland Place, London, which they called "The Adelphi," and soon everything Adam was the fashion in England. From that time on he had a greater influence upon architecture and decorating than even Inigo Jones or Sir Christopher Wren.

France slowly superseded England as the source of architectural influence in the new Republic. The people were irritated with England and sympathized with France in her struggle for freedom. This spiritual separation from the mother country was felt less in New England than in the South with its Thomas Jefferson. At this time, however, the carpenters and architects of the new Republic began to contribute something to their work not inspired by either England or France but entirely American— not original in concept, perhaps, but in interpretation. What is usually considered originality at any time is often nothing more than a matter of interpretation. This slight beginning of independence grew throughout the entire Federal period and that of the Greek Revival, a style that became important in America much earlier than a similar return to Greek classicism in either England or France and which grew to much greater proportions in this country. Never before or since has there been less dependence upon Europe for inspiration.

In Federal New England architectural history the two most important men were Charles Bulfinch of Boston and Samuel McIntire of Salem, both ardent disciples of Adam. Samuel McIntire, the less important of the two, was born in Salem in 1757. We know little of his early life. He came from a family of carpenters and wood carvers, and it is probable that during his youth he carved figureheads and other parts of ships being constructed in the Salem shipyards. Suddenly, however, in 1782, he came into prominence as the architect and builder of the lovely Peirce-Nichols house. Part of this building was not completed until 1801, and in this the details are in McIntire's charming Adam-influenced style. The earlier part is in the Georgian manner. This is a three-story white-clapboarded house with a delicate balustrade atop a nearly flat roof. A one-story addition in the rear has a series of broad doors with elliptical fanlights. Along the street is an exquisitely executed fence with urn-topped gateposts. The entire group of house and outbuildings followed the Adam ideal of design and proportion and was the finest architectural group in wood in New England at that time.

McIntire's home was at 29 Summer Street, and in the rear of this he opened a large woodworking shop, employing several of his brothers —without intent, perhaps, following in the footsteps of his English master, Robert Adam. It is probable that he drew the simple designs for his houses and that some of his brothers did the actual building. He himself did the carving of the beautiful doorways, mantels, and interior trim.

In the years between his first house in 1782 and his last in 1810 McIntire confined his work almost entirely to Salem, and during that time Salem was at the peak of its prosperity. So McIntire, the outstanding builder in his town, was commissioned by the wealthy merchants and shipowners to build their mansions. By the time of his death, in 1811, he had designed and constructed some twenty, many along Chestnut Street, and not one was destroyed by the disastrous fire of 1914. The Gardner-Pingree house, built in 1810, was his last and most beautiful.

McIntire was a simple man, never attaining the position of social equality with those for whom he built such beautiful homes, but he evidently was not without a desire for recognition as more than a carpenter builder, for we find him entering the competition for the National Capitol in Washington, and his design was that of a competent architect. We do not know how keen was his disappointment when his plan was not selected, but neither was that of Thomas Jefferson, for that matter, a man to whom is assigned much credit for architectural advance in America, particularly in the South.

Throughout his career McIntire remained a follower of Adam as interpreted by Bulfinch, a man but a few years younger than he but possessing the social position, the education, the wealth, and a national prominence never attained by McIntire.

Charles Bulfinch was born in Boston in 1763, the son of a prominent physician. He graduated from Harvard in 1781 and shortly afterward went to Europe to study architecture. In 1787 he returned to Boston and became a part owner of the *Columbia*, the first ship to make the trip around Cape Horn to China with a cargo of furs.

At first Bulfinch worked as a dilettante, designing houses for friends without remuneration. His first important undertaking was the designing and building, partly financed by himself, of the first block of houses in New England. This was the Tontine Franklin Crescent on Franklin Street in Boston, no longer in existence. This block was built in the crescent form not uncommon in England, following the style initiated by the Adam brothers in The Adelphi in Portland Place, London. In the building of this Tontine, however, Bulfinch lost much of his money and was forced to become a professional architect, the first in America.

In New England Bulfinch was largely responsible for the introduction of the new style as developed by Adam in England—a style almost too delicate for this growing people in a new country; a style with great charm consisting, as it did, of slender columns, light cornices, chaste balustrades, fanlights and side lights, metal traceries, and beautiful mantels with festoons, urns, swags, classical medallions, and paterae. Although Bulfinch lived until 1844, he seems never to have succumbed

Federal Square House

to the influence of the Greek Revival which swept the country during his lifetime. His only building which shows this influence to any degree is the Maine State Building at Augusta, Maine, constructed in 1828. From 1818 to 1830 he spent most of his time carrying out the design of Dr. William Thornton for the rebuilding of the Capitol in Washington, which had been burned by the British in 1814. Among the best of his buildings are the State House in Boston and some of the houses still standing around Beacon, Park, and Tremont streets in the same city.

In addition to these two outstanding men in New England there were innumerable architects all over the eastern seaboard designing and building along the same general lines but differing in each locality from the baroque of Russell Warren of Bristol, Rhode Island, who designed so many houses there around 1810 for the prosperous merchants, to the handsome Greek houses of Belfast, Maine, designed and built by unknown men but men of good training.

One of the most important persons—and there were many others—in the spreading of architectural designs, particularly throughout New England during this period, was Asher Benjamin (1773–1845). He published several books on building, and his *The American Builder's Companion* went through fourteen editions between 1830 and 1857. These had a widespread distribution, and their influence lasted at least until the middle of the century in conservative New England. Like Bulfinch and McIntire, Benjamin was little influenced by the new Greek classicism with its temple-form ideal. By the time of his death this had become almost a national style.

In New England, then, during this period, dominated by Bulfinch and in Salem by his devoted pupil Samuel McIntire, the typical house was square and of three stories. At times, in the cities, some were built four stories high, and in Boston one even reached the height of five stories, a veritable Federal skyscraper. In the country districts, however, the usual house was still two stories high.

In Salem these four-square houses were commonly of white pine, although brick was becoming more popular, with a low-pitched roof edged about with a wooden balustrade. Often there was a cupola with a captain's walk atop the roof from which the shipowner or the master's family could watch for homecoming boats. However, it was the doorway which held one's attention, as this was the important feature of the house and located in the center of the front façade. McIntire put his love of beautiful carving, his very soul, into his doorways. Occasionally a Salem house was built at this time with the gable end facing the street.

A portico, and porticoes were of great variety, became almost universal in New England after 1790. Although the semicircular fanlights of Adam were common until about 1800, Bulfinch and McIntire were using an elliptical type as early as 1793, and these remained popular until about 1820. These fanlights and side lights were often of rare beauty and many were elaborately leaded.

Some of the pretentious houses in New England now had their façades covered with smooth boards with the edges matching instead of clapboards or shingles. This was a favorite treatment of Bulfinch, and McIntire added such a front to the Pickman house in Salem as early as 1789. Brick became more common for houses in New England at this time although the vogue for stucco, which appeared in other parts of America around 1800, never became popular. Instead, the New Englanders built the house of brick and painted it gray.

Within the house the change was not too great from that of the Colonial period. The oval, round, or elliptical room, so much a favorite

House with Gable End Facing Street

of Robert Adam, was introduced by Bulfinch. The main stairway was usually in a separate compartment to insure more privacy to the upper floors, although Bulfinch and McIntire built an occasional elliptical stairway in the entrance hall, sometimes extending through two floors. This stairway was a thing of simple beauty and is often used today by modern architects who perhaps would have one believe it of their particular inspiration. The former elaborate twisted balusters—so appropriate in the Jeremiah Lee mansion in Marblehead—were replaced by simple tapered shafts often of remarkable delicacy.

The floor plan of this Federal house continued to have four rooms to a floor as its usual arrangement, with a transverse hall and at times a bisecting, less important hallway. Secondary stairways were more common.

On the upper floors smaller rooms to be used as dressing rooms were often included as well as alcoves for beds. Ceilings remained high and were decorated with delicate cornices, sometimes carved but often of "compo," a composition introduced by Adam.

The interior decoration became simplified. Paneling tended to disappear and the wall surfaces were usually of painted plaster above a simple wainscot capped by a delicate chair rail or covered with imported wallpaper or rich brocade. At times even the wainscot was omitted. Wallpapers were scenic, Chinese, or of delicate colors with a French influence. Stripes, swags, medallions, or other designs popular in the French Directoire and Empire were usual. As fashionable as wall coverings, however, were plain painted walls in shades of white, gray, buff, pale rose, or Adam green. Pure-white woodwork was more common in this period than the deep blues, greens, reds, and yellows of the Colonial period.

Windows were large, with panes of glass usually 10 x 12 inches or 10 x 14 inches. The effect was one of lightness and delicacy. Gone was the Chippendale style with its suggestion of rococo heaviness. The styles of Hepplewhite and Sheraton, influenced greatly by Adam and brought to America by means of books of furniture designs, became the rage. Simple and delicate elegance was the keynote of all decoration, and the finely tapered or turned legs and the chaste chair backs of these two styles fitted well into the simpler interiors.

In Salem, Samuel McIntire and other good cabinetmakers were constructing beautiful sideboards and desks from the West Indian mahogany, following the designs of Sheraton. In New York City, Duncan Phyfe was making his finest furniture at this time, influenced by both Hepplewhite and Sheraton and later by the Directoire styles from France. Following the French Revolution there was an inpouring of French aristocrats and many good artisans into America, bringing with them as many of their possessions as possible, and this had a definite influence upon furniture making, less, perhaps, in New England than elsewhere in the country. At this time the cabinetmakers were using lighter woods in addition to the rich mahogany, and many fine pieces of furniture were made of satinwood, cherry, maple, and rosewood. There was also much veneering and inlay.

With the declaration of war against England in 1812 a wave of patriotism swept the country, and this was used to advantage by furniture makers as well as other manufacturers. The eagle of Roman and Napoleonic imperialism became Americanized and was used to decorate all manner of articles, from clocks and mirrors to tables and chairs. One house built by Warren in Bristol, Rhode Island, had eagles at regular intervals along the roof balustrade. Stars and stripes were also used in wallpapers and fabrics and in innumerable other decorative accessories.

In these beautiful houses of Salem, as elsewhere in America, the wealthy shipowners and merchants and their families lived a luxurious life surrounded by exquisite furniture and treasures from all over the world, clothed in rich fabrics, and served by innumerable Negro servants. And yet with all this luxury there was no central heating, no plumbing, and no electricity. Cooking was still done at the huge fireplaces and candles and whale-oil lamps were the chief sources of light.

GREEK REVIVAL—1820–1850

T HE SO-CALLED Greek Revival began during the last years of the Federal period and overlapped the Victorian by almost two decades.

In 1801 Thomas Jefferson became President of the United States. In 1787 he had returned from France filled with admiration for the classic —abhorring, as always, the English Palladianism of Inigo Jones and Sir Christopher Wren as expressed in the American Colonial or Georgian— and two years after his return he designed the Virginia State Capitol, using the Maison Carrée at Nîmes, France, as his model. For the first time in America a building was constructed using the temple form in its Jeffersonian or Roman interpretation. About the same time Benjamin Henry Latrobe, a Frenchman who had studied architecture in London where he had been well instructed in the Greek ideal, arrived in America. Shortly thereafter he designed the Bank of Pennsylvania in this same temple design but going back to Greek architecture for his inspiration rather than to the Roman.

Shortly after his election to the presidency, Jefferson created the position of Surveyor of the Public Buildings of the United States and appointed Latrobe to fill it. And with this appointment the temple style of architecture was used almost exclusively for the new buildings constructed by the federal government. This new style, sponsored by Jefferson and furthered by Latrobe, was quite distinct from the architectural style popular in New England at the time, based as it was on English Regency and the delicate designs of the Adam brothers as interpreted by Bulfinch and McIntire.

If this were the story of architecture we would go into the details regarding this new classicism and explain that it was simply another interpretation of the Greek ideal which was at the basis of the English Renaissance, or Georgian, of Inigo Jones and Sir Christopher Wren. You will remember that the English Renaissance had been a part of a so-called rebirth which had begun in Italy in the fifteenth century and had slowly spread over Europe during the sixteenth. This had been a turning away from the Gothic and Romanesque which had held sway in architecture for a thousand years. This English Renaissance was the very basis of our American Colonial. However, during the many years since it had been introduced into England by Jones and embellished by Wren, who was so much influenced by France, it had gathered unto itself much that was English, much that was French, and some that was entirely American. Under Adam's influence it had become emasculated.

Jefferson, repudiating all these interpretations and accretions, looked for inspiration directly to Rome, although it is doubtful whether he was ever entirely free from French influence. This Roman classicism, beloved by Jefferson, had been used in Europe for garden temples and for monuments but never for dwellings. By 1820, however, this classic style had developed, largely through the efforts of Latrobe, into a decided revival of Greek forms, and by the 1830s and 1840s it had become almost a national style.

There were many reasons for the wide acceptance of this new classicism in architecture. This was a period of unrest in the new Republic. The country had lived through some turbulent times. In 1812 there had been a second war with England and the colonists were considerably irritated with the English. The sympathy of the entire country had been offered the French in their revolution, and then the people had been repelled by the highhandedness of Napoleon. In 1821, when the Greeks began their struggle for freedom, the Americans felt a close kinship with them and for their cause, and everything Greek became the fashion of the day. The effect of this espousal was less immediate in the old settlements of New England—Boston, Salem, and Portsmouth—than in the newer sections of the country. Wherever a new town sprang up between 1820 and

1850, or wherever an old town became newly prosperous, there you will find the houses built during those years in the Greek Revival style.

I have mentioned elsewhere that there has always been a close relationship between architecture, furnishings, customs, and costumes, but in this instance no such parallel occurred to any great degree. The Greek Revival fad was most apparent in the construction of buildings and in the naming of towns. There was no important classic revival in the arts, and there is no reason to believe there was any return on the part of many people to

Greek Revival House

the ideals of the classic Greeks in their way of thinking or in their manner of life. Indeed Mrs. Trollope, an Englishwoman who spent some years in America at this time, records with characteristic British candor her distaste for the prudish, smirking women at an art exhibition and the whisky-drinking, tobacco-chewing and -spitting men she met. She remarks caustically of their complete lack of interest in or knowledge of the fine arts. She describes them as a people of loud and vociferous patriotism with a lust for money and ostentation. Obviously she did not meet the other half. She was also completely dissatisfied with this country in which her effort to make a livelihood had failed. At any rate, we can believe that her description of America at this time was true of the masses and thus accept it as indicating no great return to the arts, to the thinking, or to the manners of the ancient Greeks.

And yet there was a developing trend which Hamlin says was "perhaps more completely aesthetic than any American culture before or since." A culture such as he describes, however, would be that of the few and not of the masses. Even in conservative New England as early as 1815 there was a striving for personal freedom and individualism by many people, and there developed many strange groups proclaiming various types of moral and aesthetic tenets.

What were the characteristics of this new house type found wherever a new town arose and along the coast from Maine to Baltimore in the older settlements, where the maritime prosperity of this early nineteenth century created a new moneyed class? Probably the outstanding feature was the portico. In the previous houses a portico, when used, had been a one-story affair. Now it became free-standing, extending the height of the house with four, six, or eight columns. This projecting portico was usually from the front, but in rare instances it extended completely around the building. If, by chance, a house was built without a portico, it had at least corner pilasters or boards. The latter, however, were never mitered, as in the Colonial building.

The door in the Greek Revival house was no longer confined to the center of the front façade. It might be at one side or it might be at the corner. It was square-headed with a rectangular transom above and with narrow vertical side lights. Clapboards or siding were joined with no overlapping. If brick was used for the building, it was generally painted gray. Windowpanes became larger and windows often extended to the floor. The roof was low-pitched, following the Greek temple ideal. Cast-iron balconies, balustrades, window grilles, and various other ornaments were customary.

These Greek Revival houses were of greater variety than those of the Colonial period but called for little originality on the part of the builders, as the Greek models were copied with much care.

Within the house the change was not too great, as the designers did not follow the Greek temple plan for their interiors. There was, however, a new simpleness. Paneling and wall coverings were not used, and the walls were of plain painted plaster. Even the dado was discarded. Ornate plaster decorations were used as cornices, to form panels, and as rosettes from which center-ceiling chandeliers could be suspended. Rooms were high, doorways wide, and principal rooms were often separated by columns, giving a new spaciousness. The architraves of both windows and doors were either reeded or fluted. The fireplace was no longer the important feature of a room. It was very much smaller in size, with marble facing and mantel—sometimes black—and usually carved. Classical figures similar to those used by Wedgwood on his jasper ware were popular for this carving. A gold-framed mirror, rectangular and often divided into three vertical sections, replaced the former overmantel. In fact mirrors were used throughout the house wherever possible.

In many of these simple and severe houses furniture of the Hepplewhite, Sheraton, and early Duncan Phyfe was used, but this was often replaced by the fashionable French Directoire and Empire, and, toward the end of the period, by the more massive American Empire with its huge dressers, secretary desks, wardrobes, enormous sofas, and Gargantuan beds with four tall heavily carved posts.

Beautiful materials were used for upholstery and hangings, many with narrow stripes and some with designs symbolizing the patriotism of the new Republic or the Empire of Napoleon. Although much of this material was of silk, cotton prints from both England and France were very popular, and since the manufacturers of both countries were shrewd enough to print these cottons with designs celebrating the independence of America, they found a wide acceptance among the home decorators. In like manner the potteries of Staffordshire, England, poured quantities of earthenware decorated with similar designs in rich cobalt blue into the American markets. Today these plates and platters decorated with the arms of the states, the landing of Lafayette, and similar subjects bring prices that would stupefy the potters of those days.

With some nostalgia we leave this Federal period and its Greek Revival phase which continues on into the next decades with an ever-waning popularity. In spite of the heaviness which slowly developed in furniture and in the decorative scheme generally, there was a spaciousness and beauty about it that soon disappeared in the clutter and confusion of the following years, 1830 to 1880.

Dickens visited America about this time and in his *American Notes*, published in 1842, he says about Boston:

When I got into the streets upon this Sunday morning, the air was so clear; the houses were so bright and gay; the sign boards were painted in such gaudy colors; the gilded letters were so very golden; the bricks were so very red; the stone was so very white; the blinds and area railings were so very green; the knobs and plates upon the street doors so marvellously bright and twinkling; and all so slight and unsubstantial in appearance—that every thoroughfare in the city looked exactly like a scene in a pantomime. . . .

The city is a beautiful one, and cannot fail, I should imagine, to impress all strangers very favorably. The private dwelling houses are for the most part large and elegant; the shops extremely good; and the public buildings handsome.

In reading this excerpt from Dickens it must be kept in mind that Boston had succumbed very little to the Greek Revival, and that the houses described are those of the Colonial period and the more recent buildings around Beacon and Tremont streets designed by Bulfinch and the other men of his time.

VICTORIAN—1830-1880

HOUSES

In America, as abroad, classicism was followed by romanticism. Here, however, there were several economic factors involved not present in the English scene. America had expanded enormously. Until 1850 her population was predominantly of English stock, but at that time a horde of immigrants, needed in the growing mills and factories, poured into the country from all over Europe. Until the middle of the century the economy of the country had been largely on an agricultural rather than an industrial basis. About then, however, and especially after the Civil War, industry developed at an astounding rate, and with it a society based upon the profits of commercialism. The Colonial tradition and culture of former years were swept away before this industrial expansion, and following the Civil War the entire country was dominated for a long time by the industrial North.

In spite of this new business development and a new social order, much more aggressive and individualist than in earlier periods, fashion in architecture, furnishings, and costumes was still sought abroad. And in spite of protested freedom from English domination, the period has been assigned the name of the English ruler, Victoria. The Greek Revival, which had become almost a national style, was no longer popular. Its simplicity, its severity of line, and its dependence upon the early Greek temple as a model, and its continuance needing an intellectual understanding, placed too many restrictions upon a people demanding only the ostentatious or the quaint.

At this time decorative taste in England had dipped to a very low point, in spite of a goodly number of articulate men and women who should have been able to sway the public trend, but they, too, seem to have capitulated to the fashion of the day without question. Those were the days of the Brownings, George Eliot, Dickens, Thackeray, and Ruskin.

The romantic movement had begun in England with Horatio (Horace) Walpole, 1717–97 and his Gothic villa, Strawberry Hill, and was furthered after 1800 by such men as Byron, Shelley, and Scott, true romantics. But the final impetus was given by Ruskin, who had returned from Italy enamored with Gothic architecture.

Victorian Gothic House

In America, then, we have a growing industrial society where money could be made so easily that the vast majority possessing it had little traditional background, no education, and small experience in handling what they had so quickly acquired—a people eager for every new conceit and invention and looking to Europe and England as the leaders in fashion.

Before 1830 there had persisted in lessening degree a code of restrictions regulating, to a marked extent, the lives and customs of the people. The builders and carpenters, the cabinetmakers and other artisans, had followed certain precedents in their various trades. In architecture, even though the builders and carpenters were not specially trained in the subject, the buildings they constructed were along good architectural lines, with the many books of building designs used as guides. In those days workmen were satisfied to build well without trying stunts of their own. But by 1830 every man in America felt himself an individual and wanted to prove it. And in building and furnishing his house he let his fancy roam far and wide. The country became dotted with Italian villas, Moorish cottages, Swiss chalets, the Queen Anne cottage of William Morris of England, who introduced this type for small houses at the Centennial in 1876, and those sorry houses of Charles Locke Eastlake, F.R.I.B.A., also of England. Eastlake published a book entitled *Hints on Household Taste*, which preached the "honest use of material," a cliché so popular today. If the styles in his book and if his dicta had been followed, his reputation might not be what it is in America today—if he is remembered at all—but his designs and suggestions were taken by a careless people and distorted beyond recognition.

Out of the welter of designs imported and then changed by the desire for something different and bigger than the other fellow had, two general types emerge: the Victorian Gothic and that based upon the contemporary French Renaissance. It is not necessary to go into a lengthy description of these general building types. Suffice it to say that the English Gothic novel, the influence of Ruskin, and the publication of Andrew Jackson Downing's *Cottage Residences* all played their part in popularizing this style with its steep roof, gables, latticed windows, vine-clad eaves, and of course a view. It was given further sanction by Washington Irving, who remodeled Sunnyside at Irvington on the Hudson in this manner.

Contemporary with this picturesque cottage type was the mansard-roof building of the French Renaissance of this period. Survivals of this style today are the brownstone houses of New York City, which were built by the thousands, many of them still standing. Later came the mansions of upper Fifth Avenue and Newport designed by Richard Morris Hunt, using the châteaux of France as his models. Neither must we forget to mention Henry Hobson Richardson, another of the many Americans of his generation trained at the Ecole des Beaux Arts, who, after the financial debacle of 1870, forsook the Victorian Gothic for the Roman-esque with its square towers and solid masonry.

It would be unfair if we did not say that some few builders and some few homeowners during this period did not succumb to the wave of vulgarity. But they were few and far between. The average builder whose only guide was whimsey and a desire for opulence was even helped along his downward course by the industrial development of the age. The scroll saw came into use, and this enabled the homemaker to ornament his house within and without with elaborate brackets, panels, and trim of scroll-work. And the rapidly growing ironworks provided him with cast iron of all kinds to be used on the house for balconies, balustrades, trim and ornaments and for garden seats and garden animals.

INTERIORS

It is not necessary to spend much time describing the interiors of these houses of the Victorian era. Whether it was a rustic cottage, an Italian villa, or a brownstone front, the general effect was the same. The lightness and spaciousness of the Federal period and even of the Greek Revival interior gave way to a somber, heavy feeling in which woodwork was of mahogany, black walnut, or perhaps stained cherry. The most popular interior colors were dull brown, deep blues, strong reds, and greens, and after 1859 a new color named magenta was added to the list, so called after the important battle of that year in the Italian war.

The power loom had been developed and this made carpets and rugs available to everyone. Although hooked and braided rugs on a painted floor remained common until about 1850, after that date practically every home had carpet, usually ingrain with large floral patterns, from wall to wall. Stoves were now obtainable, but there was usually a fireplace in each principal room. Fireplaces had shrunk in size, were of white or black marble with back and sides of cast iron and with an iron basket for burning cannel coal.

Window draperies and curtains were elaborate and heavy. Lace curtains from Birmingham, England, covered the windows, and these were supplemented by draperies of thick cotton weave in sharp green, somber red, or some other deep color, usually tied back with thick cords ending in huge tassels.

As early as 1830 the massive American Empire furniture was competing for popularity and losing with that showing the Gothic influence and after 1840 the rococo Belter. Much of this new furniture was made of black walnut and upholstered with horsehair in plain or patterned weaves. The Jacquard loom was developed, and this caused the market to be flooded with much inexpensive material in complex patterns for decorative purposes. Broad stripes, large florals, and huge medallions were popular. Wallpapers were heavy in design and color and often embossed to represent leather.

Plumbing had lately been introduced, and the homeowners were proud of their luxurious bathrooms with the huge marble washbasin and the tin tub encased in varnished wood.

Ceilings were high, and the murky gaslight from the large chandelier suspended from the center of the ceiling or from side lights added little in the way of enchantment to the room. This feebly flickering light had none of the charm of candles or even of oil lamps.

Let us describe a typical parlor in an average home of the period, a parlor kept tightly closed except on very special occasions—a wedding, a funeral, or a pastoral visit. The woodwork is dark and shiny from many coats of varnish, the paper gay with a garden of flowers. The floor is carpeted from wall to wall with an ingrain carpet with large sprays of roses. The windows are smothered behind coarsely woven lace curtains from England and swathed in dark green draperies and swag bordered with little yellow tassels. From the ceiling hangs an oil lamp with flowered shade and sparkling prisms. Gas is not yet available in this village. In one corner is a reed organ, the pride of the household, and, awaiting the family musician, a whirling organ stool upholstered in red plush. Over the black marble fireplace hangs a portrait of an ancient dame. On the marble shelf is a collection of Staffordshire ornaments, and at either end a Bristol vase containing dried flowers. The furniture is of black walnut, upholstered in horsehair. There is a sofa, with many fancywork pillows and a Paisley shawl, an armchair, several side chairs, and a platform rocker. Under the hanging lamp in the center of the floor there is a round marble-top table holding a musical picture album, some seashells, and many other ornaments. Embroidered or crocheted antimacassars decorate each piece of furniture, and an elaborately embroidered and fringed scarf hangs across the bamboo easel in one corner with its life-sized picture of a child. In another corner is a whatnot with a collection of small cups and saucers. The walls are hung with innumerable pictures, cross-stitched mottoes, family portraits, and some Currier and Ives prints. And over all is the faint odor of sweet-smelling potpourri from the several rose jars filled or added to each summer.

And what about the costumes of the period? One hundred years is but a short space of time, and we still have a remembrance, I think, of the clothes and accessories of this period. There was a certain formality about them. The men might wear checked pantaloons and a derby; they might have flowing whiskers and carry a cane, but they also wore their Prince Alberts and tall silk hats with a certain accustomed air. The bonnets and bustles of the ladies were not without charm, and the satins and silks were not synthetic. Much jewelry was worn in sets of brooch and matching earrings for pierced ears. Pairs of golden bracelets and large cameo pins were popular. Mourning jewelry made from a beloved one's hair was both inexpensive and fashionable. The ladies swooned gracefully, clung gently, and let Father think he was the boss. They were not unhappy, and there was considerable gracious home life.

Today, when there is so much uncertainty about the future, many people are turning back to the traditional in building and in furnishing, or, if not to that, to the simplicity and suaveness of the new American modern. And if you study this new American modern with any degree of thoroughness, you will find in it many things adapted from the traditional, so that it is possible that as the years go on and on the traditional and the new modern will merge into a truly American style.

III

Today's Interiors

WALLPAPERS

[TOP LEFT] Chantung. Courtesy of Thomas Strahan Co. [TOP RIGHT] Italian Scenery. Reproduction from probable Zuber design. Courtesy of W. H. S. Lloyd Company, Inc. [BOTTOM LEFT] Smithfield. Reproduction of stenciled wall. Courtesy of Richard E. Thibaut, Inc. [BOTTOM RIGHT] Ipswich. Courtesy of Thomas Strahan Co.

[ABOVE] Dining room, Webb House, Wethersfield, Connecticut. Woodwork soft grayed green; cupboard painted a subdued rose shade taken from design on draperies, the hand-woven blocked material of which is over two hundred years old. Cherry Hepplewhite table; cherry and mahogany Chippendale chairs. George Washington visited here. Courtesy Webb House [BELOW] Drawing room, Jeremiah Lee Mansion, Marblehead, Massachusetts, 1768. English wallpaper panels depicting classic ruins custom-made for mansion when it was built. Panels painted in tempera in manner of eighteenth-century Italian artist, Piranesi. Colors range from cream through sepia to black. They have never been removed or retouched. Furniture of Queen Anne and Chippendale periods. Courtesy Marblehead Historical Society. Photograph by Samuel Chamberlain

Bedroom, Sir William Johnson Hall, Johnstown, New York, 1762. Original paneling painted soft apricot to complement apricot flock wallpaper. Sir William was a customer of Gilbert Ash, a New York City cabinetmaker, and while the Chippendale chair shown is not attributed to Ash, it is finely designed and executed. Courtesy of New York State Education Department, Division of Archives and History.

Matthews Room, Cape May Historical Society Museum, Cape May Court House, New Jersey. From home of Silas Matthews, Fishing Creek, New Jersey. Outstanding feature of room is wall stenciling, c. 1780. This is done directly on cedar boards, which run horizontally around the room above a paneled dado and chair rail. Stenciling is in grayed blue, and same color is used on woodwork. The mantel is of gougework. Furnishings of Cape May County provenance. Courtesy Cape May Historical Society. Photograph by George O. Timanus

THE EARLY AMERICAN HOME
OF TODAY

I F YOU have decided to use the Early American type of decoration in creating your home, you must first consider the house itself. It is, of course, possible to decorate a cottage, a Quonset hut, a cabin, or perchance a simple apartment in this period style and thus make a very attractive home, but it is necessary to set boundaries somewhere in a written discussion, so we will, perforce, take for granted that your house is of the Early American type. This means that the ceilings are low; the windows small with many panes; the fireplaces somewhat crude; the walls of sheathing or paneling, or plastered, with one wall, the chimney wall, sheathed or paneled and probably with a dado on the other three; floor boards wide and of random lengths—a simple house that seems to enfold you.

Perhaps you have felt this warmth, homeliness, and charm as you read of the Early American family living and working in its home. I have told you, also, of the exteriors and interiors of the houses of this type. I hope you have visited some of them still standing in New England (listed in the Appendix), because this is the best way, after all, of absorbing and understanding the atmosphere of the period. Now, keeping all this in mind, we shall discuss the interiors and furnishings as we prefer them today. These are bright and simple, but an Early American interior as we create it would have been one of undreamed luxury to our early settler.

WALLS AND WOODWORK

Space in this book will not be given to the details of furniture arrangement, to the types and qualities of paint and varnish, to the methods of applying stencils to walls and floors, to the making of curtains, or to the other everyday problems of decorating. There are many excellent books available on these subjects. Here I shall limit my discussion to the achievement of the general over-all picture as it differs for the four decorating periods, including only those details which are not easily found elsewhere or which I have learned from my own experience to do differently than described by others.

Color is perhaps the most determining factor in the creation of an interesting and successful home. In that of the Early American decorating period it must be good basic color: red, blue, green, or yellow. The decorating scheme in any style is usually built around the treatment of walls and woodwork and floors. In our Early American home of today this treatment may follow one of several methods:

1. The plastered walls may be left in their grayish white with the woodwork in its natural coloring, preferably waxed, or the plaster may be tinted.

2. The plaster may be as above and the woodwork painted a rich carriage blue; a similar blue but grayed (in Woodbury we call this Glebe House blue, since it is the color selected by the Metropolitan Museum of Art for one of the rooms in the old Glebe house which was restored under their direction); a deep rosy red; a mustard yellow; or some shade of green.

3. The plastered walls may be papered with one of the many small-patterned papers and the woodwork left in its natural coloring.

4. The plastered walls may be papered as above with the woodwork painted the color of the wallpaper background, usually a shade lighter or darker, or in a contrasting color. In selecting the wallpaper for Numbers 3 and 4 choose one in which the colors are those of the period. Pastels have no place in our Early American home. Always select the wallpaper

before deciding upon the color for the woodwork, unless this is to be left unpainted. It is much easier to match paint to paper than paper to paint.

5. The walls may be stenciled with the woodwork matching a color in the stenciled design, or a wallpaper may be used that reproduces the old stenciled patterns.

In these little old houses bedrooms and baths on a second floor often have irregular ceilings and walls because of the slanting roof or dormer windows. This irregularity may be made less conspicuous by choosing a small all-over patterned wallpaper for both walls and ceiling. In this case one must decide by the amount and kind of woodwork, unless it is to be left unpainted, whether to have it in a contrasting color or in one that varies very little from the background color of the wallpaper. Here it is possible to use colors a little softer than those in the living rooms. However, the effect from the use of the deeper colors is often more interesting with the simple light-colored furniture.

If all beams and corner posts in any of the rooms are exposed, it is better to have all the woodwork in the natural finish. The modern custom of exposing rough-hewn beams in ceilings and corners may be interesting to some, but our early settlers left them only in sheds and barns. They are incongruous with fine furniture, draperies, and accessories, unless, perhaps, you are doing over a barn or a mill and use them as a sharp contrasting note of amused interest. Generally in any room all woodwork should be treated alike. If painted, it should all be painted. If unpainted, then all should be in the natural finish.

When hinges and latches are of good workmanship—old handmade iron, pewter, or brass—do not paint them. Some may urge you to do this, saying that they stand out too conspicuously. Are they more conspicuous than the brasses on a Chippendale highboy? No one has ever suggested subduing their grandeur. If the hinges and latches have been replaced by subsequent generations with ordinary machine-made hardware, if they are damaged, or if the latches have been removed and there are brass or glass doorknobs, then it is well to paint the hinges so that the deficiencies and differences may not be noticeable. It is the practice of experts in the restoration of old houses to leave latches and hinges unpainted when handmade and in good condition. Indeed these are often the pride of the homeowner.

I do not agree that bathrooms should conform to any period. Enclosing the tub and basin with pine or maple, when carefully done, may be of interest, but it may also recall to mind the hideous Victorian bathrooms with their boxed-in tin tubs. It is always well to remember that the unusual or conspicuous in home decorating may be interesting at first but you soon weary of it, and most people today enjoy the luxury of an attractive bathroom. In decorating this, your imagination may have full play, because here there is no tradition to follow. This is the place to use your gayest paper and your brightest colors, keying them, of course, to your house generally, but since this is a room that lends itself to many types of decorating, it is possible to make it a dramatic spot in the house.

Ceilings in any room may be white or tinted a lighter shade than the walls. Colored ceilings may be used effectively to lend height to a room or to make it appear lower. When irregular or badly broken up, treat ceilings in the same manner as the walls.

FLOORS AND FLOOR COVERINGS

It seems hardly necessary to say that floors should be darker than walls, but many people seem to like them light and sand them until they are the color of butter. Such floors become a focal point of the room, and certainly something else might serve this purpose more successfully. I was early taught that floors should be darker than the walls and woodwork so they would stay down under foot, where they belong.

If the background of our Early American decorating scheme is a really old house, the floors will doubtless be of wide boards, of varying widths and random lengths. When these are sanded and varnished, they lack the mellowness required as a background for antiques. Can any floor be more beautiful than one of age-darkened oak, maple, chestnut, or pine, nicely waxed?

If there are stains that cannot be removed without bleaching and if the floor generally is in a condition unsuitable for waxing, why not paint it instead of sanding? Here is an opportunity for interesting effects. Use a good floor or deck paint, following the usual instructions for painting. Don't use a paint simulating wood. There are floor paints in beautiful reds, blues, greens, copper colors, yellows (mustard shades), grays, and black. The floor may be left in the plain rich paint color selected to harmonize with the general decorating scheme of the room, or it may be stenciled, grained, or spattered. All three are suitable for the Early American interior. Personally, I like the spattered floors. They can be most interesting and a real addition to the decorating scheme.

For instance, in a room with carriage-blue woodwork, plain white walls, and antique red calico curtains with little yellow flowers, the floors could be painted the same shade of blue as the woodwork and spattered with white, red, and yellow. If the woodwork is grayed green and the curtains a dull shade of yellow with copper accents, the floor could be in copper brown with spatters of black, white, yellow, and green— perhaps a bit of vermilion. If the woodwork is old red and the curtains of crewel embroidery, the floor could be a deeper red—almost mahogany —and spattered with the color in the crewel embroidery with white as an accent color.

If the wallpaper is of the toile variety, then I would leave the floor unspattered, unless the paper has a one-color design. For instance, if it has this toile-like design in red on a white background and the woodwork is painted a matching red or a contrasting color, or if it is in natural wood, then the floor would be interesting spattered. But if the paper has, let us say, a background of yellow with the design in brown and green and the woodwork is painted the yellow or the green to harmonize with the paper, then I would like the floor painted a rich deep brown or green and left unspattered. This means that if there are several colors in the wall decoration, then have but the one color in the painted floor.

It is simple to work out any color combination for these spattered floors, keeping in mind the general colors of the period. Use a deep shade of the dominant color in the room and spatter with the different accent colors. The base color should always be the darkest color in the decorating scheme. Venetian red, dark green, copper brown, and black are excellent base colors, selected, of course, with the room colors in mind. If several connecting rooms on a floor are to have spattered floors, it is well to have the base color matching or similar. In one of our houses the transverse hall floor was of mellowed chestnut but the three bedroom floors were so worn and stained that we had to paint them. On each floor I used black as the base and spattered with colors varying for the different rooms, dependent upon the decorating scheme of the room. In these bedrooms we used numdah rugs on one floor and white shaggy scatter rugs on the other two, and the effect was charming.

In spattering I have found a small stiff whisk broom more useful than a paintbrush. Protect the walls around the room up to at least three feet with newspapers, because the spatters fly briskly. I have always painted the floor first and let it dry thoroughly before attempting to spatter, although some people do it section by section, painting and spattering at the same time. For the different spatter paints I use a coffee can for each color, and spatter with one color and then another, doing small sections at a time with all the different colors, working backward toward an exit. Don't blockade yourself into a room! The size of the spatters may be regulated by the height you hold the brush from the floor. They are large if the spattering is done close to the floor and smaller as the distance increases. Use a stick held in the right hand to strike the whisk broom held in the left hand, and don't have so much paint on the whisk broom that it drips. The floor looks better if the spots are not too regular and if the different colors are not splashed on too evenly. The effect should be one of true hit and miss. After you have done one floor, you will know what to do and what to avoid, so try an unimportant floor first.

In New England we have a spattered floor which my grandmother called salt and pepper. This is excellent for halls and stairs. The floor is first painted gray (you could use beige, which is warmer) and then spattered with very small spots of black and white.

When the spattering of any floor has been completed and thoroughly dry, use a coating of spar varnish to protect it.

Rugs may be of several varieties. The loomed rug is always good. The strips may be sewed into larger rugs when these are desired, and they are excellent for hallways and stairs. Hooked and braided rugs are most suitable. When using hooked rugs, search for the more primitive designs: geometric patterns, simple scenes, peculiar little animals, houses, et cetera. The elaborate floral designs are better for the Colonial home of our next period, although some of the crudely executed florals in primitive colors are good. Here is an opportunity for the homeowner to contribute to her decorating scheme. She can make her own designs and dye the materials to be used, thus obtaining faded mellow colors so that the rugs she makes will not be conspicuous spots of newness. A hooked runner with a pictorial history of the family is interesting for a stairway. If you are not that ambitious, pads to fit the stair tread may either be hooked or braided and nailed in place. Otherwise, a strip the width of carpeting may be painted on treads and risers, the paint color matching that of the hall floor. If this floor is stenciled, the strip could also be stenciled. The braided rug, when used for the Early American interior, may be made of colors chosen to harmonize or contrast with the color scheme of any room. Only keep the colors dark enough and always have the last rows of the darkest.

For bedrooms and baths I am very fond of the modern shaggy rugs, although the loomed, hooked, and braided rugs are all desirable and effective in these rooms. The shaggy rugs are easily cared for, they are so simple, and the colors are so lovely, I am sure our early settlers would have welcomed them warmly.

I shall long remember our bedroom at a friend's house in the country where we arrived one cold, snowy night to spend Christmas. Our attention was first drawn to a softly burning fire in a small fireplace. It was just twilight, and the electric lights had not been turned on. The walls were in half shadow, but you could see the rosy red of the conventionalized flower design of a paper called Chantung. The woodwork was painted a deep but grayed blue. The furniture was mellow old maple or pine. The bed was a tester with netted canopy. The coverlet was an old appliquéd quilt of faded red on white. The curtains were simple white draw curtains, and a blue material covered a chaise longue drawn near the fire. On the floor beside the bed, in front of the chaise longue and by the entrance door, were rugs of this modern shaggy type in just the right shade of rosy red, probably dyed to match the wallpaper—bright spots of color that contrasted with the mellow darkness of the old floor boards. It was all so simple, so colorful, so cozy, and seemingly so far from the problems and irritations of today, that I longed to stay there indefinitely. The room soothed and relaxed me, it gave me a feeling of warmth and security, and that is what a bedroom should do.

WINDOWS AND CURTAINS

It is probable that few houses today have casement windows with diamond- or rectangular-shaped panes of leaded glass. Some may have the old casements with small panes of clear glass, but the small double-sash windows with twelve over eight or twelve over twelve panes will be the most usual. Many of the latter windows still contain the old bubbly, wavy, greenish glass. On many will be found the scratched initials, sometimes the full names, of those who lived in the house long, long ago. Sometimes there are little ships and other pictures diamond-scratched by would-be artists. On one window in our house is the name of a man and a woman, and today their great-grandchildren come to view it. Lovers then; ancestors now.

Sometimes you will be amazed at what you see through one of these old panes. The house across the street may suddenly become squatty and out of all proportion. The tall, thin lady next door one day appears very short and very fat. Things generally look awry, and then you realize you are looking through the wrong pane. Usually one or two old rectangles have been replaced with new glass and these are the ones to remember when looking out. Did you know that way, way back the courts would not accept a person's testimony if what was described had been seen through a window? And yet this world I view through the old window-pane is perhaps no more fantastic than the one seen through clear glass.

Curtains may be of two kinds in our Early American home. The easiest selection, the one that requires little imagination, will be those beruffled ones of white organdie or dotted Swiss. They are fresh, simple, and always appropriate. Permitting of more individualism and more color are the sill-length draw curtains of calico, chintz, crewel embroidery, or other simple material in one of the rich primary colors. Unbleached muslin may be dyed the required color and made into curtains. Our grandmother's white damask tablecloths, either white or dyed, make exquisite draw curtains.

If the woodwork is a painted color, the curtains may match it or contrast, carrying out the complementary color used in the decorating scheme. If the walls are plain, the small-figured calico, chintz, or crewel embroidery may be used. If the walls are stenciled or if a patterned paper is used, then solid colors for the windows are often better. Large-figured curtain material, as large-figured wallpaper, is not for our Early American interior.

Suppose you have chosen a wallpaper copied from an old painted wall. The background is a beige yellow. It has a narrow stripe made up of little urns and leaves in chocolate brown. The space between these stripes, some twelve inches, is broken by two stripes of white crow's-feet. With this paper the woodwork would be in its natural finish or painted one shade darker or lighter than the paper background. Can you imagine how charming and cozy this room would be with red glazed-chintz curtains? A chair could be covered to match the curtains and the couch and another chair could have a small-patterned material with the blue of old Canton china as a background, the design in the red of the curtains with some yellow, brown, and white. A pine dresser in the room might contain a collection of the old blue and white Canton or pink Staffordshire, and on the mantel shelf there could be old pewter or brass.

Once again let me urge you not to use pale blues and pinks even in the bedrooms of your Early American home. Tones may be lighter than in the living rooms, but pastels are better omitted. If you want lightness at your windows, use white. It seems hardly necessary to say that in our simple Early American interior curtains are never below sill level and only the one pair seems necessary, never glass curtains and draperies. If draw curtains are used, shades are not needed unless for privacy.

FURNITURE

The furniture of the Early American home was of age-darkened oak or of simple native wood, such as birch, maple, ash, pine, cherry, or hickory. Mahogany was not used until the Colonial period and is, of course, more sophisticated.

Traditionally, the furniture styles used in the Early American home today would be those that preceded the Queen Anne type of furniture. But today we do not carry tradition in furnishing to that extent. For one reason, there is a lack of furniture of these earlier periods. Seldom does any of the old oak become available, and I am certain that many of the young people who are furnishing an Early American home today are little acquainted with this style. They would doubtless repudiate even Jacobean and William and Mary—particularly the chairs—as unsuitable. They are so accustomed to seeing the simple cottage furniture, in most cases made by the local carpenter or joiner at some later date, some of it as late as the middle of the nineteenth century, that this alone represents Early American to them. The lines of this cottage furniture are simple, it is sturdy and usually well constructed of pine, cherry, maple, or some other light wood. It can be had in a great variety of articles, many quite unknown to the homeowners of the Early American years. It can be picked up in the rough, sometimes with many coats of paint, and refinished by the homeowner himself, who not only has the pride of ownership but of a job he has done well.

The various pieces of furniture that may be successfully and correctly used in our Early American house include Windsor, fiddleback, banister-back, some types of Sheraton fancy, painted Hitchcock, and Pennsylvania chairs; Boston rockers and settles; chests, blanket chests with one or two drawers, chest-on-chests, tall chests; butterfly, tavern, trestle, gate-leg, stretcher, and tea tables; candlestands and bedside tables; dressers; dough trays; wall cabinets and shelves; slant-top or schoolmaster's desks; simple wing-type chairs and other upholstered furniture; Windsor settees or old church benches; tall clocks and crickets. This is not an all-inclusive list by any means. The so-called Pennsylvania Dutch furniture has found its way into the New England homes as has the New England furniture into Pennsylvania houses. The old pieces in this painted furniture are much more mellow and desirable than the newly decorated. French Provincial furniture is beautiful anywhere and fits well into our Early American interiors. An occasional piece of old Chinese or Queen Anne lacquer, in either black, green, yellow, or red, gives a charming accent to a room.

Naturally you will want comfortable chairs and sofas; something, I fear, the Early American family did not have. These are today's concession to comfort and are highly desirable and necessary. Fabrics on chairs and sofas must be in accord with the other furnishings in color and quality. Hand-woven materials, simple, small-patterned chintz, calico (and in the days of the Early American family this cost as much as $30 a yard and was made into the best dress lined with silk), gingham, and other simple cotton should be used. Woven coverlets, quilts made from an interesting old fabric and quilted, plain or checked blankets, and plain, coarsely textured material are all good for upholstering furniture of this period. One of the best-looking wing chairs I have ever seen was covered with a hand-woven woolen blanket (no longer prickly because of long use) in two-inch checks of faded blue and creamy white. With a little searching you can find old blankets, quilts, tablecloths, and draperies in beautiful soft colorings; worn, perhaps, but still strong enough to be used for upholstering or for slip covers.

One word of warning about modern chairs and sofas. Select those of the simplest construction, and the less wood that shows the better. The so-called reproductions made of a reddish-type maple never harmonize in line or color with the old furniture. The Lawson sofa or love seat, the Chippendale or Queen Anne wing chair, and a barrel armchair, among others, are good. Key the size and design of these pieces to the other furniture in the room and if the legs and underbracing are too conspicuous and look too new, resort to slip covers. Always remember that it is what is different but not standing out as inappropriate that makes a room interesting.

LIVING ROOM

In this room you may have in addition to the chairs, sofa, and tables, a dresser for your hobby collection, whether it be of pewter, brass, copper, Staffordshire, or pattern glass. A desk is often desirable

Pine Dresser

and may be of the slant-top variety, for some unknown reason called a Governor Winthrop, or one of the schoolmaster's type. Even a small rectangular table with a drawer may be used for this purpose. One of the Victorian commodes or washstands that had a place in every bedroom may be refinished to serve as a bar or to house the radio and Victrola. Coffee tables may be made of a doll's table of good size, of a rectangular nursery table, of a large tole tray on a luggage rack, of an old pine or maple breadboard with a simple base of old wood, or of some other table of simple construction cut down to the right height. Little wooden crickets make nice footstools. Undoubtedly you will build the shelves for your books, although some hanging shelves are available and are good for both books and ornaments. In a small library, a commode as described above could be used under the window of a long wall for the radio, with bookshelves extending along the entire wall on either side, their tops even with that of the commode and all painted the same.

DINING ROOM

Few of the early settlers had a separate room for eating, and since there were no sideboards before the days of Adam and Hepplewhite, side tables were used in their place. The dining room of today's Early American home will be one of choosing and assembling, and in the choosing will be demonstrated the ingenuity and artistry of the home-owner.

The table should be selected first. It may be a stretcher or trestle table of pine or maple. It may be a gate-leg of oak. It could be a drop-leaf of cherry, maple, or pine. With the stretcher or trestle table Windsor, banister-back, or ladder-back chairs will doubtless be used. Pennsylvania or Hitchcock chairs are also suitable. A hunt board, a small tavern table, or one of the mid-nineteenth-century cottage chests of four drawers may be used. This chest may be refinished in the natural wood, or if painted chairs are used it could be painted to key with them. (Don't have your refinished wood or your painted furniture with a high enamel-like finish. Have it rubbed down and waxed until it has the soft patina of old furniture.) Chests of drawers are convenient to hold linens, and the top drawer may be divided by partitions for flat silver. A Welsh dresser is desirable, since it has storage space below for large serving pieces as well as the shelves and top for other pieces. A commode might be refinished to use as a bar. If the inside of the top section is painted to carry out the color scheme of the room, the cover may be left open, and this is most attractive filled with potted plants.

If a drop-leaf table is used instead of the trestle or stretcher, the room will be a more formal room. With this type of table Windsor, cane, or rush-seat Hitchcocks, chairs with the Queen Anne back and turned or cabriole legs with underbracing, or the simple, painted fancy Sheratons would be pleasing.

In the dining room of our Early American home Staffordshire in any desired color to harmonize with the room decoration, Canton, or even modern pottery are better than fine china. Pewter is more suitable than silver, but if silver is used, let it be simple and chaste. The old coin-silver flatware, although fragile, is appropriate. Any of the early pressed glassware, called Early American pattern glass but never made before 1826,

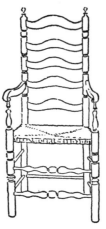

Ladder-back Chair

fits well into this dining room. Such patterns as Ashburton, Moon and Star, Horn of Plenty, New England Pineapple, Huber, Bigler, or any of the other heavy patterns may be used. Amber or ruby glass also fits into the color scheme. Old colored tablecloths, or place mats made from them, are most attractive, and the white or red embroidered square pillow shams with wide hems or little ruffles are charming as card table coverings when these are used for dessert bridge. They are also attractive when having dinner at a small table in front of the living-room fire on a cold winter night—much more cozy for two than the dining-room table.

Let's picture a dining room of this period. The walls are of white plaster. The paneled chimney wall and the other wood trim, including the chair rail, are painted the old red so common in the period. Draw curtains at the many-paned windows have a white background well covered with a small stencil-like design in the red of the woodwork with touches of bright yellow and blue. On the dark wood floor there is a large oval braided rug combining all these colors, interspersed with rows of black. The table is a long, narrow trestle, agleam from much rubbing. On it is a pewter basin piled high with brightly colored fruit, and small pots of flowering plants fill the sill of a sunny window. Around the table are fanback Windsors. Near the fire is a small yellow Windsor settee on rockers. By the window a wing chair, slip-covered in a quilted material of small pattern in which a soft old blue is the predominant color, invites you to relax. A collection of ancient pink and white Staffordshire lines the shelves of a Welsh dresser. Between the two front windows hangs a collection of pine-framed silhouettes, and over a chest of drawers nearby a pine spoon rack with its pewter spoons. The mantel, too, holds an array of old pewter plates and tankards. This room, charming by day, is even lovelier at night with its firelight and many lighted candles.

BEDROOMS

Bedrooms are more intimate and more expressive of their occupants than any other room in the house. The bed may be the tall or low four-poster or one of the later spool beds, often called Jenny Lind. The beds of this period have sturdier posts than those of the Colonial, are usually high up from the floor, and are much more attractive when supplied with a ruffle or skirt that reaches to the floor. If it is a tester, the canopy may be of a material to match the skirt, or it may be netted. Bed skirts or ruffles may be attached or removed easily today, since it is possible to buy a double tape that snaps together. One part of this is tacked to the bedframe and the other sewed to the completed bed ruffle. Thus it is an easy matter to snap the ruffle on or pull it off for laundering. Woven coverlets, pieced and patched quilts, candlewick spreads, and old Marseilles bedspreads, white or dyed, are all appropriate for counterpanes.

Dressing tables—and every woman covets a dressing table—may be simple homemade affairs draped with the material used at the windows or as skirts for the bed. I myself prefer one of the many rectangular stands of pine or maple, always with one drawer and sometimes with a row of small shallow drawers on top. I also like the draped, mirror-top dressing tables in the bathroom, but of course this is a matter for individual choice.

Wall mirrors for use with the dressing tables are not easy to find in pine. It is not difficult, however, to secure any quantity of old mahogany veneered frames of many sizes. The more chipped and broken the veneer, the cheaper the frame. This veneering was always done on a pine base and when it is all removed and the base refinished, you have a nice frame for a mirror. Such frames are also good for samplers, flower prints, fashion prints, *Vanity Fair* caricatures, maps, and Currier and Ives prints.

A modern chaise longue covered to match the curtains or bed skirt is a modern luxury appropriate for even our Early American bedroom. Small tables come in a great variety and most rooms can use two or more. Small oil lamps, wired and with simple shades, are charming for the dressing table or for bedside stands. Here as elsewhere in the house lamps made from a variety of articles at small cost are decorative assets. Don't, however, have such lamps made carelessly. If you are using even a blown-glass bottle, have a base made for it and have the rod through the bottle so that the cord comes out inconspicuously from the base. In old oil lamps it is not feasible to do other than have the wire coming from the adapter, but otherwise objects made into lamps should be well mounted. In the bedrooms use the woven rag rugs, the braided or hooked, as well as the modern shaggy ones, which fill so admirably today's requirements for color and comfort.

KITCHENS

When we come to kitchens, I can imagine one in the Early American home with a huge fireplace, a tavern or trestle table, a Boston rocker and settle by the fireside, rag rugs, red-and-yellow curtains at the windows, lots of copper or pewter, a recessed stove, a dresser with Early American pottery and much old blue and white Canton or colorful Staffordshire, but no white sink, no icebox. These most necessary modern conveniences can be installed in such a way as not to be noticeable or in a sort of buttery at one side. A cast-iron range may have its legs removed and a brick foundation and backing built for it so it looks appropriate. Even in its usual state, it is a cozy asset to any kitchen, especially during a cold winter.

Pine Settle

The nicest breakfast in the world is a lazy, leisurely one on a snowy Sunday morning in such a kitchen. The log fire blazes and crackles, the wind howls, and the snow whirls in drifts outside, the smell of coffee and cigarette smoke is everywhere, sausages sizzle in the background, and you feel it makes no difference if it snows forever. More wood is piled on the fire, someone makes more coffee, the cigarette stubs mount on the ash trays, conversation is desultory, as everyone watches the fire, time passes—but who cares?

One kitchen I shall always remember with nostalgia. It was large and rambling. There was an adjoining buttery to house the electric stove, the icebox, and the sink, as well as cabinets for brooms, for first-aid supplies, and a huge coat closet for gardening clothes, riding clothes, and those for stormy weather. In the kitchen, as well as in the buttery, cabinets and corner cupboards had been made of old chestnut boards from the floor of a disreputable barn. These boards had been planed to a soft honey color and the finished cabinets lightly waxed. Even the little wooden knobs had been made by hand. The walls and ceiling were painted a deep shade of bluish green. We had taken a gallon of Williamsburg blue paint, squeezed into it three tubes of chrome green, a bit of Venetian red, and some burnt umber. The contrast between this and the chestnut cabinets was delightful. We made draw curtains for the top half of the window of an Indian-red calico with little yellow flowers, almost pinhead in size, with touches of blue. These took away the bare look from the windows but did not spoil the view. In the summer we used crisp white organdie tie-backs for the upper half of the windows. These had narrow ruffles embroidered in red. There was no fireplace, but the old black stove with oil burners kept us cozy during the winter months. We used a long pine trestle table and painted chairs. Everyone loved this room, and it was impossible to keep guests from sauntering out to it even when they were supposed to stay in the drawing room before a dinner party.

If it is not possible for you to have an old-fashioned kitchen, your problem is to make yours individual. Many of you doubtless prefer the very efficient modern kitchen anyway, and yet most of you, I am sure, will want color in it. This can be done in at least two ways. If there is no wall space, do something about the ceiling. This can be painted a chosen color or papered. There are many papers that have no apparent up and down and this is the type to choose for ceilings. If the ceiling is low, choose a paper with a light background with the desired colors in the design. Such a paper having a gray background with an open all-over design of fruits in various colors is called "The Talleyrand." If this is used, the curtains could pick up the orange red in the paper for a north or east room, or the bluish green for a south or west room. If the kitchen needs brightening up, why not use a Chinese tea-leaf paper in red and silver? This is charming and not too commonly used. The red is a terracotta red rather than a Chinese red and the silver is the accent color. In this kitchen the curtains could match the red of the paper and you could work in accents in imperial yellow or lettuce green.

If there is a free wall in the kitchen, paper this with a really interesting wallpaper. All woodwork may be painted to match the wallpaper background, a contrasting color, or be left in the natural wood tones. I will suggest two among a great many suitable wallpapers for this purpose. "Visiting Soldiers" has a charcoal background with primitively designed houses, ships, and soldiers. Trees and clouds are olive green, the houses are red, and there is considerable white. The soldiers have touches of royal blue on their uniforms. With this the woodwork could be olive green, red, or a lighter gray than charcoal. A second paper, "Maritime News," comes with a curry background and is most intriguing since it reproduces notices and advertisements from old newspapers. With this one could use the curry color for woodwork and olive green, brown, or Chinese red for accessories. This same paper comes with many background colors if some other is more desirable—cream, gray, light brick, sky blue, and bark green.

Then again, if you do not want to use paper, the walls and ceilings may be painted. Teal and buttercup yellow, a deep grayed green and raspberry, cocoa and pomegranate are all good color combinations. The possibilities of any kitchen are infinite, and it is lots of fun to see what you can do with paper and paint.

BATHROOMS

Bathrooms should key with the rest of the house in color and in feeling, that is in formality or informality. Other than that there will probably be little difference whether the house is Early American or Victorian, unless someone wishes to experiment with these two periods. In the first case, you would use a simple pine table and stool for a dressing table and other items in pine to carry out the early feeling. In the Victorian there would be red and white fringed towels, a black walnut towel bar with its cross-stitched motto in red, black walnut towel stands, perhaps even an iron coat rack painted white or some other chosen color to hold bathrobes or bath towels.

In old houses in the country a small bedroom is often converted into a bathroom, and the result is a fairly large room. In one house where we have been guests there was a fireplace and a chaise longue in the bathroom. That was one of the most comfortable bathrooms I can remember. When decorating such a room as this, it is much easier to carry out the period theme than in the usual bathroom of today. Such a room, however, is in the minority, and generally the homeowner's problem is to make a very functional room as attractive as possible. To a large extent this must be achieved with wallpaper, paint, and accessories. The general result will be little different, whether the house itself is Early American, Colonial, Federal, or Victorian. If the house is Early American, the colors will be more basic and the paper simpler than if it is Victorian, when the paper and fittings may be exotic. For instance, for an Early American house you would use, perhaps, a little all-over chintz pattern with rather pure colors, whereas in a Victorian one you might use a paper with a white background splashed over with big American Beauty roses. Some suggestions for bathrooms follow.

For a rather simple bathroom there are two charming papers, if you like the traditional white fixtures. In this instance we shall combine them with red accessories. The first paper is called "Paisley," and has a charming all-over design in a rosy red on a white background. The use of this paper would call for white woodwork, white tiles, white floor, white fixtures, and rosy-red towels and mats with monograms in white. The second paper is "Pointe de Perse," and is a small all-over design in old red on a cream background. If this paper is used, the woodwork, tiles, floor, and fixtures could be an off white—cream—and the monograms on the red towels and mats could also be in the off white. One could, of course, use a similar all-over-patterned paper of blue, green, or yellow on a white background, with towels and bath mats matching the chosen color.

If the bathroom is a large one but only a small portion of wall is available for paper—and if you like charcoal, mauve, and pink—use a paper such as "Westchester." This has a charcoal background with a somewhat conventionalized floral design in grayed mauves and pinks. This could be used with white or warm gray woodwork and fixtures. Charcoal or mauve towels and amethyst accessories would be interesting. If any bathroom is large enough, I suggest having a dressing table.

For a rather formal bathroom in a Colonial or Federal house you might try a paper called "Colonist." This has a luscious Venetian rose background with fairly good-sized rectangles outlined in a narrow ribbon of gray and white. In each rectangle there is a gold eagle and in each corner a gold star. Narrow gray and white ribbon scrolls form a design between the rectangles. With this paper you could use gray wall tiles, gray fixtures, gray woodwork, and a gray floor. Towels and bath mats could be of a matching gray with monograms of Venetian rose, or of the latter color with gray monograms. Cranberry glass could be used effectively for accessories.

The "Colonist" also comes in other color combinations—brown and beige or green and chartreuse—if one of these fits your color scheme better than the Venetian rose and gray.

For a really beautiful bathroom you might use a wallpaper called "Peacock." This has a chocolate background with a small India print design in gold and a blue green. The woodwork could match the green. Since it is now possible to get real Italian marble cut to individual specifications for walls and floor tiles, it would be interesting to use this for wall tiles, floor, and lavatory counters in a color similar to the gold in the wallpaper. Bath towels and mats could be gold, chocolate brown, or green, as desired. Or have the marble the shade of the lovely Talisman rose. This would be a good color with the "Peacock" paper since it has tones of the gold, but with a pinkish tinge, and would be warmer-appearing than the plain gold. In this case have the bath towels and mats, if possible, in this shade of golden pink.

Of course, if you do not want wallpaper, many interesting results may be achieved with paint and tiles. You need not hesitate to use wallpaper because you fear it will be quickly damaged by steam from the bath, since there are several available preparations for protecting the paper, and it simply means painting over it with this preparation after it has been put on the wall. Many wallpaper companies will plastic coat any paper ordered at a small extra charge.

As in the kitchen, a bathroom will give the home decorator infinite opportunity to demonstrate her imaginative and creative skill.

HOW TO CREATE A COLONIAL INTERIOR

IN DECORATING a home, as in painting, sculpture, or writing, it is necessary to learn the basic rules, but those once learned you are on your own, and what you do depends upon whether you are a follower only or a creator with imagination.

The Colonial period in architecture, decorating, customs, and costumes was the most luxurious, the most picturesque, and probably the most gracious era in American history. It saw the development of the beautiful so-called Georgian house, the magnificent and rococo furniture of the Chippendale style, and of a society patterned closely upon that of England. It saw also the growth of bitterness against a country that treated its colonists as a subject people, a bitterness that grew into the Revolution and a hard-won freedom to form a new government.

In New England during this period there was the simple country Colonial home as well as the elaborate Colonial mansion. Also, there was a continuing of the central chimney house and even of the older overhang. There was no definite line of demarcation between styles in architecture or in decorating. One slowly developed beside the other but never immediately superseded it, and new styles reached the seaports more quickly than the inland towns. The same applies to furniture. Queen Anne, and doubtless also some William and Mary, continued popular in the homes of the country people long after Chippendale was a must for those of fashion in such towns as Boston, Salem, and Portsmouth. Some few pieces of Hepplewhite and Sheraton appeared in the colonies before the Revolution, but even the fashionable did not possess much of this new style until the next period, when it became the vogue.

One of the chief differences between an Early American interior and a Colonial one is in its formality. In the latter there is a more formal arrangement of furniture and accessories and they, themselves, are more formal.

In the Colonial period of 1720 to 1790 architecture, decoration, furniture, and costumes followed closely the styles current in England, allowing, as always, for the usual time lag owing to distance from the mother country. In furnishing homes in this period today it is possible to follow the interiors of that day much more closely than it was in the Early American home. In the first place more furniture of the period is available and in styles with which we are familiar and which we like. By 1720 the settler in America, especially in or near the seaports, was able to have whatever was available to members of his class anywhere, and the Colonial home was filled with beauty, comfort, and color. It is only necessary to visit some of the houses of this period in Boston, Massachusetts, and Portsmouth, New Hampshire, or the Governor's Palace in Williamsburg, Virginia, to recognize this.

The furniture in the fashionable house of the period was of the Queen Anne and Chippendale styles with some carry-overs from the William and Mary, particularly in the simple homes and in the more isolated parts of the country. Then, too, even in the most pretentious dwelling this carry-over might be found in bedrooms and unimportant rooms, though the principal rooms on the first floor had the most fashionable furniture available in mahogany. As I have said before, little of the Adam, Hepplewhite, or Sheraton, popular in England for many years, reached the colonies until after the Revolution, and in America we find no great quantity of furniture made from walnut, the chosen wood in England for the Queen Anne style. Although walnut was used by the Colonial cabinetmakers, particularly around Philadelphia and along the Delaware River, maple, cherry, and the other local woods were much more popular.

Today, however, in furnishing the Colonial interior, Queen Anne, Chippendale, Hepplewhite, and Sheraton are used indiscriminately both in mahogany and in the other woods; some oak, some walnut, but more maple and cherry. Sideboards did not appear until the days of Hepplewhite, and so today, unless you use one of the Chippendale type serving tables you should use Hepplewhite, Sheraton, or even early Duncan Phyfe sideboards with Chippendale chairs and table. Indeed Chippendale chairs for dining-room use are most popular whether the other furniture is Hepplewhite, Sheraton, or Chippendale, since they are sturdy, comfortable, and give you a feeling of greater security than do the more fragile-appearing Hepplewhite and Sheraton. The combining of these various styles is not a difficult one for the homemaker if she chooses those pieces having the same general feeling. After all, the Chippendale evolved from the Queen Anne, and both Chippendale and Hepplewhite worked from designs of Adam. As in the choice of wallpapers and colors, select the furniture and accessories that together create the required effect. Again I say study good interiors and your decisions will be made without conscious effort.

Often a piece of Queen Anne or Chippendale in walnut, maple, or other light wood will be included in a room furnished with mahogany, or vice versa. In like manner a highboy, a secretary, or a desk of Chinese or Queen Anne lacquer in a room furnished with rich mahogany in Chippendale, Hepplewhite, and Sheraton will add interest. A house completely furnished with the finest Chippendale in the richest mahogany would be stilted and monotonous.

Again a house furnished with mahogany in the principal rooms on the first floor will be more interesting if some of the bedrooms—perhaps even a less important room on the first floor—are furnished with pieces of the period in light woods. And the articles of furniture have increased enormously in this period. They now include highboys, lowboys, sofas, day beds, footstools, chests of drawers, desks, tables of all kinds, night stands and candlestands, tall clocks, wall brackets, mirrors, long side tables, and untold numbers of accessories. Your own decorating instinct will tell you into which rooms you will place your choice pieces.

In the Colonial interior the fireplace is still the important feature of any principal room. In such a room the chimney wall is usually paneled, with a dado or at least a chair rail on the other three walls. The wallpapers may be Chinese, floral, scenic, of the toiles de Jouy type, or even architectural. Or the walls may be stenciled. The colors to be used are slightly different from those of the Early American period. They have increased in number and are softer. No longer is pure red, green, blue, or yellow common. Now there are cream, grayed blue, primrose yellow, soft green, robin's-egg blue, mustard or chamois yellow, and buff, but white for woodwork did not become usual until the Federal period.

For curtains use damask, brocatelle, brocade, chintz, and similar materials, richer and more formal than those used in the Early American home. In most rooms draperies will be floor length rather than to the sill, as in the preceding period, although the sill length is still suitable for the less formal Colonial room. White organdie tiebacks may be used, and the length of these will depend upon the general treatment of the room. Someone may wish to use Venetian blinds, and for this there is ample authority. George Washington installed them at Mount Vernon and they were popular in many Colonial houses. They should, however, be painted to match the woodwork.

To the loomed, hooked, and braided rugs we now add Orientals and Aubussons. While scatter rugs on a painted floor were still common in the period, the large rug, one to a room—but never covering the floor from wall to wall—made its appearance. The hooked rug reached its greatest perfection of workmanship and design in the handsome florals of the period, and these are most desirable in the less formal, less important rooms. Today rugs with a solid color, either plain or textured, are also used successfully.

Keeping in mind the above suggestions as to types of furniture, wallpapers, curtains, floor coverings, colors, and the formal arrangement of the furnishings, today's homemaker has but to follow general rules of decorating to achieve successfully a Colonial interior. However, let us consider briefly a few problems that may arise.

In decorating the Early American home it was possible to treat the small rugs as accessories rather than as a background for the decorating scheme, but with the use of a large and often expensive rug it is important to recognize this as the source of the room's color scheme. So study the rug to be used, and then select wallpaper and paint with it in mind. Re-

member that floor coverings and wall coverings are the two most important factors in the decorating effect, since they are the main backgrounds
against which will be displayed the furniture and accessories, and don't
select a rug so interesting or exciting or a wallpaper so exotic that they
become the centers of interest in the room rather than the backgrounds.

Never overcrowd a room with furniture and accessories and don't
select furniture too large or too small. A small room with a low ceiling in
an Early American type house becomes a source of irritation and confusion when filled with massive American Empire. Arrange the important
pieces of furniture first. That done, the smaller pieces and the accessories
will fit in easily. It is well to remember that these small pieces as well as
the larger are important, and that accessories can make or spoil a room.
In the Colonial interior they must be chosen with more care than in the
less formal Early American and they should be used with more restraint.

There will be more silver than pewter and more fine china than earthenware and pottery. Lamps will be more formal in character. They may
still be assembled from many interesting articles, but these will be quite
different from those of the Early American interior. For instance, you
could use lamps made of painted tin—canisters, urns, et cetera—but the
designs would not be the somewhat garish Pennsylvania Dutch, which
are more suited to the earlier period. You could also use a lamp made
from a blown-glass demijohn in some interesting color, such as chestnut
or emerald green, but it must be carefully mounted. It is not probable
that the critical homemaker would use a ginger-beer bottle or an ordinary
whisky bottle for a lamp base, although such might be done in an Early
American interior. Pottery could be used for a lamp, but not a gray iron-
stone jug or an iron coffee grinder. Chinese vases, ginger jars, Staffordshire figurines, parian vases, Bristol vases, Dresden or Sèvres figurines or
vases, and all such similar articles may be converted into beautiful lamps.
Shades may be made of silk, shantung, linen, organdie, and other materials; of parchment, of the opaque metallic papers which come in color
as well as gold and silver; of wallpaper, of marbleized papers, and of
Chinese tea-leaf paper. Always have some unity between the various
shades in a room. They need not be entirely alike, but don't have one of

silk, one of gingham, and one of marbleized paper. Rather have most of them of silk with a pair, perhaps, of opaque paper, or all of parchment. Too great a diversity is confusing.

Simple oil lamps of the nineteenth century of various kinds are still desirable, particularly for bedrooms. These come with base, standard, and font measuring from eight to fifteen or eighteen inches high, or the small hand lamp of five or six inches tall, and are easily wired for electricity by the use of an adapter. Many of the Sandwich lamps in colored glass or overlay are exquisite bits of color and should never have to compete with ornate shades.

Pictures and mirrors assume real importance in this period. Portraits in oil and large canvases of many genre in simple gold-leaf frames are most acceptable. Mirrors in Queen Anne, Chippendale, Adam, or others similar in type add much to the richness and spaciousness of a room, or handsome gold-leaf frames may be fitted with mirrors. Crystal chandeliers, candelabra, and lustered sconces add to the brightness of the formal Colonial home.

No room can be successfully decorated unless it has at least one focal point. In any room with a fireplace this is usually the main center of interest. If the room is small, it is possible to treat it as a unit with but one dominant note, but if it is large, it will be a more attractive room if there are one or two secondary focal centers. Have such a secondary point of interest—or the main focal point if there is no fireplace—between two windows, in front of an important window, on a long wall facing the entrance, or at some point that will serve the purpose well. And then be sure to make it a center of interest. The grouping might consist of a large sofa with chairs, side tables, lamps, and pictures to complete the setting. It might be a desk or lowboy over which hangs your finest picture or mirror, and the group completed by a couple of important chairs. It might even be one large piece of furniture, such as a distinctive secretary holding a collection of *objets d'art* on its shelves.

If you have an interesting hobby, this might well serve as a secondary focal point. For colored glass, shelves could be built in a window better to display it; for several pieces of Sunderland luster or Liverpool pitchers, a corner cabinet; for little Staffordshire figurines, a hanging cabinet with mirror back; or for a number of silhouettes a group arrangement on a suitable wall space. Have such collections in rooms appropriate for them. Bennington bowls and pitchers have no place in a formal Colonial drawing room and yet might be delightful in a library. An unused doorway may be fitted with shelves in the upper section and doors at the bottom. These shelves are excellent for books or ornaments and the cabinets below for storage. Bookcases to key with the room are suitable in almost any room of any period and add interest. I have also seen an unused door from a living room to a sunroom or even a porch fitted with plate glass on the outside and a glass door on the inside. With shelves between and indirect lighting for night, this made a wonderful display cabinet for old glass paperweights and paperweight bottles. It would serve equally well for colored glass, figurines, or other collections.

In the beginning of this section I said there were two types of houses in the period: the simple country home and the elaborate Colonial mansion. The picture of a New England bedroom about 1750 facing page 65, and that of the dining room in the Wentworth-Gardner house, Portsmouth, New Hampshire, around 1760, facing page 193, will show this difference better than a lengthy discussion. The bedroom gives a picture of formal simplicity not present in the Early American home, while the dining room is one of formal elegance totally unlike that of the most pretentious dwelling of the earlier period. While the bedroom would not be out of place in a house having the beautiful dining room, one would be surprised to see a room of such formal beauty as this in a simple country residence. In the country home of the period, as today, the simple home would have less elaborate wood trim; more chintz than damask; more hooked and braided rugs than Orientals or Aubussons; more light wood than mahogany; and simpler wallpaper and accessories.

Let's take the bedroom pictured and with a few changes demonstrate how it could be made more formal. Instead of the stenciled walls we will use a paper called "The Wentworth." This has a background of warm chamois yellow and a simple stripe design. One stripe, about four inches wide, is composed of small flowers in a soft blue with leaves and stems in a violet beige and brown. This alternates with another stripe of equal width in which the blue flower is worked into a small geometric design outlined in the violet beige. We would have the woodwork matching the warm yellow background. We would add floor-length draperies of soft blue, a more formal canopy and bedspread for the bed, and a wing chair of more ample width—Queen Anne or Chippendale. Instead of the joint stool for the dressing table we would use a Queen Anne side chair of light wood and would replace the painted chair beside the fireplace with a chaise longue. The coverings of this and the wing chair would carry out the room colorings of chamois yellow, soft blue, and violet beige.

It is not necessary to live in a mansion to have a formal Colonial home. A one-room apartment may be as beautiful and formal as anyone could wish. Neither is it necessary to have a formal house if you are living in a large Colonial mansion. It will be simpler, perhaps, to make the small house formal than it would be to make the mansion informal, but it can be done, and done easily. Wallpaper, paint, curtains, floor coverings, the type of furniture and accessories used will do the trick.

The living room of the Cape Cod cottage pictured is an exceedingly simple Colonial living room. You could take this same room and without changing the wallpaper or paint make it more formal by the use of one good-sized Oriental rug, floor-length draperies, the replacing of the Windsor chairs with more important ones in Queen Anne or Chippendale, a Queen Anne tea table by the window, a more elegant desk, and much more formal accessories.

The Wentworth-Gardner dining room would be somewhat less formal if the wallpaper was changed to a suitable but simple design.

As an illustration of the basic difference between the simple country Colonial and the more formal house of the same period, let's examine two suggestions for homes for today—one in each style. Both interiors will represent a home that can be created without too much difficulty and one in which the average family of the present time will be comfortable. No longer do many of us wish for the elaborate mansion of the Colonial period because of the difficulty of getting servants. Hence we shall not consider here a decorative scheme for such a formal mansion.

The simple Colonial home will show more relationship to the Early American interior than will the more pretentious one. Nevertheless, even the simple interior will be more formal than that of the earlier period.

Examine the floor plan of the central chimney house on page 99 since we shall picture our simple Colonial interior in this type of house. White woodwork is not indicated for the Colonial interior, and because it is good decorating to key the colors throughout the entire house, we shall use a group of colors in this fashion—grayed green, old gold, a soft yellow, and a light brick red.

For the hallway—upstairs as well as down—let's use a paper called "Wedgwood Stripe." This has an old-gold background, which is a soft shade somewhat akin to mustard. It is a rather formal paper, but halls and dining rooms are generally more formal than other rooms, even in a small house. The design of "Wedgwood Stripe" is composed of one-inch stripes alternating with three-and-a-half-inch stripes. In the narrow stripe there is a small design in white with dots of brown; in the wider stripe, urns and leaves in white and brown. With this wallpaper we shall have the woodwork match the old-gold background. Since the halls in these central chimney houses are small, we need not worry about furniture. Hangings may match the background of the paper. Mellow old Oriental rugs may be used or, if desired, the stair carpeting and rugs may be of a brick-red broadloom. Don't, however, have the floors covered from wall to wall.

In the dining room to the left of the entrance (marked "Keeping room" on the floor plan on page 99) we will paint all the woodwork the same color as that in the hall—fireplace wall paneling, door and window trim, wainscoting. The plaster walls will remain white. Floors may be stained or painted. If the latter, a brick red would be charming. In this simpler house it is probable the dining-room furniture will be of maple, pine, or cherry—a drop-leaf table, a chest of drawers, a hunt board or table for serving, and a corner cupboard—with Windsor or Hitchcock chairs. At the windows we will use draw curtains to the sills of "Sarelda," an American Heritage Document print, which comes in shades of green and brick. For interest and privacy, if desired, we may use lower sash curtains. These could be of old embroidered muslin such as grand-mother's embroidered petticoat or embroidered shams, or if this lovely old material is not available, new material similar in style to the old. A large oval braided rug will add to the Colonial feeling of the room. Pink or mauve Staffordshire and ruby or amber glass may be used.

Just back of the dining room is the kitchen, and this may be decorated in the colors of the dining room—brick red, old gold, and green.

The library, which occupies the space marked "Lean-to" on the floor plan, will have, of course, the largest fireplace since this was the former kitchen, and this will doubtless be the focal point of interest in the room. Have as many book shelves constructed as are necessary for your books and a few extra for the display of your favorite collection. Shelves full of colorful books are always an important decorative asset. Leave the woodwork in its natural wood tones, carefully waxed. The remaining wall space may be papered with a wallpaper having a grayed green background with a small all-over conventionalized design in soft yellow and white; or if the room is fairly large, with a reproduction of an old stenciled paper called "Old Stone House," which comes with a grayed green background, with the stenciled design in shaded yellow. Hangings in this room may be of yellow homespun, linen, or similar material, to the sill. Chairs and sofas may be upholstered with the new tweed-like materials, homespuns, or linen, keeping the colors in various shades of green, yellow, old gold, and red. Leather chairs and sofas may also be used. Rugs should be similar to those in other parts of the house.

The living room at the right of the entrance hall may be painted to match the background of the library wallpaper—a grayed green. This means walls and woodwork. This will permit the use of gay chintz or crewelwork material for the hangings, keeping them to the sills, as in other rooms of the house. Unless necessary, glass curtains are not indicated, as the draperies may be drawn for privacy. Rugs may be braided, hooked, or mellow old Oriental; the charming Orientals will give more formality.

Furniture may be of mahogany, cherry aged until it is almost indistinguishable from mahogany, some maple, but more formal in type than that used in the Early American interior—Queen Anne, and country Chippendale. Modern upholstered sofas and chairs in keeping with the other furniture will be necessary for comfort. Chintz or crewelwork material to match the hangings and simple weaves will be more suitable for upholstery than brocades and velvets. Accessories will be more formal than in the Early American interior and used with more restraint—to accent the room, not to dominate it.

Bedrooms will carry forward the downstairs color scheme, whether furnished with maple, cherry, or mahogany. Hooked, braided, small Orientals, or shag rugs are suitable for floor coverings in this simple country Colonial interior.

For our second Colonial interior—the more formal home—let us consider a house with the typical Colonial house floor plan. This will have a transverse center hall, both downstairs and up, with two rooms on either side, with fireplaces on the end exterior walls. In the house chosen, we shall assume that the wall between the two rooms on the right of the transverse hall has been removed, giving us one large room with a fireplace near the center of the long exterior wall and on the left of the hall two rooms, one to be the dining room, the other a large kitchen with its fireplace.

For this house we will use a decorating scheme based upon a grayed blue—popularly known as Williamsburg blue—gray, yellow, deep pink, rosy red, and a dulled green.

For the hall, downstairs and up, we will use a wallpaper called "the Redmond." This is an old French paper showing two alternating scenes, a lady in a French garden and a gentleman in a similar setting, both in simple costumes of the French Empire period. These scenes are separated by cartouches containing small bunches of flowers. The background color of the paper is a grayed blue, and the colors of flowers, costumes, and scenery are a soft yellow; a grayed green, dark in tone; a rosy pink; touches of brown. With this paper the woodwork will match the background blue. The stair and floor carpet will match the green in the wallpaper design. In this transverse hall there will be plenty of room for several side chairs, a lowboy or highboy, a chest on chest, a tall clock, perhaps a fine painting, and certainly a mirror. The furniture will all be of mahogany; probably Chippendale or Queen Anne in style, although Hepplewhite and Sheraton may also be used.

In the dining room at the left we will use a paper that has been a favorite for a long time, "the Whistler"; so called because it was found under layers of wallpaper in a house in Stonington, Connecticut, in which Whistler once lived. The background of this paper is of the same blue as that in the hall wallpaper, and its design of wreaths and scrolls is in gray and white. With this paper we will paint the fireplace wall paneling, the wainscoting, and all other woodwork a gray matching that in the paper. The floor covering will be a room-size Oriental chosen for its rosy reds, greens, and yellows. The hangings will be floor length, of rosy-red damask or brocade, and there will be a fitted cornice of the same material. The mahogany furniture will consist of a large table of Chippendale, Hepplewhite, Sheraton, or even the later pedestal table so popular with Duncan Phyfe; a Hepplewhite or Sheraton sideboard; chairs in one of these several styles; and other pieces, as space permits. Chair seats will be upholstered with a formal striped material having the colors seen in the hall wallpaper. We will use electrified crystal sconces on the side walls and a crystal chandelier over the table.

The adjoining kitchen, roomy and with its fireplace, can easily be made into a convenient working unit, but also one that can serve the family for breakfast. Necessary cabinets may be constructed of pine. On the walls we will use "Little Things," a charming wallpaper having a Venetian rose background with a small picture design in gray and black with touches of gold. Double sash curtains may be used of a simple cotton material having a Venetian rose background. Near the fireplace we will have a round pine or maple "Lazy Susan" table and Windsor chairs. On the floor we will use braided or hooked rugs. An antique cupboard, either corner or one to stand against the wall, would add to the charm of this kitchen and could be used to hold a collection of colorful pottery, stenciled tin, or pewter. Or one of the popular "dry sinks" could be used to hold plants or as a bar.

Many houses combine a library and living room, and in this more formal Colonial interior we shall assume that the long room at the right of the transverse hall must fill these two needs. We will have the library section at the rear of the room, and bookshelves will be constructed there. The walls and woodwork will be painted a soft yellow, toned to that in the hall wallpaper. The floor coverings will be Oriental rugs, and the hangings of yellow damask or brocade, a little darker than the walls. These should be to the floor and made with a fitted cornice of the same material. Furniture will be of mahogany. Chairs and sofas will be upholstered with formal materials carrying out the color scheme of yellow, blue, green, and rosy red. Lamps should be of the finest quality, as should accessories.

Bedrooms and baths on the second floor should be decorated to carry forward the color scheme of the first floor. Mahogany, maple, or fruit-wood furniture may be used.

A paper that carries out the color scheme perfectly for one bedroom is "the Pawling." This has a yellow background with small sprays of blue flowers with brown leaves, each medallion separated by a scrolled vine in old gold. Other bedroom colors could be Venetian rose, Williamsburg blue, or gray, with contrasts and accents of the other colors used on the first floor.

In summing up the requirements of a good Colonial interior, whether simple or more elegant, we have but to remember that it is formal in arrangement and uncluttered.

CONTEMPORARY FEDERAL
STYLE OF DECORATING

I N NEW ENGLAND the years 1790 to 1830, which we have assigned to
the Federal period, mark a slow but perceptible change from the
lavish though orderly interiors of the Colonial years to the chaste
simplicity so fashionable in the London of the Adam brothers. As the
period advances, however, this classicism is influenced by the French
Directoire (1795–99), the French Empire (1804–15), and the English
Regency (1793–1820), and as the era comes to a close, the massive
American Empire is becoming the popular furniture of the day. These
influences, however, do not have so great an effect in the New England
of Bulfinch and McIntire as they do in New York and the other fashionable centers to the South.

During this period the house type in New England changes from the
so-called Georgian of Colonial days to the square house, often of three
stories, but with many simpler houses of two stories scattered over the
countryside. There is also a continuing of the Georgian type house and
of the many houses, large and small, in all sections of the six states, of the
older central chimney and other early designs. And then, as the Greek
Revival style sweeps the country during the three decades beginning
about 1820, its temple-form dwellings are constructed throughout New
England, especially in new settlements and in older ones as well, where
a newly rich populace build houses for themselves.

In the majority of these Federal houses we find an interior differing
not too greatly from that of the Colonial. There is a new spaciousness
and symmetry. The fireplace is still present in any principal room, but it
has shrunk in size and no longer dominates the picture as it did in the

Early American and Colonial dwelling. Paneling has almost entirely disappeared, although in some instances a simple wainscot remains, capped by a delicate chair rail. Mantels, window and door trim, and sometimes cornices are beautifully carved, and often a new substance called "compo," an invention of Adam, decorates the wall panels and ceiling in raised scrolls and cartouches.

Although wallpapers showing the French or Chinese influence remain fashionable, a plain painted wall is just as popular. Colors have softened: gray, buff, pale rose, and Adam green are the favorites while pure white for woodwork is common.

The heavier and more ornate pieces of Chippendale have lost favor and have been replaced by the lighter and more graceful furniture of Hepplewhite and Sheraton inspiration. Although mahogany is still used, it is often inlaid with other woods, and satinwood, cherry, maple, and particularly rosewood are all fashioned into this new furniture. There is much veneering and inlay, using the classic motifs popularized by Adam. Furniture and accessories are paired: a pair of chairs, sofas, mirrors, et cetera.

The ceilings are high, rooms are often connected by double doorways, and windows are large. The materials used for draperies and upholstery are damask, brocade, satin, taffeta, velvet, printed linen, and chintz. The satins and taffetas are striped or dotted with medallions. New toiles de Jouy by Oberkampf in designs suitable for the period are also good. Draperies are made in the formal English and French styles with boxed cornices, swags, or fabric valances. As shown in the bedroom of the Pingree house in Salem in the illustration on page 128, cotton voile curtains with fringe for bedrooms are used with a swag valance and rosettes. The curtains in the Pingree front parlor are made of India mull and embroidered in Paris, and those in the Crowninshield memorial bedroom of the same house are the most elaborate. This bedroom also has a sofa showing the French influence and a Salem secretary topped by a brass eagle. In this period beds are usually beautifully and elaborately dressed. Chinese accessories of all kinds fit well into these spacious homes. Although the simpler home is furnished with less formal furniture and fabrics, it has the delicacy and balanced arrangement of the more elaborate dwelling. Instead of satins and taffetas for upholstery, toiles and chintzes are used, and ruffled tie-back curtains are good.

With the War of 1812 and the upsurge of patriotism, a new note enters the American decorating scheme—the use of the eagle to symbolize the new Republic. It tops mirrors and clocks and ornaments furniture in various ways. Indeed brass adornments of many kinds other than eagles are used extensively on Federal furniture. There are brass feet and casters and many types of applied embellishment. Fabrics and wallpapers with stars and stripes alone or combined are popular, and even the colors of the new American flag are used within the house.

In New York City Duncan Phyfe is making beautiful furniture influenced at first by Sheraton but later by the French Directoire and Empire, using the lyre motif for table supports, for chair backs and sofa arms, as well as Grecian curves in the backs and legs of chairs. Not yet has he succumbed to the demands of his clients for that heavy, cumbersome furniture, the American Empire.

During this period a new overmantel mirror comes into vogue as does the convex mirror surmounted by an eagle and the similar girandole with convex mirror and eagle but with the addition of candle brackets. The photograph of the Pingree dining room shows girandoles paired, as was the custom in the Federal period, as well as a pair of knife boxes on the sideboard and a pair of compotes on the table. Added to the furniture of the Colonial period are several new pieces. The Hepplewhite serpentine sideboard is a cherished possession in any home, and the Sheraton table of several parts as well as the extension dining table is introduced. The Martha Washington chair (shown in the extreme right of the Pingree bedroom), the hinged card table, tiered tables, and the drum table all make their appearance.

The floors in this Federal house are beautifully polished—sometimes of fine parquet—and are covered with handsome Oriental rugs. There are also the Aubusson rugs used in the Colonial interior, and, as the period advances, Savonnerie from France as well as Brussels and English Wiltons.

As the Greek Revival house invades New England, but not so much as in some other sections of the country, it in no way supersedes the four-square building but is constructed beside it. The interiors of this style are not too different, since the Greek temple ideal is not introduced within the house. Often, however, the windows on the main floor are room length.

Thus in considering the decorating problems of this Federal period as we interpret them today, we shall discuss two different types. The first is the simple and delicate interior inspired by Adam and the second the no-less-simple and elegant although perhaps more striking interior dominated by the French and English influence.

First we shall consider the decoration which followed so closely the Adam inspiration. The home decorator will not find it difficult to achieve the simple and delicate elegance which is the keynote of this style if she selects the soft colors used in the period, the furniture of Hepplewhite and Sheraton type, the materials indicated for draperies and upholstery, and then arranges her furnishings and accessories in the balanced, paired symmetry of the era—not, of course, carrying it to a monotonous degree.

The photographs of the Pingree house in Salem show furniture arrangement, type of furniture, and the way in which the window draperies were treated. Notice, also, the wonderful bed and its trappings. This period, like the Colonial, is one we can follow much more closely today than it is possible for us to do with either the Early American or the Victorian.

A few suggestions as to colors and furniture for this Adam-inspired home may be helpful. For the beautiful hallway of a Federal house, whether it be like the one appearing on page 218, or whether it has an elliptical staircase like the one appearing on page 2, I would suggest a paper similar to the "Ipswich." This comes with a soft gray background and a design in black and white. It is an architectural type wallpaper inspired by historical events and "portrays the exultation felt by the French nation in Britain's loss of her American colonies as a result of the American Revolution. It is believed to represent Washington, or perhaps one of the colonists, trampling British laws and chains underfoot. He is holding out to weeping Britannia a scroll inscribed '4 July 1776' symbolic of the Declaration of Independence. With his left hand he beckons America, personified by an American Indian, to come witness the humiliation of her oppressor." The original of this paper was probably made during the Federal period and undoubtedly in France. It is highly suitable for a spacious hall in a Federal home. Another paper for this purpose is very much the same in coloring, but instead of the patriotic design there is a formal garden with peacocks. This is called "Varrell." With either of these papers there should be a dado, and this and the other woodwork should be painted white. The floor could be painted, carpeted, or have inlaid linoleum in black-and-white diamonds as in the illustration on page 192, or it could be carpeted with a darker gray chenille. It could, of course, have Oriental rugs and a runner for the stairs.

For a dining room connecting with this hall you could use a paper called "Medallion," which is available in a soft green with a medallion in gold. The woodwork could be either a matching green or white. The draperies might be of slipper satin in a soft golden yellow, made with a valance similar to that in the Pingree dining room. The rug should be a mellow old Oriental, or, if one wished a more modern look, a large plain chenille in green much deeper than the wall. Chair seats could be striped green and gold. The furniture could be of Hepplewhite or Sheraton although Chippendale ladder-backs, which have a feeling of lightness, would also be appropriate. Instead of a portrait over the sideboard and the flanking girandoles one might, if desired, use an exceedingly beautiful Venetian mirror or a girandole with flanking gold-leaf wall brackets holding formal ornaments or a cache pot or cornucopia for flowers or green hanging plants.

The living room on the opposite side of the hall might be painted a yellow similar to the curtains in the dining room. The draperies could be of a striped taffeta in yellow and green or of green with a medallion in yellow. The rug would probably show these colors with a bit of rosy red and blue if it were either an Oriental or an Aubusson. One chair or sofa might be done in the drapery material and others in yellow or green, as desired. A bit of blue or red might also be introduced.

Another less formal living room might have the walls painted an olive-green with the woodwork an off-white. Curtains could be an off-white material similar to brocatelle—a material with a dull surface whether patterned or plain. The sofa and perhaps a chair might be upholstered with a glazed chintz showing a black background with a floral design of white flowers and green leaves. The other upholstery material in the room should be informal—no satin or damask. It could be of the drapery material, it could match the wall in color, or some lemon-yellow or cherry-red might be introduced for accent. Don't hesitate to use mirrors; they are even more acceptable than pictures, since they add spaciousness and formality. Lamps should also be formal, often of white and gold and with silk shades.

Bedrooms in houses of this Federal period may be done in softer colors: shrimp pink, warm gray, beige, off-white, and several shades of green. For example, a bedroom could use a delicate wallpaper called "Empire," which comes with a lovely shell-pink background and a small spot design in gold consisting of a conventionalized flower. With this I would have the woodwork matching. If you own as beautiful a bed as that in the Pingree bedroom and wish it as elaborately dressed, I would suggest satin for draperies and bed in a deep powder blue. Even a bed with a simpler canopy and curtains at the head only could use this blue satin. If a less formal material is desired, a toile de Jouy in a blue on white would be appropriate. Another suitable material would be a narrow striped taffeta in the same colorings. With the plain blue satin for draperies and bed, an olive-green-and-white-striped material might be used on a chaise longue or chair. If the toile or striped taffeta is used for draperies and bed, a plain material in powder blue with a small medallion in gold or cherry red might be used for the chaise longue and chair. If the room needed more light, voile curtains with only the valance of the material used on the bed would be appropriate. If you did not wish the Oriental rugs, a large shaggy rug covering much of the floor in a much deeper shade of the wall pink would be very attractive. And every room in this Federal house will be brightened by beautiful mirrors.

The exquisite beauty of the Federal interior is well shown by the photograph facing page 193 of the entrance hall of the Pierce Mansion, Portsmouth, New Hampshire built in 1799. This shows the archway, the circular wall space, the elliptical fanlights and side lights of the period; the paired tables on either side of the entrance door with their matched plants; a circular Hepplewhite settee, and a center hanging light with eagle.

However, this classicism of Adam was almost too delicate and beautiful for a growing, robust people. It had already felt the effect of the French Directoire with which it had something in common, and then both suffered the impact of the French Empire and the English Regency. In

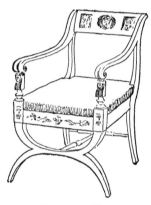

Regency Chair

England as well as in America the influence of Napoleon's France was seen in both decorating and in the making of furniture. In the England of the Regency wall surfaces were usually plain and painted in deep colors, such as red, brown, and green. While simplicity remained, it no longer was the somewhat effeminate simplicity of Adam. The balanced arrangement of furniture and accessories continued, and the interiors decorated in this new style had much of dignity and charm. Furniture became heavier and was upholstered in plain and patterned silk in vivid colors. Leather was also used for this purpose.

In France during these days of the Empire the general trend in decorating became more and more opulent. The favored colors were royal purple, emerald green, wine red, and brilliant yellow and blue. These colors were used for walls and woodwork as well as for the heavy silk draperies and upholstery. Designs on fabrics were symbolic of Napoleon's victories. There were rosettes, victory wreaths, bees (his chosen symbol), cornucopias, urns, torches, and honeysuckle. Much furniture was made of ebony and rosewood, often carved or decorated with sphinxes (after the campaign into Egypt), swans, acanthus, and similar objects, and embellished with ormolu mounts.

Although these influences were not felt so quickly in New England as in other parts of the country, they did have an effect. Much of this furniture and the newly vivid fabrics found their way to America for the homes of the fashionable and were copied by the cabinetmakers and manufacturers of the new Republic.

A few color suggestions—and only suggestions—as backgrounds for this imported style will follow. In most cases they would be used for the American Empire also if this formal, dignified style was desired.

Let us imagine we are entering a hall of medium size. The stairs face the entrance door, and a narrow hallway extends back for a short distance. The space permits very little furniture. Above a dado we will use a wallpaper called "Portsmouth Pineapple." This has a soft gray background with conventionalized pineapple design in grayed pinks and greens and a scrolling white vine between pineapples. We will paint the dado and woodwork white. On the wall opposite the staircase we will have a black-and-gold console table; over it, a large Venetian mirror. On the table we will place a pair of gold-and-black candelabra holding geranium-red candles. On either side of the table will be a Regency bench with a cushion of geranium-red-colored velvet. Floor and stairs will be covered with soft gray carpeting or with old Oriental rugs. From the ceiling we will hang a Venetian crystal chandelier.

At the left we enter a dining room with plain walls above a simple wainscot dado. We will use a wallpaper called "First Empire." It has a stone-gray background with a three-inch stripe of flowers and leaves in white with touches of gold. The space between these stripes is about fifteen inches wide and contains two large medallions about eight inches in diameter, one directly over the other to form another vertical design.

The first medallion is composed of two cornucopias spilling out flowers to form a victory wreath. The second is in the shape of a square. Bows form the corners and arrows divide the square into quarters. Flowers fill the interspaces. Between the stripes and the medallions, at regular intervals, is a bee. The entire design is in white with touches of gold. With this we would paint the dado and wood trim about one tone lighter than the gray background of the wallpaper. The draperies would be of emerald-green satin and the chair seats of a striped satin in the emerald green, wine red, and white. The table and sideboard may be of the early Duncan Phyfe style and the chairs similar to those shown on pages 82 and 202. Over the sideboard would be hung the most beautiful French or Venetian mirror available. On either end of the sideboard we would place a gold-and-black candelabrum holding tall green candles the same shade as the draperies. In front of each of the two end windows would be a tiered table, matching if possible, holding as many white flowering plants in white pots as their several tiers will accommodate. Between these windows there could be a Regency cabinet in mahogany or in the more dramatic black and gold. *Objets d'art* in the cabinet and on the fireplace mantel would add a further touch of red.

In the living room on the opposite side of the hall let us have emerald-green walls and woodwork with off-white draperies and rug. The main center of interest is a beautiful pinkish-brown marble fireplace. On one side of this would be placed a coral-red leather armchair with table and lamp beside it. Opposite would be two side chairs, the seats upholstered in a striped satin in green, yellow, and coral. Over the fireplace we would hang a large gold-framed mirror, or, if you prefer, a plain sheet of mirror from mantel to ceiling the width of the fireplace. The only mantel ornaments would be a matching pair of old French tole urns in dark red and gold. A second grouping on a long wall at the end of the room opposite the entrance door could consist of a large sofa upholstered in the off-white drapery material. Over it would be hung a group of four architectural drawings in red and green in simple gold-leaf frames. At either side of the couch a table would hold a tall Empire lamp in gold and white with white shade. To complete this grouping there would be a sizable chair at right angles to the couch at either end upholstered in a patterned material of off-white and coral.

In addition to the plain dark walls or wallpapers just suggested for hall, dining room, and living room, flock papers and three-inch stripes are good either for this furniture influenced by the English Regency and French Empire or for the American Empire. Gold-and-white, green-and-white, and rose-and-white-striped wallpapers are all good, or try a white flock paper with the furniture upholstered in emerald green or crimson.

Although this house of the late Federal period is more striking in color than the early Federal house of Adam inspiration, with furniture heavier than the Hepplewhite and Sheraton, it is still a house of classical balance and dignity, and this balance gives a simplicity not present in the Colonial home and certainly not in the Victorian.

VICTORIAN AS WE LIKE IT

WHETHER you like Victorian or not, it cannot be denied that it was the most lusty, perhaps the most human era of the American scene. It ran its course in a manner not unlike the life of a person, beginning as a rollicking young lady of the Fröhlich's syndrome type, rather plump, but certainly intelligent. As the period ends this young lady has developed into an unseemly old woman with false curls of a questionable reddish tinge, much paint on her cheeks, well-padded hips and bosom, and with a penchant for overdressing.

Since we make no pretense today of following the Victorian as it was in the period of 1830 to about 1880, there is no point in reviewing any of its aspects. We shall select for our homes in this modern Victorian some furniture from its fast-changing fashions. This will include pieces made by John Henry Belter, the New York City cabinetmaker, as well as love seats, lady's and gentleman's armchairs, and side chairs in the finger-, rose-, and grape-carved black walnut or rosewood. We shall choose, also, some of the Duncan Phyfe and a few pieces of the so-called American Empire, particularly sofas, chairs, secretaries, small sideboards, and chests of drawers. For informal bedrooms we shall not overlook the spool furniture made for country homes around the middle of the century nor the Hitchcock chairs and settees and the Boston rockers, all of which have already been indicated as appropriate for our Early American and Colonial interiors. With these items from the period itself modern sofas and chairs may be used as needed for comfort, and accessories from the Victorian years as well as modern items that seem appropriate and necessary.

During the Victorian years colors were somber and deep. Today we shall use them in their softer but no less heady shades: rose, mauve, violet, hydrangea blue, rich green and red, and yellow.

With the Victorian as a basis for our decorating scheme we must dramatize the furniture or its backgrounds to make it interesting. This may be done in either a formal or informal manner. An interior in this style should be a full-furnished one but not confused or cluttered, as were so many of its ancestors. This is one decorating scheme in which the homemaker may permit herself a certain amount of "stunt" decorating not advisable in the three preceding periods. It might be well, however, to confine this to one room in a house, and it should never be carried to a point of shock or irritation. I know one woman who kept a decorating scrapbook in which she noted every smart idea that appealed to her. When it came time to redecorate her house, she tried to use every idea in the book. Any individual room was not uninteresting, but by the time you had gone through the entire house, you realized that there were simply too many different "stunts" incorporated within the walls of one building. Even in "stunt" decorating there should be considered choice, and it is best to confine it to some room not in constant use—say a dining room, hall, game room, or guest room.

A Victorian room today should have the effect of cozy comfort. It is, I am sure, possible to decorate a home in this period style for less money than either the Colonial or the Federal, and since none of this furniture has entered the price brackets of Queen Anne, Chippendale, Hepplewhite, and Sheraton, it is still possible to find bargains.

To illustrate today's Victorian we present a number of rooms for a country home and a second group more suitable for a town apartment. Color pictures of these interiors would be a great help, but since that is not possible, word pictures will have to suffice.

For a country living room use a wallpaper called "Early Victorian." This has a gray background with six-inch stripes composed of small flowers in rosy red and blue with deep green leaves. These stripes are twelve inches apart and between them is a scattered spot design of bud and leaves in deeper grays than the paper background. Paint the woodwork to match the gray of the background. Floor coverings may be either scatter Oriental rugs, hooked floral rugs, or a dark gray carpet. Have the draperies the rosy red of the wallpaper flowers and loop them high over white organdie curtains. Place a gentleman's and a lady's chair upholstered in the red of the draperies on either side of the fireplace. In front of the fireplace have a coffee table made from a large shadow box mounted on a proper base and still showing beneath its glass top a wreath of old-time wax flowers. On either side of the fireplace have a console table made from an oval marble-top table cut in half. On the wall opposite this grouping have a large Belter love seat upholstered in a blue material with a small floral pattern in yellow and red, and at either end a couple of side chairs in lemon yellow. At the far end of the room place a modern baby grand piano with needlework-covered bench, and at the opposite end a game table of Victorian papier-mâché with its painted decoration and mother-of-pearl inlay and four matching chairs. Bookshelves, desk, accessories, and lamps make this a colorful, comfortable room.

For a man's bedroom we will paint the walls mocha and the woodwork oyster white. The furniture will be some old black walnut bought at a country auction for the proverbial song. The harsh, glossy finish has been removed and the wood refinished in a soft, gleaming walnut. The bed has had the high headboard cut down to a more modern height; the footboard has been discarded. The bedspread is of coarsely textured material in the mocha color of the walls, and the draperies are of the same material. On the floor is a large mocha-colored shag rug. If a contrast is desired, bedspread, draperies, and rug may be several shades lighter than the walls. There is a marble-top chest of drawers, and the mirror, formerly attached to it, hangs on the wall over it. Over the bed hangs a group of old *Vanity Fair* caricatures in narrow lacquer-red frames. On either side of the bed are small tables, each with its lamp made from a fairly large yellow tole canister with shade of plaid taffeta in red and green with some yellow. A library table also bought at the auction has been refinished and stands at right angles to one of the windows to serve as a desk. On this we will use desk fittings of brown or red leather and a double student lamp with yellow ribbed shades. A wastepaper basket made from a top-hat leather case stands beside the desk. A comfortable chair in red leather with its glint of brass nailheads completes the picture of a dignified, comfortable room achieved at little cost.

For the most feminine room in the house, either for the mistress or as a guest room, use a wallpaper called "Windsor Rose." This has a cream background with an all-over design of large luscious roses in beautiful shades of rose pink. Paint the woodwork to match one of the colors found in the roses—a shade almost a rose beige with a hint of mauve. A mauve rug covers most of the floor. For the headboard of the bed use the back of a Victorian rose-carved love seat. Paint this white and antique it with burnt umber and then upholster it in hydrangea-blue linen, tufted. Do not use a footboard but have this headboard attached to a Hollywood-type bedspring. Make the bedspread of blue linen piped with rose beige. The curtains may be of very fine Swiss embroidery in rose that exactly matches the woodwork, even if they have to be dyed. Make them very full and to the floor, with a ruffled valance and ruffles. Have them criss-cross and tied very high up, about the middle of the upper sash. Between the two front windows a dressing table has a skirt of the curtain material and a mirror top. Over it hangs a large oval mirror made from a very ornate Victorian picture frame painted the color of the woodwork. The dressing-table accessories are silver and amethyst, and all lampshades in the room are of the curtain material, with little picot ruffles top and bottom. A chaise longue is slip-covered in the material used for the bedspread, and a small boudoir chair upholstered in mauve with little Dresdenlike flowers in blue and pink.

Perhaps you have inherited, or in a rash moment bought, a Victorian painted bedroom set of furniture, a creamy white with touches of pink and blue. Use this for a young lady's room. The wallpaper should have a soft blue background with spot bunches of pink flowers. Have the draperies of blue glazed chintz the color of the wallpaper background with white chintz ruffles over white organdie curtains. The bedspread could be in the same blue chintz with white chintz center panel and bindings. Have the pillow covers square and of the blue chintz with perky white ruffles and stand them up straight against the headboard. The rug could be a deeper blue than the walls, or white, and a chaise longue might wear a pink slip cover.

Let's have the dining room the most striking room. We will use a flock paper called "Verona." This has a compact white flock design on a lemon-yellow background. The woodwork will be painted white. The hangings will be of heavy silk to match the paper background, with white glass curtains, both floor length. The floor covering will be olive green. We will use a round mahogany table and Victorian chairs, having padded back and seat. We will upholster these in persimmon-colored satin. A mahogany sideboard will have a pair of crystal candelabra, and there will be a crystal chandelier over the table.

If one wishes a different color scheme, this same paper comes in a soft sea-green combination—the flock design slightly deeper than the background. With this one could have the woodwork and hangings similar to the deeper tone in the paper, an Oriental rug, and chairs upholstered in rosy-red satin. Furnishings could be similar for both rooms.

And now let us do a few rooms in a town apartment—a bit more formal, perhaps. The apartment is in a converted brownstone house in New York City.

The living-room walls, woodwork, and ceiling may be painted smoke blue. The floor will be covered completely with a rosy red velvet carpet. The draperies will be of blue linen to match the wall color, patterned with large white flowers and made with a plain blue swag. By the fireplace there will be two overstuffed chairs upholstered in the drapery material. Between them and the wall on either side of the fireplace have a round table for lamps with a circular cover of olive-green satin, made like that in photograph shown on page 90. Over the fireplace hang a large mirror made from a wide ornate gold frame, painted with the blue wall paint and then rubbed while still wet so that glints of gold show through the blue. On the white marble fireplace mantel have a pair of cranberry lusters. On the wall opposite place a sofa upholstered in olive green and a couple of Victorian side chairs covered in blue and cranberry striped satin, one at either end of the couch. Lamps may be of cranberry overlay or crystal

with white shades. A secretary or whatnot may hold a collection of cranberry glass and bisque figurines.

In the adjoining dining room use American Empire furniture: an oval
pedestal table, a Duncan Phyfe type sideboard, and a pier table. The
chairs will be the comfortable Empire side chairs. There are two windows
at the end of the room opposite the large doorway from the living room.
This wall—windows and space between—will be treated as is that pictured on page 80 with a mirror panel between the windows and
the curtain swag carried over it. We will use a three-inch stripe gold-and-
white wallpaper, and the draperies will be a golden-yellow satin. A pier
table will be between the windows and will hold a large pair of French
ormolu candelabra. The rug will be old needlepoint, and the chair seats
of a striped material in wine, green, and yellow.

The bedroom in this apartment might have watermelon-pink walls,
dark green rug, and lime-green curtains. The bed might have a pink bedspread a little deeper than the wall. The dressing table between the windows could be a converted spinet, its worn-out innards removed. On a
dressing-table bench use a cushion to match the bedspread and a boudoir
chair upholstered in a pink-and-green-stripe material.

These rooms have been suggestions only, given in the hope that they
may spur you to work out color schemes and arrangements for your own
Victorian interiors and to help you solve the problem of using what may
seem to be uninteresting odds and ends of furniture. So much of this can
be adapted and beautified at little cost but more time and effort. It should
not be done carelessly. Unless done carefully and well, it will be apparent
to everyone that it is just a tawdry makeshift.

Entrance hall Gideon Tucker house built by Samuel McIntire at 126 Essex Street, Salem, Massachusetts, in 1805 (now demolished), showing French scenic paper. Courtesy The Essex

Lower front hall of Pingree House, Salem, Massachusetts. Designed by Samuel McIntire, 1804. Courtesy The Essex Institute

Appendix

APPENDIX

HISTORIC HOUSES

MAINE

Augusta—*Fort Western.* Original building, now a museum, was built in 1754, the start of Arnold's march on Quebec. *Open:* May 1 to September 30. *Exhibits:* invaluable historical pieces. *Admission:* 25c.

Brunswick—*Harriet Beecher Stowe House.* The home of the author of *Uncle Tom's Cabin. Open:* daily. *Admission:* no charge. Now an inn.

Columbia Falls—*Ruggles House.* Built in 1810. Noted for delicate detail of fine interior wood carvings. *Open:* daily. *Admission:* voluntary contribution.

Ellsworth—*Black House,* Surry Rd. Built about 1820. *Open:* weekdays May 30 to October 31 from 10 to 5; otherwise by appointment. *Exhibits:* furnishings of the period. *Admission:* 60c.; children 30c.; including tax. *Colonel Black Mansion. Open:* May 30 to November 1, weekdays from 10 to 5. *Exhibits:* period furniture, china, glass, beautiful garden. *Admission:* small charge for guide service.

Gorham—*Baxter House,* South St. Built in 1790s. Formerly the home of Dr. Elihu Baxter, presented by his son James Phinney Baxter. *Open:* July and August on Wednesday and Saturday from 2:30 to 5. *Admission:* 10c.

Kittery—*Fort McClary Blockhouse.* Original foundation built about 1715, then called Fort William, rebuilt in 1864. *Open:* June 1 to September 3. *Admission:* no charge. *Sparhawk Mansion.* Built in 1742, probably by Sir William Pepperell. *Open:* daily except Monday and Friday from 2 to 5. *Exhibits:* Georgian paneling, ballroom. *Admission:* 50c., tax included.

Kittery Point—*Lady Pepperell House.* Built in 1760. *Open:* June 18 to September 25, weekdays from 2 to 5. *Exhibits:* fine period furniture and furnishings. *Admission:* 50c., tax included S.P.N.E.A.

Machias—*Burnham Tavern,* corner of Main and Free Sts. Built in 1770, restored in 1907. *Open:* June 1 to October 1 on Saturday from 2 to 5; otherwise by appointment. *Exhibits:* relics from the Revolutionary period. *Admission:* 10c.

Key to Abbreviations.

S.P.N.E.A.—Property of the Society for the Preservation of New England Antiquities.

T.P.R.—Property of Trustees of Public Reservations (a private organization).

E.I.—Property of the Essex Institute.

N.P.S.—Property of the National Park Service.

N.S.C.D.—Property of National Society of Colonial Dames (followed by state).

Compiled by and reprinted with permission of The New England Council, The Museum of Fine Arts, Boston; The Society for the Preservation of New England Antiquities.

NORTH EDGECOMB—*Fort Edgecomb Blockhouse*. Built in 1809. *Open:* May 30 to September 15 from 9 to 9 daily. *Admission:* no charge.

PEMAQUID BEACH—*Fort William Henry*. Built in 1630. *Open:* May 30 to September 30 from 9 to 12 and from 1 to 5 daily. *Admission:* 10c. fifteen years or older.

PORTLAND—*Old Tate House*, 370 Westbrook St. Built in 1755 by George Tate. *Open:* July 1 to August 31 from 10:30 to 5:30 on Tuesday and Friday and 2 to 5 on Sunday. *Admission:* 35c. N.S.C.D., Me. *L.D.M. Sweat Mansion*, 105 Spring St. Built in 1800. *Open:* year round except Monday from 10 to 4:30 on weekdays; 2 to 4:30 Sunday; closed on Sunday during July and August. *Admission:* no charge. *Victoria Mansion*, corner of Park and Danforth Sts. Built in 1859. *Open:* daily except Monday from 2 to 5. *Exhibits:* excellent examples of Victorian art, architecture, and decoration. *Admission:* 60c. *The Wadsworth-Longfellow House*, 485 Congress St. Built in 1785. *Open:* June 16 to September 13 from 9:30 to 4:30 daily except Sunday. *Exhibits:* memorabilia of Longfellow and Wadsworth families. *Admission:* 40c.; children 30c. including tax.

SOUTH BERWICK—*Sarah Orne Jewett Memorial*, 101 Portland St. Built in 1774. *Open:* all summer on weekdays from 9 to 5. Sundays by appointment. *Exhibits:* fine example of Colonial interior with antique furnishings. *Admission:* 25c. S.P.N.E.A.

THOMASTON—*Montpelier House*, a reproduction built in 1929 of the original General Knox Mansion (1795). *Open:* May 30 to October 31 from 10 to 6 daily. *Exhibits:* antique furnishings and possessions of Major Gen. Henry Knox. *Admission:* 50c.

WATERVILLE—*William Redington House and Museum*, 64 Silver St. Built in 1813. The museum was built later by Miss Ada Redington. *Open:* year round daily from 2 to 9, except Sunday. *Exhibits:* articles connected with the early life of Waterville and vicinity. *Admission:* no charge.

YORK VILLAGE—*Old Gaol Museum*, Main St. Built in 1653. *Open:* June 25 to September 25; weekdays 9:30 to 5:30; Sunday 1:30 to 5:30. *Exhibits:* American Colonial Relics. *Admission:* Adults 30c., children 12c., including tax.

NEW HAMPSHIRE

CORNISH—*Saint-Gaudens Memorial*. Built in 1800, originally a country tavern. *Open:* May 30 to October 15 from 10 to 6 daily. *Exhibits: The Little Studio*, personal workshop of Saint-Gaudens, contains a large collection of bas-reliefs, portraits, busts, and reductions. Such work as *Sherman Monument, The Pilgrim*, and the seated *Lincoln* was done here. *The New Studio* contains casts of Saint-Gaudens' larger works. *Admission:* 25c.

DOVER—*Dame Garrison House*, 182 Central Ave., on the grounds of the *Woodman Institute*. Built about 1675. *Open:* year round from 2 to 5. *Admission:* no charge.

EXETER—*Cincinnati Hall* (former Ladd-Gilman House), Governor's Lane. Built in 1721. *Open:* year round on Thursday from 2 to 4 by application to the caretaker. *Exhibits:* relics of the Revolutionary period, antiques, portraits, and engravings. *Admission:* no charge.

FRANKLIN—*Daniel Webster's Birthplace*, on Rt. 127. Built in 1780, restored in 1913, maintained by the state of New Hampshire. *Open:* year round (guide in attendance). *Exhibits:* antique furnishings, arts and crafts shop. *Admission:* no charge.

HILLSBORO—*Franklin Pierce Birthplace*. Built in 1804 and restored in 1925. *Open:* June 15 to October 15 from 1 to 5 daily. *Exhibits:* scenic wallpaper and stenciled walls, period furniture. *Admission:* no charge.

PETERBOROUGH—*"Bleakhouse,"* Wilton Road. Built c. 1796. Guest house the year round. *Exhibits:* some original finish and restored wall stenciling. S.P.N.E.A.

PORTSMOUTH—*Thomas Bailey Aldrich House,* 386 Court St. Built in 1790, scene of *The Story of a Bad Boy. Open:* daily from 10 to 5 except Sunday. *Exhibits:* restored as an eighteenth-century home with family touches everywhere. *Admission:* 50c.; children under twelve years 25c. *Richard Jackson House,* Jackson Hill St. Built in 1664. *Open:* June 18 to September 25, weekdays from 11 to 5. *Exhibits:* seventeenth-century architectural details, leaded-glass windows, furniture. *Admission:* 25c. S.P.N.E.A. *John Paul Jones House,* State St. Built in 1758. *Open:* June 15 to September 15 from 10 to 5 weekdays. *Exhibits:* china, silver, books, documents, furniture, portraits, and costumes. *Admission:* 50c. *Governor John Langdon Mansion Memorial,* 143 Pleasant St. Built in 1784, described by Washington as the "handsomest house in Portsmouth." *Open:* June 18 to September 25, Friday and Saturday from 2 to 5. *Exhibits:* antiques, paneling, gardens. *Admission:* 75c., tax included. S.P.N.E.A. *Moffatt-Ladd House,* 146 Market St. Built in 1763. *Open:* June 15 to September 15 weekdays from 10 to 5. *Exhibits:* china, pewter, silver, antique furnishings, bedspreads, portraits, and other relics of interest. *Admission:* 50c. N.S.C.D., N. H. *Warner House,* Daniels and Chapel Sts. Built in 1718. *Open:* June 15 to September 15 from 10 to 5 on weekdays. *Exhibits:* antiques and portraits. *Admission:* 50c. *Wentworth-Gardner House,* Gardner and Mechanics Sts. Built in 1760. *Open:* June 15 to September 15 from 10 to 5 on weekdays. *Exhibits:* perfect example of Georgian architecture; carving, scenic wallpapers. *Admission:* 50c.; children under five no charge.

SHARON—*Laws House.* Built c. 1800. *Open:* by appointment. *Exhibits:* part of Sharon Arts Center. *Admission:* no charge.

VERMONT

BROWNINGTON—*Old Stone House.* Built in 1836. *Open:* May 1 to October 30, from 9 to 4. *Exhibits:* brick oven, spinning wheel, loom, handmade tools, and simple, homely articles of the Vermont pioneer home. *Admission:* 50c.

BURLINGTON—*Grassmount,* 411 Main St. Built in 1804, and regarded as the best example of Georgian architecture in Vermont. The house is now a dormitory for women. The public rooms may be seen upon request and during vacations the whole house is open. *Open:* year round from 10 to 6. *Admission:* no charge.

FERRISBURGH—*"Rokeby,"* one mile north of Ferrisburgh Center. Built before 1784, with additions in 1812. *Open:* May 1 to November 1 from 2 to 8 daily. *Exhibits:* possessions of Rowland Evans Robinson; furnishings of early America. *Admission:* 25c.; children, no charge.

GRAND ISLE—*Hyde Log Cabin.* Built in 1787. *Open:* June 1 to October 31, daily. *Exhibits:* antiques, historical relics of the Islands. *Admission:* no charge.

KENT CORNERS (Calais, 10 miles north of Montpelier)—*Kent Tavern,* country museum of the Vermont Historical Society. Built in 1835, restored in 1948. *Open:* June 1 to October 31, daily. *Exhibits:* old tools, agricultural implements, and home industries. *Admission:* no charge, by card from Vermont Historical Society, Montpelier.

MIDDLEBURY—*Middlebury Community House.* Built in 1815, known as the *"Battell House." Open:* year round from Tuesday through Saturday from 2 to 5. *Exhibits:* beautiful Adam mantels, circular staircase. *Admission:* no charge.

WINDSOR—*Old Constitution House,* 15 North St. Built about 1768 and restored in 1912. *Open:* year round. *Exhibits:* antiques, portraits, grooved beams; house in which the

Vermont Constitution was drawn up and signed in 1777, and used for the first session of the state legislature. *Admission:* no charge.

MASSACHUSETTS

ADAMS—*Eleazer Brown Homestead,* Orchard St. Built 1778, partly refurnished with period furniture. *Open:* all summer, daily. *Admission:* no charge.

AMESBURY—*Macy-Colby House,* Main St. Built about 1650. *Open:* June 1 to August 31 from 2 to 5, Wednesday. *Exhibits:* typical pioneer home. *Admission:* voluntary contribution. *John Greenleaf Whittier Home,* 86 Friend St. Purchased by the poet in 1836 and occupied by him for fifty-six years. *Open:* year round from 10 to 5 daily, Sunday by appointment. *Exhibits:* memorabilia of Whittier, antiques. *Admission:* voluntary contribution. Special consideration for children and parties.

AMHERST—*Nehemiah Strong House,* 67 Amity St. Built in 1774. *Open:* June 1 to October 1 from 2 to 5 on Tuesday and Friday. *Exhibits:* collection of local interest. *Admission:* 25c.

ANDOVER—*Deacon Amos Blanchard House,* 97 Main St. Built in 1819. *Open:* daily 2 to 5, and by appointment. *Exhibits:* local furnishings of the period. Staffordshire, glass. *Admission:* voluntary contribution.

ARLINGTON—*Jason Russell House,* 7 Jason St. Built around 1680. *Open:* April 1 to November 1 from 2 to 5 daily except Sunday and Monday (other times by appointment). *Exhibits:* holes made by British bullets on April 19, 1775; souvenirs of the Revolutionary period. *Admission:* voluntary contributions.

ATTLEBORO—*Peck House.* Built before 1776. *Open:* year round by appointment. *Admission:* no charge.

BERNARDSTON—*Ryther House.* Built in 1745. *Open:* year round when convenient. *Exhibits:* murals on plaster walls supposedly done by a British spy during the War of 1812; Indian shutters, early furniture, pewter, glass, tools, prints, and relics. *Admission:* no charge.

BEVERLY—*Balch House,* 448 Cabot St. Built in 1638, by the Old Planter, John Balch. *Open:* year round daily except Sunday and holidays, from 10 to 6 (summer) and 10 to 4 (winter). *Exhibits:* house furnishings, especially of Colonial days. *Admission:* no charge. *Cabot House,* 117 Cabot St. Built in 1781. *Open:* July 1 to August 31 from 10 to 4 daily except Sunday; other months same hours Monday, Wednesday, Friday, and Saturday. *Exhibits:* articles of historic interest by sea and land in great variety. *Admission:* no charge. *Hale House,* 39 Hale St. Built in 1694 by the Rev. John Hale, the first minister in Beverly. *Open:* June 15 to September 15 from 10 to 12 and 2 to 5 daily except Sunday and Monday. *Exhibits:* furnished as the home of generations of an American family; a notable collection of lamps, both foreign and American; the Loring Family Museum. *Admission:* no charge.

BILLERICA—*Billerica Historical Society,* Concord Rd. Built before 1723, now restored. *Open:* year round; caretaker usually in residence. *Exhibits:* antiques and manuscripts revealing Billerica history. *Admission:* no charge.

BOSTON—*Faneuil Hall.* Built in 1742. Armory of the Ancient and Honorable Artillery, the oldest military organization in the country (top floor). *Open:* year round daily from 10 to 4 weekdays, Saturday from 10 to 12 and Sunday from 2 to 5. The Armory is closed on Sunday. *Admission:* no charge. *Harrison Gray Otis House,* 141 Cambridge St. Built in 1795. *Open:* on weekdays from 9 to 4:45; Saturday from 9 to 12:45.

Exhibits: furnished house and New England Museum containing historical collections of glass, pottery, silver, costumes, ship models, Shaker objects, pewter, painted ware, dolls. *Admission:* 25c. S.P.N.E.A. *Paul Revere House,* 19 North Square. Built about 1676 and restored in 1908. *Open:* 10 to 4 daily except Sunday and holidays. *Exhibits:* original furnishings. *Admission:* 30c.; special rates for student classes.

BOURNE—"*Aptucxet,*" Gray Gables Road. A 1930 reproduction of Plymouth Colony's first trading post, built in 1627. *Open:* April 1 to November 1 daily except Monday. *Exhibits:* historical relics from the Pilgrim period. *Admission:* 25c.; children, 10c.

BOXFORD—*Holyoke-French House.* Built in 1760. *Open:* summer, Sunday from 3 to 5, or on request to custodian. *Exhibits:* pre-Revolutionary furnishings, primitive paintings, shoemaker's equipment, and farm tools in barn. *Admission:* 25c.

BROOKLINE—*Edward Devotion House,* 347 Harvard St. Built about 1680. *Open:* year round Saturdays from 2 to 4; other times by appointment. *Admission:* 25c.; children accompanied by an adult, no charge.

CAMBRIDGE—*Cooper-Frost-Austin House,* 21 Linnaean St. Built about 1657. The oldest house in Cambridge. *Open:* from 2 to 5 on Thursday only. *Exhibits:* early furniture. *Admission:* 25c. S.P.N.E.A. *Harvard University,* 5 Weld Hall in the Harvard Yard. Arrangements for free guide service. *Open:* year round weekdays from 9 to 5. *Admission:* no charge. *John Hicks House,* Boylston and South Sts. Built in 1762. Formerly used by General Putnam as an army office, now a library. *Open:* year round by application to Kirkland House superintendent; office in "H" entry on Dunster St. *Admission:* no charge. *The Longfellow House,* 105 Brattle St. Built in 1759 by Maj. John Vassell, a British Tory. Headquarters of General Washington from July 1775 to April 1776. Enlarged in 1793 by its new owner, Andrew Craigie. Home of Longfellow from 1837 until his death in 1882. Here most of his poems were written. *Open:* year round from 2 to 4 daily. *Exhibits:* marble busts, oil paintings, portraits, furniture and china, books and manuscripts; house is today as Longfellow left it; Longfellow Garden. *Admission:* 30c. including tax. *Wadsworth House,* Massachusetts Ave. Built in 1726. Here Harvard presidents resided for 125 years. *Open:* year round weekdays from 9 to 5. *Admission:* no charge.

CHATHAM—*Old Atwood House,* Atwood St. Built in 1752. *Open:* July 1 to August 31 from 2 to 5 Wednesday and Friday and by appointment. *Exhibits:* antiques and relics and the Joseph C. Lincoln Memorial Room. *Admission:* voluntary contribution.

CHELSEA—*The Bellingham-Cary House.* Built in 1659 by Gov. Richard Bellingham. Enlarged, 1791. Here Washington placed the last outpost of the left wing of the Continental Army besieging Boston. *Open:* year round on Thursday from 2 to 5. *Admission:* 25c.; children, 10c.

CONCORD—*Emerson House,* Cambridge Turnpike. Built in 1828. Occupied by Ralph Waldo Emerson from 1835 until his death in 1882. *Open:* April 19 to December 1 from 10 to 11:30 and 1:30 to 5:30 weekdays except Monday, and 2:30 to 5:30 Sunday; large groups by appointment. *Admission:* 25c.; children, 15c. *Grapevine Cottage,* Lexington Road. Built before 1690 and restored in 1896. *Open:* June 15 to September 15 from 12 to 8:30 daily. *Exhibits:* the original Concord grapevine; antiques. *Admission:* no charge. *The Old Manse.* Built in 1769 by Rev. Wm. Emerson, Concord's pastor who was succeeded by Rev. Ezra Ripley. Ralph Waldo Emerson here wrote his essay "Nature." Nathaniel Hawthorne home from 1842 to 1845. *Open:* April 19 to November 11 from 10 to 5 weekdays except Monday; Sunday 2 to 5. *Exhibits:* memorabilia of Ripley family. *Admission:* 35c.; children, 20 c. including tax. T.P.R. *Old Orchard House,* Lexington Road. Built in 1650 and 1730, formerly comprised two houses, remodeled and brought together by the Alcotts (*Little Women*) for their home. *Open:* April 19 to November 1 from 10 to 5 weekdays except Monday and 2 to 6 Sunday. *Admission:* 30c.; children under seven, no charge. *The Wayside*, Lexington Road. Built before 1717, remodeled in 1845 and again in 1860. Occupied by Nathaniel Hawthorne, Louisa May Alcott, and "Margaret Sidney," author of *The Five Little Peppers*. *Open:* May 1 to June 15 week ends and by appointment; June 16 to October 4 daily except Tuesday; October 5 to 30 week ends and by appointment. *Admission:* 30c. including tax; children between eight and eleven years, 18c.

CUMMINGTON—*William Cullen Bryant Homestead*. Mr. Bryant wrote his *Thanatopsis* here at the age of eighteen years. *Open:* year round from 2 to 5 Monday, Wednesday and Friday. *Exhibits:* memorabilia of the family, furnished just as it was when Bryant lived there. *Admission:* 25c. T.P.R.

DANVERS—*Rebecca Nurse House*, 149 Pine St. Built in 1678. *Open:* weekdays 10 to 5 during summer months; other times by appointment. *Exhibits:* rooms of the seventeenth century. *Admission:* 25c.; children free. S.P.N.E.A. *Page House*, 11 Page St. Built in 1754. *Open:* April 1 to November 30 on Saturday afternoon and by appointment. *Exhibits:* antiques and historical relics. *Admission:* small charge.

DANVERSPORT—*Samuel Fowler House*, 166 High St. Built in 1810. *Open:* Wednesday 3 to 5; Saturday 10 to 5; other times by appointment. *Exhibits:* antiques, wallpaper, woodwork, in original condition, and some pewter. *Admission:* 25c. S.P.N.E.A.

DEDHAM—*Fairbanks House*, at Eastern Ave. and East St. Built by Jonathan Fayrebanke in 1636, still stands in its original form, now generally accepted today to be the oldest wooden framed house in this country. Occupied continuously by Fairbanks kin 1636 up to 1903, when it was acquired by the Fairbanks Family in America, Inc. *Open:* May 1 to November 1 daily from 9 to 6. *Exhibits:* antiques, objects handed down in the family for generations. *Admission:* voluntary contribution.

DEERFIELD—*Parson Ashley House*. Built in 1733, restored in 1948. *Open:* May 1 to November 1 daily, except Monday and Thursday, from 10 to 12 and from 2 to 4, Sundays from 2 to 4:30; November 1 to May 1 by appointment. *Exhibits:* antique furnishings, fabrics, pewter, china, and belongings of the Tory parson. *Admission:* 60c., including tax. *Frary House*. Built in 1689 with eighteenth-century additions including a Colonial ballroom. *Open:* May 1 to October 1 daily from 10 to 4. *Exhibits:* rare example of tavern of Revolutionary period. *Admission:* 48c., including tax. *Indian House Memorial*, Old Deerfield St. Reproduced in 1929 as an exact replica of John Sheldon's Old Indian House, dating from 1698. In the garden is the Bloody Brook Tavern, built in 1700 and moved to Deerfield in 1932. *Open:* from 9 to 12 and 1 to 5 weekdays except Tuesday, and 1 to 5 Sunday. Both houses open for season May 10. *Admission:* 25c.; children under twelve, no charge. *The Old Manse*, or *Willard House*, Main St. Constructed in 1694 and restored in 1768. *Open:* upon application at the Deerfield Academy office. *Exhibits:* antiques, wallpaper, ironworks, and old fireplaces. *Admission:* no charge. *The John Williams House* (1707), the *Ephraim Williams House* (1760), and the *Nims House* (1710). *Open:* upon application at the Deerfield Academy office. *Admission:* no charge.

DOVER—*Miller-Cary House*. Built in 1777. *Open:* by appointment. *Admission:* no charge.

DUXBURY—*John Alden House*, Alden St. Built in 1653 by Jonathan Alden, third son of John and Priscilla Alden. *Open:* April 15 to November 15 daily. *Admission:* 25c.

FAIRHAVEN—*Captain Thomas Bennett House*, 199 Main St. Built in 1810. *Open:* weekdays from 9 to 5, Sunday by appointment. *Exhibits:* good old mahogany furniture. *Admission:* 25c. S.P.N.E.A.

FALMOUTH—*Julia A. Wood House*, Palmer Ave. Built about 1790. *Open:* July 1 to September 30 from 2 to 6 weekdays except Monday, and 10 to 12 on Saturday. *Exhibits:* possessions from whaling ships, portraits, old glass, and china. *Admission:* 25c.; children, 15c.

FRAMINGHAM CENTER—*The 1812 House*, on Rt. 9. Built in 1812. *Open:* year round. *Exhibits:* much of the house, especially the stairway and the old fireplaces where the cooking was done, is unchanged. *Admission:* no charge. House is now an inn.

GLOUCESTER—*James Babson Cooperage Shop*, between Gloucester and Rockport. Built in 1658. Believed the oldest building on Cape Ann. Built and used by James Babson. *Open:* year round from 3:30 to 5:30 on Saturday. *Exhibits:* early American tools and furniture. *Admission:* no charge. *Beauport*, Eastern Point Boulevard. *Open:* weekdays, except Saturday and holidays. Guided tour at 2:30, 3:30, and 4:30 from June through September. *Exhibits:* over 50 rooms of different types and periods, beautifully furnished with all kinds of antiquities. *Admission:* $1.00; children, 50c. S.P.N.E.A. *The Riggs House*. Oldest house in Gloucester. Log cabin built in 1638, main house in 1700. *Open:* by appointment. *Exhibits:* first schoolhouse; old household equipment. *Admission:* 50c. *Sargent-Murray-Gilman-Hough House*, 49 Middle St. Built in 1768 and remodeled in 1916. *Open:* July 1 to September 25 from 11 to 5 weekdays. *Exhibits:* portraits, furniture, wood paneling. *Admission:* 30c. including tax.

GROTON—*Governor Boutwell House*, Main St. *Open:* June to October, Saturday from 3 to 5. *Admission:* no charge.

HADLEY—*Old Hadley Farm Museum*. Built in 1782, present building remodeled from the original. *Open:* May 1 to November 1 from 2:30 to 5 on Saturday and Sunday. *Admission:* no charge.

HANOVER CENTER—*Samuel Stetson House*. Built about 1694 and enlarged before 1716. *Open:* weekdays from 10 to 5, Sundays by appointment. *Admission:* 25c. S.P.N.E.A.

HARVARD—*Fruitlands and the Wayside Museum, Inc.* Built before 1717. The group includes Shaker House (1781), the "New Eden" of A. Bronson Alcott, the American Indian Museum, and gallery of American paintings. *Open:* May 29 to September 26; 12:30 to 6 daily. *Exhibits:* picture galleries showing work of American primitives and Hudson River artists. *Admission:* 10c. to each house.

HAVERHILL—*The Buttonwoods*, Water St. Built in 1814. *Open:* year round from 2 to 5 on Tuesday, Thursday, and Saturday. *Exhibits:* household furnishings of the eighteenth and nineteenth centuries; very fine collection of Indian relics; articles connected with the life of Justice William H. Moody; Hannah Dustin relics. *John Ward House*, 240 Water St. Built before 1645. *Open:* year round from 2 to 5 on Tuesday, Thursday, and Saturday. *Exhibits:* complete seventeenth-century furnishings. *Admission:* voluntary contribution. *John Greenleaf Whittier Homestead*. Built in 1688. The scene of the poem *Snowbound*. *Open:* year round daily from 10 to 6 except Mondays. *Admission:* 25c.; children accompanied by an adult, 10c.

HINGHAM—*Old Ordinary* (Hingham Historical Society), 19 Lincoln St. Built in 1650. *Exhibits:* antique furniture and Americana. *Samuel Lincoln House*, 182 North St. Built about 1741, later additions at back. *Open:* Monday from 2 to 5. *Exhibits:* two rooms as Lincoln family memorial. S.P.N.E.A.

IPSWICH—*Emerson-Howard House*, Turkey Shore Road. Built about 1648. *Open:* at reasonable hours the year round. *Admission:* 25c. S.P.N.E.A. *Hart House* on Line Brook Road, 0.7 of a mile off Rt. 1A. Built in 1640. *Open:* May to December. *Exhibits:* early American antiques, fine example of early seventeenth-century architecture. *Admission:* no charge. Now an inn.

Ipswich—*Preston-Foster House*, 6 Water St. Built about 1640. *Open:* year round, daily except Monday, 10 to 5. *Exhibits:* mainly structural interest. *Admission:* 25c. S.P.N.E.A. *John Whipple House*, 53 South Main St. Built about 1640 with additions by Captain John Whipple (1670) and Maj. John Whipple (1700). *Open:* year round from 10 to 6 weekdays except Mondays, and 1 to 6 Sunday. *Exhibits:* genealogical records, documents, china, early interiors, seventeenth- and eighteenth-century furniture. Inquire also about *Hurd House. Admission:* voluntary contribution.

Kingston—*Major John Bradford House.* Built in 1674, remodeled in 1720, and restored in 1921. *Open:* July 1 to September 6 from 9:30 to 5:30 weekdays and Sunday by appointment. *Exhibits:* the interior is a replica of an authentic Pilgrim home. *Admission:* 25c.; children, 10c.

Lexington—*Buckman Tavern.* Built in 1690. Meeting place of the Minute Men, April 19, 1775. *Open:* April 19 to October 1 from 10 to 5 weekdays; 2 to 5 on Sunday. *Exhibits:* antiques and historical relics, old bar. *Admission:* 25c. *Hancock-Clark House*, 35 Hancock St. Built in 1693. Samuel Adams and John Hancock were sleeping here when aroused by Paul Revere April 18, 1775. *Open:* May 22 to October 12 from 10 to 5 weekdays, and 2 to 5 Sunday. *Exhibits:* valuable collection of relics of early days. *Admission:* 25c. *Munroe Tavern*, 1332 Massachusetts Ave. Built in 1695. British Earl Percy used as his headquarters and care for his wounded soldiers April 19, 1775. Washington was entertained here in 1789. *Open:* April 19 to November 11 from 9:30 to 5 weekdays; Sunday 2 to 5. *Exhibits:* collections of historical articles. *Admission:* voluntary contribution.

Lincoln—*William Hartwell House.* Built between 1636 and 1639. *Open:* year round daily from 12 to 8. *Admission:* no charge. Now an inn called Hartwell Farm.

Lowell—*Whistler's House.* Built in 1823. Birthplace and former home of James McNeill Whistler. *Open:* year round except during August, from 10 to 5 weekdays except Monday, and 1:30 to 5 on Sunday. *Exhibits:* etchings, et cetera, works pertaining to Whistler, works of contemporary artists; at times arts and crafts. *Admission:* no charge.

Lynn—*Hyde-Mills House.* Built in 1839. *Open:* year round from 9 to 11 and 1 to 4; Saturday 9 to 11. *Exhibits:* furniture, silver, and documents. *Admission:* no charge.

Manchester—*Manchester Historical House*, 12 Union St. Built around 1830 and restored in 1933. *Open:* July 1 to August 31 from 2 to 5 on Wednesday. *Admission:* no charge.

Mansfield—*Fisher-Richardson House.* Built in 1704, enlarged in 1800, and restored in 1930. *Open:* June 15 to October 1 from 2 to 5 on Saturday and Sunday. *Exhibits:* interiors and furnishings of the period and examples of early American industries. *Admission:* no charge.

Marblehead—*Colonel Jeremiah Lee Mansion*, 161 Washington St. Built in 1768. *Open:* year round from 9 to 5 weekdays. *Exhibits:* one of the finest examples of Colonial architecture. Noted for finely carved staircases, original hand-painted wallpaper and collection of antique furniture. *Admission:* 30c. *King Hooper Mansion*, Hooper St. Built in 1728. Now headquarters of Marblehead Art Association. *Open:* year round from 2 to 5 daily except Monday. *Exhibits:* paneled rooms, with period pieces; monthly art collection. *Admission:* no charge.

Marshfield—*Historic Winslow House*, corner of Careswell and Webster Sts. Built in 1699 and remodeled about 1756. *Open:* June 15 to September 15 from 10 to 6 daily. *Exhibits:* children's room, Daniel Webster's room. *Admission:* 25c.; children under ten years, 10c.

MEDFORD—*Peter Tufts House,* 350 Riverside Ave., near Spring St. Built about 1678. *Open:* at any reasonable hour. *Exhibits:* Gambrel-roof brick house with superb oak beams exposed inside and early staircase. *Admission:* 25c. S.P.N.E.A. *Royall House,* 15 George St. Built in 1637 by Governor John Winthrop, additions made by Lt. Governor John Usher around 1690 and Colonel Isaac Royall in 1732. *Open:* May 1 to October 1 from 2 to 5 daily except Monday and Friday. *Exhibits:* furnishings of the period. *Admission:* 30c.; children, 15c.; groups of twenty or more, 10c.

MILTON—*Governor Belcher House,* 401 Adams St. Built in 1777 by the widow of Governor Jonathan Belcher. *Open:* year round on application to custodians, Mr. and Mrs. Nathaniel Lord. *Admission:* no charge.

NANTUCKET—*Jethro Coffin House,* Sunset Rd. Built in 1686 by John Gardner for his daughter, who became the wife of Jethro Coffin. It is the oldest house on the island. Restored in 1926. *Open:* June 20 to September 10 daily. *Admission:* 25c. *Lydia S. Hinchman House,* Vestal St. *Open:* June 15 to September 15 from 10 to 5 daily except Sunday. *Exhibits:* island birds, shells, insects, plants, and daily fresh flowers of season. *Admission:* no charge. *Maria Mitchell Memorial House,* 1 Vestal St. Built in 1790. Birthplace of Maria Mitchell, pioneer astronomer and educator. *Open:* June 15 to September 15 from 10 to 12 and 2 to 5 daily except Sunday. *Exhibits:* period furniture, "widow's walk" on roof, children's room. *Admission:* 25c. *Old Jail,* Vestal St. *Open:* June 20 to September 10 daily. *Admission:* 25c. *Old Wind Mill,* Mill Hill. Built in 1746. *Open:* June 20 to September 10 daily. *Admission:* 25c.

NEWBURY—*Tristram Coffin House,* 14 High Road. Original ell built about 1651. *Open:* Monday, Wednesday, Friday, 2 to 5, the year round. *Exhibits:* period furnishings and interiors. *Admission:* 25c. S.P.N.E.A. *Jackman-Willett House,* "The High Road." Built in 1696 by Richard Jackman. *Open:* upon request. *Exhibits:* early relics of Newbury. *Admission:* voluntary contribution. *Short House,* 33 High Road. Built in 1733. *Open:* weekdays from 10 to 5 during summer months; Sunday by appointment. *Exhibits:* antiques and original paneling of the period. *Admission:* 25c. S.P.N.E.A. *Swett-Ilsley House,* 4 and 6 High Road. Built before 1670. *Open:* March 19 through Christmas; closed Saturday and Monday. Partly used as a tearoom. *Exhibits:* old woodwork and fireplaces. *Admission:* 25c. S.P.N.E.A.

NEWBURYPORT—*Bradbury-Spaulding House,* 28 Green St. Built about 1788–91. *Open:* Monday, Wednesday, Friday, 10 to 5; other times by appointment. *Exhibits:* some furniture, paintings, and prints. *Admission:* 25c. S.P.N.E.A. *Pettingill-Fowler House.* Built in 1793. Museum of History of Old Newbury. *Open:* June 1 to September 30, daily except Sunday and holidays. *Exhibits:* furniture, china, oriental curios, combs, guns, et cetera. *Admission:* 10c., except Wednesday, no charge.

NORTHAMPTON—*Cornet Joseph Parsons House,* 58 Bridge St. *Open:* Wednesday, Friday, and Sunday from 2 to 5 and by appointment; telephone 990. *Exhibits:* antiques presented to Northampton Historical Society. *Admission:* voluntary contribution. *Isaac Damon House,* 46 Bridge St. *Open:* summer by appointment. *Exhibits:* antiques, collection of Jenny Lind articles.

NORTH OXFORD—*Clara Barton Birthplace,* on Clara Barton Road (between Rts. 12 and 20). Built in 1805 by Stephen Barton, Clara's father. *Open:* year round. *Exhibits:* possessions and souvenirs of Clara Barton. *Admission:* no charge.

NORTH SWANSEA—*Martin House,* Fall River Ave., on the highway between Providence and Fall River. Built in 1728. *Open:* May 15 to November 1 from 10 to 6 daily. *Exhibits:* old pewter, china, silver, antiques, household utensils, clocks, needlework, portraits. *Admission:* 25c.; children 15c. N.S.C.D., Mass.

NORWELL—*Jacobs Farmhouse*, Cor. Main St. and Jacobs Lane, Assinippi. Built in 1726. *Open*: Monday and Thursday 2 to 5, June through September. *Exhibits*: collection of fire apparatus from 1760 to early 1900s in barn. *Admission*: voluntary contribution. S.P.N.E.A.

PEABODY—*General Gideon Foster House*, 35 Washington St. Built in 1800. *Open*: July 1 to September 30 from 2 to 5 on Wednesday. *Exhibits*: antiques, pottery. *Admission*: no charge.

PLYMOUTH—*Antiquarian House*, 126 Water St. Built in 1809. *Open*: June 15 to September 15 from 10 to 5 daily except Monday. *Exhibits*: completely furnished mansion of the early Federal period, formal garden, collection of dolls, costumes, toys, books, porcelains, laces, fans, et cetera. *Admission*: 25c. plus tax. *Harlow Old Fort House*, 119 Sandwich St. Built in 1677 and restored in 1921. *Open*: June 1 to September 30 from 10 to 5 daily. *Exhibits*: collections of seventeenth-century relics, furniture, and early utensils; demonstrations of early household occupations, such as spinning, weaving, candle making, dyeing, preparation of flax, fireside cooking. *Admission*: 25c.; special rates for schools and groups. *Headquarters of General Society of Mayflower Descendants*. *Open*: May 1 to November 1 daily except Monday. *Admission*: no charge. *John Howland House*, Sandwich St. Built in 1667 and restored in 1913. The oldest house in Plymouth. *Open*: May 18 to October 12. *Admission*: 30c.; children 10c.

QUINCY—*Adams Mansion*, 135 Adams St. Built in 1731 and enlarged several times during the nineteenth century. Occupied by four famous generations of the Adams family, 1787–1927, including Presidents John and John Quincy Adams. Became the Adams Mansion National Historic Site 1946. *Open*: April 19 to November 1, 9 to 5 daily, except Mondays. *Exhibits*: family furnishings, portraits, interiors, library and garden, complete as when occupied by the Adamses. *Admission*: 25c. N.P.S. *Birthplace of President John Adams*, 129 Franklin St. Built in 1659 and restored in 1896. *Open*: year round from 10 to 5 daily. *Exhibits*: early Colonial furnishings and antiques. *Admission*: 25c.; children 10c.; groups over twelve, 15c. ea. *Birthplace of John Quincy Adams*, Franklin St., on the corner of President's Ave. Where the Constitution of Massachusetts was written. Built in 1663. *Open*: April 1 to November 1, 10 to 5 daily. *Admission*: 30c.; children 12c.; including tax. *Dorothy Quincy Homestead*, Hancock Ave. and Butler Rd. Built 1636–1700 by William Coddington and remodeled in 1706 by Judge Edmund Quincy. *Open*: April 19 to November 1, 10 to 5 daily. *Exhibits*: period furniture. *Admission*: 25c.; children 15c. N.S.C.D., Mass.

READING—*Parker Tavern*, 103 Washington St. near the railroad station. Built in 1694. *Open*: June 1 to October 1, Sunday from 2 to 5, and by appointment with Mr. or Mrs. Warren Southwick. *Exhibits*: example of American Colonial home with some furnishings. *Admission*: voluntary contribution.

ROCKPORT (Pigeon Cove)—*The Old Castle*, Old Castle Lane, corner of Granite and Curtis Sts. Built in 1678, with addition of a lean-to in 1792. *Open*: July 1 to August 31 from 2 to 5 Saturday and Sunday. *Exhibits*: early American utensils and furniture. *Admission*: no charge.

ROXBURY—*Dillaway-Thomas House*, 183 Roxbury St. Built in 1750. *Open*: April 1 to October 1 from 2 to 4 on Wednesday. *Admission*: no charge.

ROWLEY—*Chaplin-Clarke-Williams House*, Bradford St. (Route 133) between the Newburyport Turnpike and Old Bay Road. Built about 1671. *Open*: apply to occupant for appointment. *Admission*: 15c.; S.P.N.E.A. *Platts-Bradstreet House*, Main St. Built in 1670 and restored in 1919. *Open*: June 1 to October 1, upon request. *Exhibits*:

an English garden, relics from early life of Rowley and an old-fashioned New England shoemaker's shop with benches and tools.

RUTLAND—*Rufus Putnam House,* Revolutionary home of General Rufus Putnam, friend of Washington, who planned fortification of Dorchester Heights. The Ohio Movement was planned here. *Open:* June 1 to October 1 daily from 2 to 5. *Exhibits:* Revolutionary relics and antiques. *Admission:* 25c.; children 10c.

SALEM—*Retire Beckett House,* 54 Turner St. near House of Seven Gables. Built in 1655 and restored in 1924. *Open:* June 15 to October 1 from 10 to 6 weekdays. *Exhibits:* early period furniture. *Admission:* no charge. *Derby House,* 168 Derby St. Built in 1762. Oldest brick house in Salem. Part of Salem Maritime National Historic Site which also includes the historic Derby Wharf and the Salem Custom House, built in 1819. *Open:* year round from 10 to 5 daily. *Exhibits:* painted paneling and staircase, furnishings of the period, and Derby family portraits. *Admission:* 25c. N.P.S. *Hathaway House,* 54 Turner St. on the ground of the House of Seven Gables. Built in 1682, and restored in 1911. *Open:* June 15 to September 1 from 10 to 5. *Exhibits:* two chambers with seventeenth-century furnishings. *Admission:* 16c. Proceeds go for settlement work. *House of Seven Gables,* 54 Turner St. Built in 1668 and restored in 1910. *Open:* year round from 10 to 5 except Thanksgiving and Christmas. *Exhibits:* secret staircase, antiques, paintings, early china, and kitchen utensils. *Admission:* 50c. Proceeds go to settlement work. *Lye Shoe Shop,* 132 Essex St. in the Institute Garden. *Open:* May 1 to October 31 from 9 to 4:30 weekdays. *Exhibits:* shop of tools of the 1830 shoemaker. *Admission:* no charge. E.I. *Peirce-Nichols House,* 80 Federal St. Built in 1782; designed by Samuel McIntire. *Open:* year round from 3 to 5 on Wednesday and Saturday. *Exhibits:* fine example of a Salem merchant's home; period furnishings. *Admission:* 30c.; children, if accompanied by an adult, no charge. E.I. *Pickering House,* 18 Broad St. Built in 1651, home of ten generations of Pickerings. *Open:* May through July, Thursday from 11 to 4. *Exhibits:* antique furnishings and heirlooms. *Admission:* small charge. *Pingree House,* 128 Essex St. Built in 1804. Designed by Samuel McIntire. *Open:* year round daily. *Exhibits:* fine example of a Salem merchant's home; complete in period furnishings; McIntire wood carving. *Admission:* 60c.; children, if accompanied by an adult, 25c. E.I. *Pioneers' Village.* Built by the city in 1930 as a replica of the wilderness village of Salem in 1630. *Open:* June 1 to October 31, daily. *Exhibits:* the village includes the "Governor's Fayre House," thatched and weatherboarded houses, wigwams, dugouts. The oldest house in Salem, the Ruck House, is now part of the group. *Admission:* 25c.; children 15c. *Ropes Mansion,* 318 Essex St. Built in 1719 with additions in 1804 and 1894. *Open:* year round during the afternoon except Sunday, Monday, and holidays. *Exhibits:* antiques, portraits, old manuscripts, laces, silver, double set of Canton china. *Admission:* 25c.; garden, no charge. *Vaughn Doll and Toy House,* in the Essex Institute Garden. Built in the late seventeenth century. *Open:* weekdays from 9 to 4:30. *Exhibits:* collection of over 500 dolls and toys dating to the Revolution. *Admission:* no charge. E.I. *John Ward House,* 132 Essex St. Built in 1684, moved here and restored in 1909. *Open:* May 1 to October 31 from 9 to 4:30 weekdays. *Exhibits:* furniture of the seventeenth and eighteenth centuries, early nineteenth-century apothecary shop. *Admission:* 30c., children, if accompanied by an adult, no charge. E.I. *Witch House.* Built in 1642. *Open:* year round. *Admission:* 30c.

SAUGUS—*Old Iron Works House,* 237 Central St. Built in 1636 by Thomas Dexter, and was the home of Richard Leader, the first proprietor of the Iron Works, which is noted for being the first successful ironworks in America. Except for small repairs, the house is much as it was when first built. *Open:* June 1 to September 30, from 1 to 5 daily. *Exhibits:* original seventeenth-century furniture. *Admission:* 30c., including tax. *"Scotch" Boardman House,* Howard St. Built in 1651. *Open:* by appointment. *Exhibits:* original sheathing, period staircase, early sponge painting. *Admission:* 25c. S.P.N.E.A.

SCITUATE—*Cudworth House,* opposite the schoolhouse in Scituate Center, on First Parish Rd. Built in 1723. *Open:* July 5 to September 17 from 1 to 6 daily, except Monday. *Admission:* no charge. *Old Grist Mill.* Built around 1640, the first water grist mill in the Old Colony and the inspiration for the poem "The Old Oaken Bucket," now partially restored. *Open:* on request to Scituate Historical Society. *Admission:* voluntary contribution.

SOUTH EGREMONT—*Blacksmith Shop.* Built in the eighteenth century. *Open:* year round. *Admission:* no charge. Now an inn. *Egremont Tavern* built in 1730, *Mount Everett Inn* in 1780, and the *Old Grist Mill* in 1790. These three buildings are together and in the center of the town. It was at the *Tavern* that Sir William Johnson stopped on his trips from New York and Connecticut. Plans for Shay's Rebellion were made at the *Inn* and the wounded were returned. It was also used by troops during the Civil War. *Open:* year round daily. *Admission:* no charge. Still operated as inns.

SOUTH LEE—*Merrell's Tavern,* Main St. Built about 1760. *Open:* Saturday and Sunday afternoons from July to September. *Exhibits:* some original furniture, old bar, taproom. *Admission:* 25c. S.P.N.E.A.

SOUTH SUDBURY—*Leonard P. Goulding House.* Built about 1700 in Wayland, Massachusetts; moved and restored in 1925. *Open:* year round. *Exhibits:* antique furnishings, British redcoat uniform. *Admission:* no charge. *Longfellow's Wayside Inn,* on Rt. 20. Built in 1683. *Open:* year round from 8 A.M. to 9 P.M. daily. *Exhibits:* authentic interiors and furnishings of an early eighteenth-century inn. Other interesting buildings in the same vicinity are: the *Coach House,* the *Red Stone Schoolhouse, Grist Mill,* and *Martha-Mary Chapel. Admission:* 25c.; children and students, no charge. It is still an inn.

SPRINGFIELD—*Alexander House,* 284 State St. Built in 1811 from designs by Asher Benjamin. *Open:* on application the year round. S.P.N.E.A.

STOCKBRIDGE—*Mission House,* Main St. Built in 1739 by John Sergeant, first missionary to the Indians of the vicinity. *Open:* April 1 to November 1 from 10 to 12:30 and 2 to 6 weekdays; 2:30 to 6 Sunday during the summer months; during the winter, visitors may obtain admittance by ringing the bell at the Cobbler's Shop. *Exhibits:* complete interiors of early America, Indian room, weaving room, courtyard, old-fashioned garden, et cetera. *Admission:* 35c. T.P.R.

STURBRIDGE—*Old Sturbridge Village.* A reproduction of a New England village of the early 1800s. Contains 26 buildings, many original and moved here from Massachusetts, Rhode Island and Connecticut. *Open:* May 15 to November 1. *Exhibits:* weavers, printing press, and shoe shops; antiques, early household utensils, mechanical gadgets, toys, woodware; over 4000 pieces of lighting devices. *Admisssion:* $1.00; children under twelve, 60c.; groups of 20 or over, 80c. ea.; educational groups and school children accompanied by a teacher, and servicemen in uniform, fed. tax only.

TOPSFIELD—*Parson Capen House,* just off the Village Common on Howlett St. Built in 1683. *Open:* June 21 to September 21 from 10 to 4 daily, except Saturday. *Exhibits:* seventeenth-century furnishings. *Admission:* 10c.

TOWNSEND HARBOR—*Conant House.* Built about 1720. *Open:* only by prior appointment. Address: *Old Mansion. Exhibits:* early sheathing, hinged partition between parlors, stenciled dado, furnishings. S.P.N.E.A.

WAKEFIELD—*Colonel James Hartshorne House*, on Lake Quannapowitt, Church St. Built about 1681 with several additions in the eighteenth century. *Open:* year round daily; private parties by appointment. *Exhibits:* antiques of the period; garden featured. *Admission:* voluntary contribution.

WALTHAM—*Gore Place*, corner of Main and Gore Sts. Built in 1804 by Governor Christopher Gore. Country seat of the Honorable Christopher Gore, governor, statesman, and first United States district attorney, appointed by George Washington. *Open:* from 10 to 5 daily. *Exhibits:* extensive grounds with stable, farm cottage, interior furnished in the period. *Admission:* 50c. including tax.

WATERTOWN—*Abraham Browne, Jr., House*, 562 Main St. (Route 20). Built about 1698. *Open:* weekdays 2 to 5, year round. *Exhibits:* seventeenth-century interiors. *Admission:* 25c. S.P.N.E.A.

WENHAM—*Claflin-Richards House*, opposite the Village Green on Main St. Built in 1664. *Open:* June 1 to September 30 from 1:30 to 5:30 weekdays; Sundays by appointment. *Exhibits:* collection of 2000 dolls and figurines, quilts, costumes, textiles, and research library. *Admission:* no charge.

WEST SPRINGFIELD—*Josiah Day House*, on Town Green, corner of Hanover and Park Sts. Built in 1754 with interior restorations in 1903. *Open:* June 21 to September 21 from 9 to 6 on Tuesday, Thursday, and Saturday. *Exhibits:* relics from Colonial days, antiques, costumes, crockery. *Admission:* 10c. (Storrowton)—*New England Colonial Village*, a village of New England Colonial houses assembled with restorations (on the Eastern States Exposition grounds). Included in the town are: the *Atkinson Tavern* (1798), the *Chesterfield Blacksmith Shop* (1750), the *Eddy Law Office* (1806), the *Gilbert Homestead* (1794), the *Little Red Schoolhouse* (1810), the *Phillips House* (1767), the *Potter House* (1777), the *Salisbury Meeting House* (1834), and the *Town House* (1822). *Open:* May 15 to November 1 daily. *Admission:* 60c.

WINTHROP—*Deane Winthrop House*, 40 Shirley St. Built in 1637. Home of Governor Winthrop's younger son, Deane Winthrop, from 1647 to 1703. *Open:* year round from 2 to 5 Tuesday, Wednesday, and Friday. *Exhibits:* documents and records of the house, portraits, relics of the period. *Admission:* 10c.; school children 5c.

WOBURN—*Rumford House*, 90 Elm St. Built in 1714. *Open:* year round daily. *Exhibits:* antiques of the period, portraits, cradles, English garden, the "Rumford Roaster." *Admission:* no charge.

WOLLASTON—*Col. Josiah Quincy House*, 20 Muirhead St. Built in 1770. *Open:* weekdays 9 to 5; Saturday 9 to 1, May to October. *Admission:* 25c. S.P.N.E.A.

YARMOUTHPORT—*Colonel John Thacher House*, corner of Thacher Lane and King's Highway. Original part built in 1680. *Open:* during the summer on weekdays from 10 to 5. *Exhibits:* antiques, furnishings of the period, relics. *Admission:* 25c. S.P.N.E.A.

RHODE ISLAND

ANTHONY—*The General Nathanael Greene Homestead*, 20 Taft St. Built in 1770 by General Greene, second in command to General Washington in the Revolutionary War. *Open:* year round from 2 to 5 Wednesday, Saturday, and Sunday. *Exhibits:* furnished complete in furniture of the period. *Admission:* no charge.

CUMBERLAND—*Elder Ballou Meeting House*, on Elder Ballou Meeting House Road. Built in the late seventeenth century. *Open:* year round by obtaining key from Adelbert H. Whipple, RFD 1, Woonsocket. *Admission:* no charge.

EAST GREENWICH—*General James Mitchell Varnum House and Museum*, 57 Peirce St. Built in 1773. *Open:* Sundays, June 1 to November 1 from 3 to 6; also by appointment. *Exhibits:* collection of historical pieces and furnished in the period. *Admission:* no charge.

JOHNSTON—*Clemence-Irons House*, 38 George Waterman Road, Manton. Built about 1680. Finely restored. *Open:* at reasonable hours upon application. *Admission:* 15c. S.P.N.E.A.

MIDDLETOWN—*Whitehall*, 4 miles from Newport, off Green End Ave. at Paradise Road. Built in 1729 by George Berkeley, British philosopher, Dean of Derry, Ireland, and later Bishop of Cloyne. *Open:* June 25 to August 31. *Admission:* 25c. See also *Old Colony House*, Newport. N.S.C.D., R. I.

NEWPORT—"*The Breakers*," Ochre Point. Built for Cornelius Vanderbilt in 1894. *Open:* daily all summer from June 25, from 10 to 5. *Exhibits:* exterior and interior decoration rivaling the magnificent Italian palaces after which it was modeled. *Admission:* See *Old Colony House. Hunter House.* Built in early eighteenth century. *Open:* daily all summer from June 25 from 10 to 5. *Exhibits:* fine paneling and decorative details. *Admission:* See *Old Colony House. Old Brick Market*, on the Parade. Built in 1762. *Open:* year round from 9 to 4:30 weekdays; 9 to 12 Saturday. *Admission:* no charge. *Old Colony House*, on the Parade. Built in 1739. First state house in Rhode Island. *Open:* year round from 10 to 5; closed briefly in July before opening of special exhibit of oriental wares brought to Newport by china traders. *Admission:* a combination ticket (adults $2.50; children $1.00) admits visitors to *Old Colony House, Wanton Lyman Hazard House, Trinity Church, Whitehall* (Middletown, R. I.), *Touro Synagogue, Hunter House,* and "*The Breakers*." Single admissions to each house may also be purchased. *Redwood Library*, Bellevue Ave. *Open:* year round from 10 to 6 weekdays, closed Sundays and holidays. *Exhibits:* portraits by Gilbert Stuart, Sully, and other early American painters. *Admission:* no charge. *Vernon House*, Clarke St. Rochambeau's headquarters. Built in 1758. *Open:* by appointment, year round. *Admission:* no charge. *Wanton Lyman Hazard House*, 17 Broadway. Built about 1675 and restored in 1928. Scene of Stamp Tax riot, 1765. *Open:* June 25 to August 31 from 10 to 5. *Exhibits:* period furniture, Colonial garden. *Admission:* See *Old Colony House.*

NORTH KINGSTON—*Birthplace of Gilbert Stuart*, and *eighteenth-century Snuff Mill*, Hammond Hill Road. Built about 1751–1752. *Open:* year round. *Exhibits:* gristmill and snuff mill, fireplaces, relics of 1700; small Indian graveyard and "buckies" running in season. *Admission:* 25c.; children no charge.

PROVIDENCE—*John Brown House*, 52 Power St. Headquarters of the Rhode Island Historical Society. Built in 1786. John Quincy Adams wrote in his diary about the house: "the most magnificent and elegant private mansion that I have seen on this continent." *Open:* year round from 9 to 5 Monday through Friday, from 3 to 5 Sunday; closed Sundays and holidays in July and August. *Exhibits:* special monthly exhibits. *Admission:* no charge. *Carrington House*, 66 Williams St. Built in 1810–11. It was the home of three generations of a distinguished Rhode Island family. *Open:* April 1 to October 1 daily except Monday, from 1 to 5. *Exhibits:* furnished as the family had lived in it, and contains many pieces of Chinese art and Lowestoft china. *Admission:* no charge. *Governor Stephen Hopkins House*, corner of Hopkins and Benefit Sts. Built in 1743 and the first ell constructed in 1741. *Open:* year round from 2 to 4 on Tuesday and Thursday. *Admission:* no charge. N.S.C.D., R. I. *Betsey Williams Cottage*, Roger Williams Park. Once owned by a descendant of Roger Williams, who gave the land to the city for the Roger Williams Park. *Open:* year round from 9 to 5 daily except Thursday. *Exhibits:* cottage kept as a museum of Colonial furniture. *Admission:* no charge.

WAKEFIELD—*Perry House.* Home of Commodore Oliver Perry and Commodore Matthew C. Perry.

CONNECTICUT*

ANSONIA—*Richard Mansfield House. Open:* May 30 to November, from 2 to 5 except Monday. *Admission:* 25c.

CLINTON—*Stanton House,* Main St. Near the Congregational Church Green. Built in 1789. *Open:* year round from 2 to 5 weekdays. *Exhibits:* Governor Buckingham's room, court cupboard, post-Revolutionary country store, Abraham Pierson well, old wallpaper, costumes. *Admission:* no charge.

DANBURY—*St. John House.* (Danbury Historical Society.) *Open:* Wednesday and Thursday afternoons or on request. *Admission:* no charge.

EAST HADDAM—*General Epaphroditus Champion House. Open:* June 1 to September 15 from 2 to 6 except Tuesday. *Admission:* 50c.

EAST LYME—*Thomas Lee House.* (East Lyme Historical Society.) Built in 1660. *Open:* summer, from 10 to 5 except Monday. *Exhibits:* china, pewter, utensils, *Little Boston Schoolhouse. Admission:* voluntary contribution.

GREENWICH—*Putnam Cottage.* General Israel Putnam is supposed to have escaped from the British here in 1779. *Open:* year round, Monday, Thursday, Friday, and Saturday from 10 to 5. *Exhibits:* antiques of eighteenth and nineteenth centuries. *Admission:* no charge.

GUILFORD—*Hyland House,* Boston Post Road. Built by George Hyland in 1660. *Open:* June 15 to October 1 from 11 to 4 except Monday. *Exhibits:* furnishings and antiques of the period. *Admission:* 25c.

HAMDEN—*Jonathan Dickerman House. Open:* July 1 to August 31 Saturday afternoon. *Admission:* no charge.

LEBANON—*Trumbull House and Lebanon War Office.* Built about 1704. *Open:* Monday and Wednesday, 10 to 5; Saturday, 2 to 5. Will be opened upon request on other days during this period for 25c. per person. *Admission:* 25c. D.A.R.

LITCHFIELD—*Tapping Reeve House and Law Office,* South St. Built in 1773. Restored in 1930. *Open:* June 1 to November 1 from 2 to 5 except Wednesday. *Exhibits:* documents, and records of law students, Colonial furniture; America's first law school was founded here. *Admission:* 30c. including tax.

MADISON—*Nathaniel Allis House,* Boston St. Built in 1739. *Open:* July to October from 10 to 4 weekdays. *Exhibits:* excellent example of a typical eighteenth-century home, with period furnishings. *Admission:* 25c.

MARLBOROUGH—*Marlborough Tavern.* Built in 1740. *Open:* year round. *Exhibits:* old furniture and fittings. *Admission:* no charge. Tavern is now a hotel.

MILFORD—*Eells-Stow House,* 32 High St. Built in 1689 and restored in 1930. *Open:* on request, daily. *Admission:* no charge.

NEW HAVEN—*Pardee-Morris House,* 325 Lighthouse Road. Originally constructed by Eleazer Morris around 1680–85, with the addition of a wing in 1767. Opening up of the old fireplaces in 1940 proved the house was partially burned by the British in 1779, but was restored the same year. *Open:* May 1 to November 1 from 10 to 5 weekdays

*Compiled by and used with permission of Development Commission, State of Connecticut.

except Monday, and 2 to 5 Sunday. *Exhibits:* period antiques, coach and gig; colonial herb garden. *Admission:* no charge.

NEW LONDON—*Joshua Hempstead House.* Open: May 15 to November 1 from 1 to 4 daily except Monday, Sunday 2 to 5. *Admission:* 25c. *Shaw Mansion,* 1 Blinman St. Built in 1756. *Open:* year round from 1 to 4 weekdays. *Exhibits:* the room where Washington slept; antiques, china, whaling relics, portraits. *Admission:* 25c.; children 10c.

NORTH HAVEN (Clintonville)—*Rising Sun Tavern,* Todd Pace off Middletown Ave. Built in 1732. *Open:* June 1 to September 30 from 1 to 5 Sunday. *Exhibits:* old doorways and wainscoting, paneling, cupboards, 9 fireplaces. *Admission:* no charge.

OLD LYME—*Florence Griswold House,* on Post Road. Built in 1818. First summer art group started here. *Open:* June 1 to September 30 from 2 to 5, except Monday. *Exhibits:* architecture, furnishings and particularly the paintings reveal romantic history of the house. *Admission:* 25c.

SOUTH COVENTRY—*The Hale Homestead.* Open: June to October, except Monday, 1 to 5. *Exhibits:* unusual collection of Nathan Hale memorabilia. *Admission:* 50c.

STONINGTON—*Denison House (Pequotsepos Manor).* Built about 1811, Open: December and January, from 1 to 4 daily; February to May, from 1 to 5 daily; June to September, from 10 to 5 daily; October and November, from 1 to 5 daily. *Admission:* 30c.

STRATFORD—*David Judson House,* 967 Academy Hill. Built in 1723 and restored in 1885. *Open:* May to October from 2 to 5 Friday and Saturday, and by appointment, telephone. Bridgeport 7-0395. *Exhibits:* good example of a New England home with fine interiors and slave quarters. *Admission:* 25c.; children 10c.

WALLINGFORD—*Samuel Parsons House,* 180 South Main St. Built in eighteenth century. *Open:* July 1 to September 30, from 2 to 5 Sundays, or by appointment; telephone 965 or 543. *Exhibits:* manuscripts, historical pictures, and other relics. *Admission:* no charge. *Nehemiah Royce House,* 538 North Main St. Built in 1672. *Open:* weekdays 9 to 11, and 3 to 5, July and August. *Admission:* voluntary contribution toward maintenance. S.P.N.E.A.

WETHERSFIELD—*Webb House,* 211 Main St. Built in 1673 with a front addition in 1752 and restorations 1916. *Open:* year round from 10 to 5 weekdays and 1 to 5 Sunday with the exception of winter months when closing hour is 4 P.M. *Exhibits:* old furniture, china, fine woodwork; scene of Washington's and Rochambeau's work on the plans for the siege of Yorktown. *Admission Fee:* N.S.C.D., Conn.

WINDSOR—*Ellsworth Homestead,* 778 Palisade Ave., between Windsor Locks and Windsor. Built in 1740. *Open:* year round from 9 to 5 weekdays except Wednesday, and 1 to 6 Sunday. In winter the Homestead closes at dusk. *Exhibits:* housed Presidents Washington and Adams on their visits to Ellsworth, contains excellent antiques of the Colonial period; heirlooms. *Admission:* 25c.; Connecticut Daughters, no charge. *Lieutenant Walter Fyler House,* 96 Palisade Ave. Built in 1640 with addition of four rooms in 1773. *Open:* two rooms open by appointment, telephone 461-M. *Admission:* no charge. *Loomis Homestead,* Loomis School. *Open:* by appointment; telephone 58. *Admission:* no charge.

WINSTED—*Solomon Rockwell House,* corner of Lake and Prospect Sts. Built in 1813. *Open:* June 1 to October 1 afternoons daily except Sunday. *Exhibits:* antiques, portraits, woodwork. *Admission:* no charge.

WOODBURY—*Glebe House,* "Birthplace of American Episcopacy," on Hollow Road. Built around 1690 and enlarged in 1740. *Open:* year round from 10 to 5 weekdays and 1 to 5 Sunday. *Exhibits:* original paneling, documents, and pictures of historical interest, early American furnishings. *Admission:* voluntary contributions.

BIBLIOGRAPHY

ACKERMAN, PHYLLIS, PH. D. *Wallpaper, Its History, Design, and Use.* Frederick A. Stokes Co., New York, 1925.

ADAMS, JAMES T. *Album of American History, Colonial Period.* Charles Scribner's Sons, New York, 1944.

BARBEAU, MARIUS. *The Origin of the Hooked Rug. Antiques* magazine, August 1947.

BOSSERT, HELMUTH. *An Encyclopaedia of Colour Decoration from the Earliest Times to the Middle of the XIX Century.* With explanatory text. Victor Gollancz, Ltd., Covent Garden, 1928.

BRIGGS, MARTIN S. *The Homes of the Pilgrim Fathers in England and America.* Oxford University Press, London, 1932.

BULFINCH, ELLEN SUSAN. *The Life and Letters of Charles Bulfinch.* Houghton Mifflin Company, New York, 1896.

BURRIS-MEYER, ELIZABETH. *Historical Color Guide.* Wm. Helburn, Inc., New York, 1938.

CANDEE, HELEN CHURCHILL. *Decorative Styles and Periods in the Home.* Willy Book Co., New York, 1938.

CAULKINS, FRANCES MAINWARING. *History of Norwich, Connecticut, from Its Possession by the Indians to the Year 1866.* Published by the author in 1866.

CHAMBERLAIN, ALLEN. *Beacon Hill: Its Ancient Pastures and Early Mansions.* Houghton Mifflin Company, New York, 1925.

CHAMBERLAIN, SAMUEL. *Boston in Four Seasons.* Hastings House, New York, 1942.

———. *Cape Cod in the Sun.* Hastings House, New York, 1937.

———. *The Coast of Maine.* Hastings House, New York, 1941.

———. *Historic Salem in Four Seasons.* Hastings House, New York, 1938.

———. *Nantucket.* Hastings House, New York, 1939.

———. *Portsmouth, New Hampshire.* Hastings House, New York, 1940.

———. *A Small House in the Sun.* Hastings House, New York, 1936.

———. *New England Doorways.* Hastings House, New York, 1939.

———. *Beyond New England Thresholds.* Hastings House, New York, 1937.

CHANDLER, JOS. E. *The Colonial House.* Robert M. McBride and Company, New York, 1916.

CHESKIN, LOUIS. *Colors—What They Can Do for You.* Liveright Publishing Corporation, 1947.

CONGDON, HERBERT WHEATON. *Old Vermont Houses.* Alfred A. Knopf, New York, 1946.

CORNELIUS, CHARLES OVER. *Furniture Masterpieces of Duncan Phyfe.* Doubleday, Page & Company, New York, 1922.

COUSINS, FRANK AND RILEY, PHILIP M. *The Colonial Architecture of Salem.* Little, Brown and Company, Boston, 1920.

———. *The Woodcarver of Salem—Samuel McIntire.* Little, Brown and Company, Boston, 1919.

DAVIS, DORSEY, RALPH HALL. *Georgetown Houses of the Federal Period, 1780–1830.* Architectural Book Publishing Company, New York, 1944.

DOW, GEORGE FRANCIS. *The Arts and Crafts in New England, 1704–1775.* The Wayside Press, Topsfield, Massachusetts, 1927.

DOW, JOY WHEELER. *American Renaissance.* William T. Comstock Company, New York, 1904.

DREPPERD, CARL W. *Handbook of Antique Chairs.* Doubleday & Company, New York, 1948.

DYER, WALTER A. *Early American Craftsmen.* The Century Company, New York, 1915.

EBERLEIN, HAROLD D. *The Architecture of Colonial America.* Little, Brown and Company, Boston, 1915.

EBERLEIN, HAROLD D. AND CORTLANDT, VAN DYKE HUBBARD. *Colonial Interiors, Federal and Greek Revival,* 3d Series. Wm. Helburn, New York, 1938.

EVANS, RALPH MERRILL. *An Introduction to Color.* J. Wiley, New York, 1948.

FOX, JOHN A. Selected by *Classical Architecture.* Geo. H. Polley & Co., Boston and New York.

FRARY, IHNA THAYER. *Thomas Jefferson: Architect and Builder.* Garrett & Massie, Inc., Richmond, Virginia, 1931.

FRENCH, LEIGH, JR. *Colonial Interiors.* William Helburn, Inc., New York, 1923.

GIEDION, SIGFRIED. *Space, Time and Architecture.* Harvard University Press, 1941.

HALSEY, R. T. H. AND CORNELIUS, CHAS. O. *A Handbook of the American Wing.* Printed and sold by the Metropolitan Museum of Fine Arts. Fifth Edition, 1932.

HALSEY, R. T. H. AND TOWER, ELIZABETH. *The Houses of Our Ancestors, as Shown in the American Wing of the Metropolitan Museum of Art.* Doubleday, Page & Company, 1925.

HAMLIN, TALBOT FAULKNER. *Greek Revival Architecture in America.* Oxford University Press, New York City, 1944.

———. *The American Spirit in Architecture,* Vol. xiii of The Pageant of America series. Yale University Press, New Haven, Connecticut, 1926.

HAYWARD, ARTHUR H. *Colonial Lighting.* B. J. Brimmer Co., Boston, 1923.

HOLLOWAY, EDWARD STRATTON. *American Furniture and Decoration, Colonial and Federal.* J. B. Lippincott Company, Philadelphia, 1928.

HOWE, LOIS AND FULLER, CONSTANCE. *Details from Old New England Houses.* Architectural Book Publishing Company, Inc., New York, 1913.

HOWELLS, JOHN MEAD. *Lost Examples of Colonial Architecture.* William Helburn, New York, 1931.

ISHAM, NORMAN M. AND BROWN, ALBERT F. *Early Connecticut Houses.* Preston and Rounds Co., Providence, Rhode Island, 1900.

———. *Early Rhode Island Houses.* Preston and Rounds Co., Providence, Rhode Island, 1895.

KELLY, JOHN F. *Early Conn. Architecture.* First Series, 1924, Second Series, 1931. William Helburn, Inc., New York.

———. *Early Domestic Architecture of Connecticut.* Yale University Press, New Haven, Connecticut, 1924.

KENT, WILLIAM WINTHROP. *The Hooked Rug.* Tudor Publishing Company, New York, 1937.

KETTELL, RUSSELL HAWES. *Early American Rooms.* Southworth-Anthoensen Press, Portland, Maine, 1936.

KIMBALL, FISKE. *American Architecture.* Bobbs-Merrill Company, 1928.

———. *Mr. Samuel McIntire, Carver, the Architect of Salem* for the Essex Institute, 1940.

———. *Domestic Architecture of the American Colonies and the Early Republic.* Charles Scribner's Sons, New York, 1922.

KINGMAN, RALPH C. *New England Georgian Architecture.* Architectural Book Publishing Company, New York, 1913.

LANGLEY, BATTY. *Examples from Ancient Masonry in the Proportions and Orders of the Most Eminent Masters of All Nations, Together with Their Most Valuable Designs.* Selected by John A. Fox, Architect, Boston. Published by Geo. H. Polley & Co., Boston and New York.

LATHROP, ELSIE. *Historic Houses of Early America.* Tudor Publishing Company, New York, 1941.

LYON, IRVING WHITALL. *The Colonial Furniture of New England.* Houghton Mifflin Company, Boston, 1925.

McCLELLAN, ELISABETH. *Historic Dress in America, 1607–1800.* George W. Jacobs & Co., 1904.

McCLELLAND, NANCY. *Historic Wall-Papers.* J. B. Lippincott Company, Philadelphia, 1924.

———. *Duncan Phyfe and English Regency, 1795–1830.* William R. Scott, Inc., New York, 1939.

MAJOR, HOWARD. *The Domestic Architecture of the Early American Republic, Greek Revival.* J. B. Lippincott Company, Philadelphia, 1926.

MILLAR, DONALD. *Measured Drawings of Old Colonial and Federal Houses.* Architects' League.

MIXER, KNOWLTON. *Old Houses of New England.* The Macmillan Company, New York, 1927.

MORSE, FRANCES CLARY. *Furniture of the Olden Time.* The Macmillan Company, New York, 1917.

MUNSELL, ALBERT. *Color Notations.* George Ellis Co., Boston, 1905.

NEWCOMB, REXFORD. *The Colonial and Federal House. How to Build an Authentic Colonial House.* J. B. Lippincott Company, Philadelphia, 1933.

———. *A Brief History of Rural Architecture in the U. S.* Vol. VII. President's Conference on Home Building and Home Ownership, Washington, D. C., 1932.

NORTHEND, MARY H. *Colonial Homes and Their Furnishings.* Little, Brown and Company, Boston, 1912.

PLACE, CHARLES A. *Charles Bulfinch, Architect and Citizen.* Houghton Mifflin Company, Boston, 1925.

POOR, ALFRED EASTON. *Colonial Architecture of Cape Cod, Nantucket and Martha's Vineyard.* William Helburn, Inc., New York, 1932.

RAMSEY, STANLEY C. *Small Houses of the Late Georgian Period, 1750–1820.* Technical Journals, Ltd., London, 1919.

RAWSON, MARION N. *Sing Old House.* E. P. Dutton & Co., New York, 1934.

ROBINSON, ALBERT G. *Old New England Doorways.* Charles Scribner's Sons, New York, 1920.

ROBINSON, THOMAS P. *Houses in America.* Viking Press, New York, 1936.

SALE, EDITH TUNIS. *Colonial Interiors*. Second Series. William Helburn, Inc., New York, 1930.

SHERRILL, WHITON. *Elements of Interior Decoration*. J. B. Lippincott Company, Philadelphia, 1944.

SYMONDS, R. W. AND ORMSBEE, T. H. *Antique Furniture of the Walnut Period*. Robert M. McBride & Company, 1947.

TALLMADGE, THOMAS E. *The Story of Architecture in America*. W. W. Norton & Company, Inc., New York, 1927.

Travels of Marco Polo. Modern Library, New York.

TROLLOPE, MRS. (FRANCES MILTON). *Domestic Manners of the Americans*. Whitaker, Trecher & Co., London, 1932.

WALLACE, PHILIP B. AND MILLER, M. LUTHER. *Colonial Houses*. Architectural Book Publishing Company, Inc., New York, 1931.

WARING, JANET. *Early American Stencils on Walls and Furniture*. W. R. Scott, New York, 1937.

WENHAM, EDWARD. *Antique Furniture for Modern Rooms*. Robert M. McBride & Company, New York, 1948.

WASHINGTON, GEORGE. *The Writings of*, ed. by Wm. Chauncey Ford, New York, 1889.

WAUGH, ELIZABETH AND FOLEY, EDITH. *Collecting Hooked Rugs*. Century Company, New York, 1927.

WEBSTER, MARIE D. *Quilts, Their Story and How to Make Them*. Tudor Publishing Company, 1943.

WHITEFIELD, EDWIN. *The Homes of Our Forefathers*. A. Williams & Co., Boston, 1917.

Index

INDEX

Accessories, 22, 26, 35, 38, 186, 187, 189, 193, 196, 214, 215; costume, 55, 115, 144, 164

Adam brothers, 25, 75, 76, 146, 147, 153

Adam, Robert, 75, 76, 78-80, 81, 85, 133, 146, 147, 151, 179; building design, 150; furniture, 61, 75, 76, 190; ideal, 146, 208, 211; style, 61, 145, 146

Advancing or active colors, 31, 32

Affleck, Thomas, 71

Afterimage or aftermirage, 31

Allston, Washington, 117

Amboyna, 84

American Empire, 26, 61, 84, 131, 157, 163, 198, 211

American Modern, 26, 119

American Notes, Charles Dickens, 158

American Revolution, 24, 135, 140, 145

American wallpapers, 44, 45

American Wing, Metropolitan Museum of Fine Arts, 73, 130

Analogous harmony, 30, 31, 35

"Anciente maides," 108

Andrade, Fernando Perez de, 39

Aptucxet, 96

Architectural and decorating periods, 19, 89

Architectural orders, 126

Architectural wallpaper, 24, 191

Architecture: brownstone houses, 161, 162, 216; Colonial, 120; Early American, 22; English Renaissance, 121, 145, 154; Federal, 145-52; French Renaissance, 161; Georgian, 121, 123, 136, 154; Gothic,

Augusta, Maine, 97, 148 120, 154, 160; Greek Revival, 155, 158; Renaissance, 120; Romanesque, 120, 154, 162; Victorian, 159-64; Victorian Gothic, 161,162

Artists, itinerant, 24

Aubusson, 24, 118, 133, 142, 192, 195, 204, 206

Background colors, 36

Bacon's Castle, Surrey County, Virginia, 100

Balusters, 128, 150

Balustrade, 125, 146, 148, 149, 156, 162

Banister-back chair, 20, 22, 65, 66, 108, 176, 179

Bathroom, 163, 169, 170, 173, 182, 185, 186, 187

Bedroom, 22, 100, 106, 169, 173, 181, 195, 199, 207, 214, 215, 217

Beds, 109, 123, 134, 199, 207, 214, 215

Belfast, Maine, 148

Belter, John H., 87, 163, 212

Ben-Hur, 95

Benjamin, Asher, 149

Bennington Pottery, 85

"Birchlands," Woodbury, Connecticut, 103, 128

Blackburn, Joseph, 116-18, 136

Blanket chest, 65, 176

Block-front furniture, 23, 71

Boardman-Marvin house, Portsmouth, New Hampshire, 136

Bolection molding, 129

Boston, Massachusetts, 67, 116, 117, 122, 123, 125, 143, 145, 155, 158, 189

Boston Museum of Fine Arts, Karolik Collection, 73

Boston rocker, 20

Boston Tea Party, 117

Braided rugs, 20, 21, 24, 57, 162, 173, 182, 191, 194

Brick houses, 100, 122, 149, 150, 156

Bricks, manufacture of, 101, 102

Bristol, Rhode Island, 148, 152

British East India Company, 39

Brocade, 59, 142, 191, 201

Brocatelle, 24, 59, 133, 144, 191, 207

Brooks, Hervey, 85

Brownings, the, 160

Brownstone houses, 161, 162, 216

Brussels carpeting, 198

Building manuals, 97, 121, 128, 145, 149, 161

Bulfinch, Charles, 146-50, 153, 158

Burlap, 59

Butterfly table, 20, 63, 176

Byron, 160

Cabinetmakers, 160; American, 72; Colonial, 24, 25; Huguenot, 65; in seventeenth-century England, 63; influx of, 70; New England, 79, 151; Philadelphia, 69, 71, 73, 79

Cabinet-Maker and Upholsterer's Guide Hepplewhite, 77, 78

Calico, 59, 171, 175, 177, 184, 185

Cambridge, Massachusetts, 123, 125, 127

Camlet, 56

Candlestands, 69, 133, 176, 191

Card table, 69, 204

Carlyle, Thomas, 41

Carsay, 56

Carter, Dagny, 39

Carver, Governor, 108; chair, 63, 108

Caulkins, Frances M., 115

Ceiling, 124, 131, 142, 151, 163, 167, 170, 203

Central chimney house, 99 100, 101, 128,

197, 202

Chairs: banister-back, 20, 22, 65, 66, 108, 176, 179; Carver, 63, 108; Chippendale, 74, 78; Cromwellian, 63; Duncan Phyfe, 84, 85; Hepplewhite, 78, 151; Hitchcock, 20, 86, 176, 179, 212; Jacobean, 63, 176; ladder-back, 22, 179, 206; lyre-back, 84; Martha Washington, 204; Queen Anne, 68; roundabout, 69; Sheraton, 81, 151; Sheraton fancy, 176; shield-back, 77; slat-back, 63, 108; Victorian, 210; wainscot, 63; Windsor, 20, 22, 69, 108, 176, 179, 181, 197, 200

Charles I of England, 62

Chenille carpeting, 206

Cherry, 133, 152, 162, 176, 189, 197

Cheskin, Louis, 29

Chest of drawers, evolution of, 65

Chestnut, 170, 172, 184

Chestnut Street, Salem, Massachusetts, 122, 147

Chimney, 106; central (house), 100, 101; construction of, 101; dimensions, 106; in Georgian house, 123; materials used in, 101; smoke chamber, 107; stack size, 101, 102, 106; "viewer," 101

China (porcelain), 22, 24, 134

China trade, 24, 67

Chinese wallpapers, 24, 25, 40, 44, 133, 151, 190, 197, 198

Chintz, 24, 59, 130, 133, 175, 177, 191, 194, 198, 203, 207, 215

Chippendale, Thomas, 23, 40, 70, 71, 75; The Gentleman and Cabinet-Maker's Director, 70, 71, 74

Chippendale furniture, 23, 61, 64, 68, 70-75, 131, 132, 133, 188-90, 196, 199, 206; chair, 74, 78; Chinese, 30, 75; country, 75; French, 75; Gothic, 75; "Irish," 73

Chroma, color, 29, 31

Circular fanlights (semi), 149; room, 127, 150

Clapboards, 96, 103, 150, 156

Clarke, Richard, 117

Coffee table, 178, 214

Coiffures, 114

Colonial period in America, 22, 23, 112-39; colors used, 24 130, 133; furniture, 132, 133; houses, exteriors, 120-27; interiors and furnishings, 127-39. Today's Colonial interiors: colors used, 192, 201; curtains and draperies, 192; fireplace, 191, 194; furniture, 188-91; lamps and lighting, 193, 194; rugs, 191; wallpapers, 191; walls and woodwork, 191. Bathrooms, 185-188 (see also Early American). Bedrooms, 186, 187-202 (see also Early American.) Dining room, 196-201. Kitchen, 200 (see also Early American). Living room, 198-201

Color and color schemes: color wheel, 30; how they affect, 32; moods in, 33-35; primary, 29; related, 32; secondary, 29; spectral, 29; symbolism, 33; tertiary, 29; use of color, 34, 35, 36, 37, 38; various harmonies, 31, 35; what is color, 28

Color: in Early American home, 21, 106; in Colonial home, 24, 130, 133; in Federal home, 25, 151; in French Empire, 83; in Victorian home, 162, 163. In today's Early American home, 168-87; Colonial 190-201; Federal, 203, 205-211; Victorian, 212-217. In bedrooms, 35. In dining room, 35, 38. In hospitals, 34. In kitchen, 38. In library, 35. In living rooms, 35, 38.

Color Research Institute of America, 29

Color theories and systems, 29

Columbus, Christopher, 39

Cool colors, receding and passive, 31, 32

Commonwealth, 62

Complementary color, 31, 35, 36

Complementary harmony, 30, 31

"Compo," 151

Composite architectural order, 126

Connecticut, History of, Trumbull, 54

Connecticut, settlement, 97

Connecticut shelf clock, 85

Console table, 182

Construction of Early American house, 20,

23, 92, 97-100; Colonial, 22, 23, 120-27; Federal, 149-52, 196; Greek Revival, 156-57; Victorian, 160-61

Copley, John Singleton, 116-18

Corinthian architectural order, 126

Cornice, 125, 126, 127, 129, 133, 148, 157

Costumes, 155; in Colonial period, 112-116; in Federal, 144; in Victorian, 164; accessories, 55, 115, 144, 164

Cottage Residences, Downing, 161

Coverlets, 20, 56, 177, 181

Cretonne, 59, 60

Crewel embroidery, 60, 175

Cromwell, Oliver, 62

Cromwellian chair, 63

Cupboards, court, press, livery, 108

Cupid and Psyche, 43

Cupola, 126, 149

Currier and Ives, lithographs by, 21, 164, 182

Curtains and draperies, 21, 27, 142, 162, 163, 174, 175, 180, 191, 197-201, 203-217

Dado, 23, 128, 133, 157, 167, 206, 209; cap, 23

Damask, 24, 60, 130, 133, 191, 194, 197, 207

Darnick, 56

Decorating, architectural and, periods in America, 19, 89

Dentils, 126

Derby, Elias Hasket, 122, 141

Desk, development, 65

Dewey, Parson Jedediah, 97

Dickens, Charles, 158, 160

Dining room, 22, 38, 179-80, 181, 197, 200, 206, 209, 217

Directoire period, 83, 84, 151, 157, 204

Documentary print, 60

Dolls, jointed, 114

Dominant or monochromatic harmony, 31, 35

Dominotiers, 40

Doors, 108, 124, 127, 129, 133, 147, 149,

156, 157

Doric architectural order, 126

Dormer windows, 124, 125

Downing, Andrew Jackson, 161

Draperies. *See* Curtains

Drawings, measured, 19

Dressing table, 133, 181, 182, 185, 187, 215, 217

Drop-leaf table, 20, 69, 177, 179

Drum table, 204

Dufour, Joseph, 43

Dutch East India Company, 39

Dyeing of homespun and yarn, 57

Dyes, aniline, 57; sources of, 57-58

Eagle, 26, 152, 203, 204

Early American family, 107, 108, 110, 167

Early American pattern glass, 177, 180

Early American period, 18, 91-111; furnishings and accessories, 107-10; houses, 91, 97-106; interiors, 100; of today, comparison, 119; restoring, 93.   Today's Early American home: ceilings, 170; color, 168-87; fireplace, 167, 182; floors and floor coverings: painted, 171; salt and pepper, 172; spattered, 171-72; rugs, 173; furniture, 107-8, 175-77; hinges and latches, 169; lamps, 182; wallpapers, 168-87; walls and woodwork, 168-71; windows and curtains, 174-75.   Bathroom, 169, 170, 173, 182, 185, 186, 187; bedrooms, 181, 182; dining room, 109, 179-81; kitchen, 107, 182-84; library, 179; living room, 178

Early pattern weaves, 55

Eastlake, Charles Locke, F.R.I.B.A., 161

Ebony, 84, 203

Ecole des Beaux Arts, Paris, 161

Edward VI of England, 61

Eliot, George, 160

Elliptical fanlights, 146, 149; rooms, 127, 150; stairway, 150

Embargo of Jefferson, 140

English Regency, 61, 153, 205

English Renaissance, 121, 145

English wallpapers, 43, 44

Essex Institute, Salem, Massachusetts, 102

Fabrics. *See* name of material

Fanlights, 124, 146, 148, 149

Farmington, Connecticut, 102

Federal period in United States, 25, 61, 140-52; architecture, 145; costumes, 144; interiors, 150-52.   Federal today: ceiling, 203; colors used, 203, 205-11; curtains and draperies, 203-10, fireplace, 202, 210; floors, 204-6; furniture, 203 205; house, 202; interior, 202; lamps and lighting, 207-10; mantels, 203; paneling, 198; rugs, 204; wallpapers, 203-211; windows, 203; woodwork, 206-11. Showing Adam influence: bathroom, 186; bedrooms, 207; dining room, 206; hall, 205, 209; living room, 206, 207. Showing Regency influence, 208-11; dining room, 208; hall, 209; living room, 210

Federalists, 141, 143

Fireplace, 20, 107, 127, 129, 133, 142, 152, 157, 162, 163, 167, 182, 191, 194, 198, 200, 202, 204, 210, 208-11, 214-17

Fleeson, Plunket, 44

Flock wallpaper, 40, 211, 216

Floor coverings. *See* rugs, carpets

Floors and flooring, 20, 92, 130, 133, 170-73, 204, 206, 214-17

Floral wallpaper, 24, 191

"Foreign devils," 39

French Empire (style), 26, 81, 83, 84, 151, 157, 211

French Provincial, 22, 177

French Renaissance, 161

French Revolution, 41, 42, 83

French wallpapers, 40-43, 151, 203

French War of 1756-63, 118

Fulford, Abraham, 54

Furniture styles: Adam, 61; American Empire, 26, 61, 84, 131, 157, 163, 204, 211; Chippendale, 23, 61, 64, 68, 70-75, 78, 132, 133, 189-206; Colonial, 132, 133; Directoire, 83, 84, 151, 157, 202; Duncan Phyfe, 61, 81, 82, 83, 157, 204, 212; Early American, 20, 107-10; English Regency, 61, 153, 211; Federal, 61; French Empire, 26, 81, 83, 84, 151, 157, 211; Gothic, 61; Greek Revival, 157; Hepplewhite, 61, 68, 75, 76, 77-79, 80, 151, 157, 179, 189, 191, 200; Jacobean, 23, 61, 62, 63, 176; Queen Anne, 23, 61, 64, 68-70, 132; Sheraton, 61, 68, 76, 80, 81, 83, 131, 133, 189, 191, 200, 201; spool, 86, 181, 206; Tudor, 61, 62; Victorian, 61, 87, 163; William and Mary, 61, 65-67, 131, 176, 189. As used in the Early American period, 20, 22, 107, 108-10; Colonial, 23, 132, 133; Federal, 25, 151; Greek Revival, 157; Victorian, 61, 163.   As used today in Early American, 175-77; Colonial, 189-91; Federal, 203, 204-11; Victorian, 212-17

Gamble, John, 44
Gardens, 136, 142
Gardner-Pingree house, Salem, Massachusetts, 147, 203, 205
Garvan Collection, Yale Museum of Fine Arts, 73
Gas lights, 163
Gate-leg table, 20, 69, 176, 179
Georgian architecture, 121, 123, 136, 154
Gibbon, Grinling, 63, 136
Gilt gesso, 69
Goddard, John, 23, 72, 73
Golden Age, The, of Furniture, 75
Gorham, Maine, 51
Gostelowe, Jonathan, 71
Gothic architecture, 120, 154, 160; Victorian Gothic, 161, 162
Gothic furniture, 61
Gothic Revival, 27, 87
Governor John Langdon Mansion Memorial, Portsmouth, New Hampshire, 136
Governor's Palace, Williamsburg, Virginia, 112, 123, 127, 190
Great House on Little Harbor, Portsmouth, New Hampshire, 112, 113, 136-39
Greek orders, 126

Greek Revival, 146, 148, 153-58, 159; fabrics, 157; furniture, 157; houses, 156, 199; interiors, 157, 202
Greek struggle for freedom, 154
"Grundsell," 93
Guilford, Connecticut, Henry Whitfield State Historical Museum, 55, 102

Halfpenny, W., Modern Builder's Assistant, 121
Halls, 98, 127, 150, 197, 199, 209
Hamilton Hall, Salem, Massachusetts, 143
Hancock, John, house, Boston, Massachusetts, 123, 125
Handrails, 128
Harewood, 76, 78
Harmony, analogous, 30, 31; complementary, 30, 31; dominant, 31; monochromatic, 31; triad, 30, 31
Hearths, 107
Henry VII of England, 61; Henry VIII, 61
Henry Whitfield State Historical Museum in Guilford, Connecticut, 55
Hepplewhite, George, 76, 77-79, 133; Cabinet-Maker and Upholsterer's Guide, 77, 78; Alice, 77; A. Hepplewhite & Co., 77
Hepplewhite chairs, 78, 151; furniture, 61, 78, 79, 80, 151, 157, 179, 189-91, 199, 200-07; influence, 75
Herculaneum excavations, 76, 77, 145
Highboy, 23, 65, 67, 133, 191
Hilton, Martha, 136
Hinges, 92, 169
Hints on Household Taste, Eastlake, 161
Historic houses, open to public, Connecticut, 235; Maine, 221; Massachusetts, 224-33; New Hampshire, 222; Rhode Island, 233; Vermont, 223.
History of Connecticut, Trumbull, 54
History of Norwich, Connecticut, Caulkins, 115
Hitchcock, Lambert, 85, 86; chairs, 20, 86, 176, 179, 197, 212
Homespun, 60; parties, 118

Hooked rugs, 20, 21, 24, 57, 133, 162, 173, 182, 192, 195, 200
House of Seven Gables, Salem, Massachusetts, 102
Houses: brick, 100, 122, 149, 150, 156; brownstone, 161, 162, 210; central chimney, 100, 101, 128, 197; Colonial, 23, 120-39; Federal, 145-52, 202; Georgian, 120-39, 154; Gothic Revival, 160; Greek Revival, 153-58; overhang, 102, 103; salt-box, 100; seventeenth-century, 97-99; Victorian Gothic, 161, 162
Houses open to public. See Historic Houses
Hue, color, 29, 31
Hunt, Richard Morris, 161
Hunter, George Leland, 73
Huts, settlers' in early America, 95, 96, 97

India print, 60
Industrial expansion in United States, 26, 159, 160
Industrial society in America, 160
Ingrain carpets, 162
Inlay, 152, 197, 214
Insurrections, 24, 25
Interiors: in Early American period, 100, 119; Colonial, 127-39; Federal, 150-52; Greek Revival, 156-58; Victorian, 162-64. Today: Early American, 169-88; Colonial, 189-201; Federal, 202-11; Victorian, 212-17
Inventories, 55, 56, 97; list ordered by Washington, 114, 115
Ionic architectural order, 126
"Irish Chippendale," 73
Irish glassware, 142
Irving, Washington, 161
Irwin, Beatrice, 34
Isinglass in Early American house, 20, 103
Itinerant weaver, 54
Ives, Currier and, lithographs by, 21, 164, 182

Jackson house (Richard Jackson), Portsmouth, New Hampshire, 135

Jackson, John Baptist, 43
Jacobean period in England, 62; furniture, 23, 61-63, 176
Jacquard loom, 163
Jacquemart and Benard, 43
James I of England, 62
Japanning, 66
Jefferson, Thomas, 124, 146, 147, 153, 154; embargo, 140
Jesuits, 39
Jewels, 115, 134, 142, 144, 164
Jones, Inigo, 120, 121, 145, 153, 154
Josephine, Empress, 114
Jouy, toiles de, fabrics, 60, 201, 203, 207; wallpapers, 171, 191
Jumel house (Roger Morris), New York City, 123, 127

Karolik Collection, 73
Kauffmann, Angelika, 76
Kelly, John Frederick, 125
Kennebec (now Augusta), Maine, 97
Kimball, Fiske, 125
King's arm (flintlock), 106
King's Woods, Portsmouth, New Hampshire, 113
Kitchen, 107, 123, 182-85, 198, 200

Lacquering, 66, 69
Ladder-back chair, 22, 179, 206
Lady of the Lake wallpaper, 136
Lafitte, Louis, 43
Lampshades and bases, 20, 21, 182, 192, 193, 207-10, 214-17
Landry, Doris, 57
Landscape wallpapers, 25, 43
Langer, 43
Lannuier, Charles Honoré, 83, 84
Latches, 92, 169
Latrobe, Benjamin Henry, 153, 154
Lean-to, 53, 92, 99, 135
Lear House, Portsmouth, New Hampshire, 136
Leather, 63, 202, 204, 208, 209
Lee Mansion, Jeremiah, Marblehead, Massa-

chusetts, 44, 126, 127, 128, 150

Le François of Rouen, 40, 43

Les Amours de Psyche, 43

Leyden Street, Plymouth, Massachusetts, 95

Lighting and lighting fixtures used in the Early American home, 21; Colonial, 134; Federal, 152; Greek Revival, 157; Victorian, 163.   In today's interiors: Early American, 182; Colonial, 193, 194; Federal, 204-10; Victorian, 214-17

Lind, Jenny, 86

Linoleum, 200

Linsey-woolsey, 53

Lithographs, Currier and Ives, 21, 164, 182

Living room, 38, 178, 196, 198, 201, 206, 210, 213, 216

Loom woven rugs, 20, 21, 53, 57, 133, 182

Longfellow, Henry Wadsworth, 136-39

Longfellow House (John Vassall), Cambridge, Massachusetts, 123, 124, 127

Loom, Jacquard, 163

Louis XV of France, 77; Louis XVI, 77, 83

Lowboy, 67, 133

Lyre-back chair, 84

Machine-made rugs and carpets, 162

Mahogany, 22, 23, 25, 73, 76, 84, 133, 151, 162, 182, 190, 191, 198, 200, 201; first use in America, 133; first use in England, 133

Maine, settlement, 97

Main State Building, Augusta, Maine, 148

Manchus, 39

Manhattan, Island of, 96

McIntire, Samuel, 26, 85, 122, 136, 142, 146-50, 153

McPhedris, Capt. Archibald (Warner), house, Portsmouth, New Hampshire, 123, 125, 135

Mantel, 142, 147, 198

Manuals of architecture and building, 97, 121, 128, 145, 149, 161

Maple, 20, 22, 23, 73, 133, 152, 170, 176, 190, 197, 198

Marblehead, Massachusetts, 126-28, 150

Marot, Daniel, 65

Marquetry, 67, 69, 130

Martha Washington chair, 204

Masks, 115

Mason, David, 66

Massachusetts Historical Society Collections, 98

Mayflower, 108

Mealtime in the Early American home, 109-11; in the Colonial home, 134; picnic in Federal period, 143

Measured drawings, 19

Measurements for wallpapers, 50

Medford, Massachusetts, 125

Metropolitan Museum of Fine Arts, New York City, 73, 130, 168

Mezzotints, 116, 134

Mirrors, 21, 109, 134, 152, 157, 181, 191, 194, 204, 206, 209, 210, 214, 216, 217

Modern Builder's Assistant, Halfpenny, 121

Modillions, 126

Moffatt-Ladd house, Portsmouth, New Hampshire, 136

Moldings, bolection, 129

Monochromatic or dominant harmony, 31, 35

Monticello, Virginia, 123, 124

Moods in colors, 33, 34, 35

Morris, Roger, house (Jumel), New York City, 123, 127

Morris, William, 44, 161

Mount Vernon, Virginia, 52, 191

Mulberry trees, 54

Munsell, Albert H., 29

Nantes, Edict of, 65

Napoleon, 83, 154, 157

National Capitol, Washington, D.C., 147, 148

Needlepoint rug, 217

Neoclassic, 77, 80

New Amsterdam, 96

New Hampshire, settlement, 97

Newport, Rhode Island, 23, 72, 117, 161

Newton, Sir Isaac, 29

New York City, 73, 123, 127, 130, 161, 204, 216

Norton, Captain John, 85

Norwich, Connecticut, History of, Caulkins, 115

Numdah rugs, 172

"Nutmeg graters," 113

Oak, 20, 107, 108, 132, 170, 176

"Oldest house" in United States, 94

"Orders" of architecture, definition, 126, 129

Oriental rugs, 24, 26, 133, 142, 191, 194, 198, 200, 201, 204, 206, 207, 209

Ormolu mounts, 203

Overhang, framed, 102; hewn, 102

Painted floors, 170, 171, 197

Painted walls, 51, 130, 175

Paired decoration (balanced), 25, 197, 208

Palace of the Governors, Santa Fe, 94

Palladian window, 124

Palladio, Andrea, 121; influence on Jones and Wren, 120

Panels and paneling: in Early American home, 20, 22, 93, 107, 167, 180; in Colonial, 23, 128, 130, 133; in Federal, 25, 151; in Greek Rivival, 157.   Today in Early American, 168, 169; Colonial, 191; Federal, 203

Paper hanging, 47

Paper, invention, 39

"Paper stainers," 43

Papillon, Jean, 40, 41

Passive or receding colors (cool), 31, 32

Patching wallpaper, 49

Patriotism in American decoration, 26

Peirce-Nichols house, Salem, Massachusetts, 146

Pelham, Peter, 116, 117

Pembroke table, 75, 133

Pendills, 102

Penn, William, house in Philadelphia, 125

Pennsylvania Dutch style, 123, 177, 193

Periods, architectural and decorating in

America, 19, 89

Perpetuana, 56

Philadelphia school of cabinetmakers, 69, 71, 73, 79

Phyfe, Duncan, 81-85, 151, 191, 200; furniture, 61, 81-83, 85, 157, 212

Pickman House, Salem, Massachusetts, 125, 150

Pier table, 75, 217

Pigment colors, 31; complementaries, 32

Pine, 20, 22, 133, 149, 152, 170, 176, 181, 185

Pingree. *See* Gardner-Pingree.

Pioneer village, Salem, Massachusetts, 95

Piscataqua River, 113

Plymouth, Massachusetts, 95; *History of Plimouth Plantation 1606-1646,* 96; men of, 97

Polo, Marco, *Travels,* 39

Pompadour, Madame de, 114

Pompeii, excavations, 76, 77, 145

Portico, 127, 149, 156

Portland, Maine, 135

Portland Place, London, 145, 147

Portrait painting, 116-18

Portsmouth, New Hampshire, 112, 113, 116, 122, 123, 125, 135, 136, 154, 190, 195

Portuguese, 39

Power loom, 53, 162

Preparation for wallpapering, 48, 49

Primary colors, 29, 32

Protectorate in England, 62

Proportion in patterns in wallpapers, 46

Proportioning colors in room decoration, 36, 37

Queen Anne, 43; death, 65; reign, 68

Queen Anne furniture, 61, 68-70, 131; characteristics of, 68, 69; chair, 68; in America, 23, 64, 132, 189-201

Queen Elizabeth, 39, 61

Queen Mary of England, 61

Queen Street, Portsmouth, New Hampshire 113

Queen's Chapel, Portsmouth, New Hampshire, 113

Quilts, 56, 177, 181

Rails and stiles in woodwork, 128

Randolph, Benjamin, 71

Rasieres, Isaack de, Governor of Manhattan, 96

Receding and passive colors (cool), 31, 32

Related colors, 32

Republicans, 141, 143

Restoration period in England, 62

Réveillon, J. B., 41, 42

Revolution in America, 24, 135, 140, 145

Revolution in France, 41, 42, 43

Rhode Island school of cabinetmakers, 72, 73

Rhode Island, settlement, 97

Richardson, Henry Hobson, 161

Rolling press, 43

Roman architectural orders, 126

Romanesque architecture, 120, 154, 162

Roof: captain's walk, 149; cupola, 126, 149; gambrel, 101, 125; hip, 125; pitched, 100; shingled, 101; thatched, 100; tiled, 101

Rosewood, 78, 84, 197, 209

Roundabout chairs, 69

Rowley, Massachusetts, 54

Royall, house, Medford, Massachusetts, 125

Rugar, John, 45

Rugs: Aubusson, 24, 118, 133, 142, 192, 195, 198, 200, 204, 206; braided, 20, 21, 24, 57, 162, 173, 182, 191, 194; Brussels, 198; chenille, 206; English Wiltons, 204; hooked, 20, 21, 24, 57, 133, 162, 173, 182, 192, 195, 198; ingrain carpet, 162; linoleum, 206; loom woven rag, 20, 21, 53, 57, 133, 182; needlepoint, 217; numdah, 172; Oriental, 24, 26, 133, 142, 191, 194, 198, 200, 201, 204, 206, 207, 209; Savonnerie, 204

Rugs and carpets as used in Early American home, 20, 21; Colonial, 24; Federal, 142; Victorian, 26, 162.   Today's interiors: Early American, 173, 174, 182; Colonial, 192; Federal, 204; Victorian, 212-17

Ruskin, 27, 160

St. Augustine Institute of Science and Historical Society, 94

St. Paul's Cathedral, London, 121

Salem, Massachusetts, 25, 26, 85, 95, 102, 103, 122, 125, 140-52; social life in, 141; gardens, 142; air of, 143; costumes in, 144, 154

Salt-box house, 100

Sampler, 21

Sandwich glass, 180, 194

Satin, 144, 203, 207, 210, 216

Satinwood, 25, 76, 78, 152, 203

Savery, William, 23, 71, 73

Savonnerie, 204

Saw, scroll, 162

Scenic wallpaper, 24, 25, 43, 133, 136, 151, 191

Scott, Sir Walter, 160

Secondary colors, 29, 32

Seventeenth-century houses, 97, 98, 99; colonists', 97

Shaggy rugs, 173, 174, 199, 207, 214

Shayes' Rebellion, 140

Shearer, Thomas, 79

Shelley, Percy, 160

Shelters, Early American, 19, 97

Sheraton, Thomas, 61, 68, 76, 77, 80, 81, 83, 131, 133, 191, 200, 203; chair, 81; Sheraton fancy, 176; influence, 75, 85, 151, 204; *The Cabinet-Maker and Upholsterer's Drawing Book*, 80

Shield-back chairs, 77

Shipbuilding, 141, 146; launching, 143

Shipping, influence in Salem, 140

Shock accent in color, 36

Shutters, 103, 125

Side table, 75

Sideboard, 79, 134, 151, 204, 217

Silhouettes, 181

Silkworms, 54

Silver, domestic, 134, 179, 193

Silversmiths, Colonial, 134

Sizes of wallpapers, 50

Sizing of walls for wallpapering, 48
Slat-back chair, 63, 108
Slaves, 25, 26, 108, 134, 142, 143
Smibert, John, 116, 117
Snuffbox, 113, 114
Source of colors, 29
Southbury, Connecticut, 85
Spattered floors, 171, 172
Spectral colors, 29
Spectrum, 32
Spinning, 52
Spool furniture, 86, 181, 212
Staffordshire pottery, 22, 157, 163, 175, 178, 180, 181, 183, 193, 195, 198
Stairways in Early American house, 98, 102; in Colonial house, 123, 127, 128; in Federal house, 150
Stars and stripes in decoration, 152, 204
State House in Boston, Massachusetts, 148
Stenciled floors, 173; walls, 24, 51, 52, 169, 175, 195. In period decoration, 52. Wallpapers reproducing stenciled walls, 52
Stiles and rails in wood paneling, 128
Stoves, 162, 182, 184
Stretcher table, 176, 179, 182
Stucco, 150
"Stunt" decorating, 213
Sumptuary laws, 55
"Swingling tow," 106
Swiss embroidery, 209
Symbolism in colors, 33
Symonds, Deputy Governor Samuel, instructions for building his house in Ipswich, 98

Tabby, 56
Tables: butterfly, 20, 63, 176; candlestands, 69, 133, 176, 191; card, 69, 204; coffee, 178, 214; console, 182; dressing, 133, 181, 182, 185, 187, 215, 217; drop-leaf, 20, 69, 177, 179; drum, 204; gate-leg, 20, 69, 176, 179; Pembroke, 75, 133; pier, 75, 217; side, 75; stretcher, 176, 179, 182; tavern, 20, 22, 176, 179, 182; tea, 69, 133, 176; tier, 204; tilt-top, 75; trestle, 20, 69, 176, 179, 184, 211; tripod, 75
Taffeta, 197, 201, 203, 207
Tales of a Wayside Inn, Longfellow, 136-39
Tavern table, 20, 22, 176, 179, 182
Tax, house, 19; new King, 112; "paper stainers," 43; wallpaper, 43; window glass, 20
Tea Party, Boston, 117
Tea table, 69, 133, 176
Tertiary colors, 32
Textiles. See Names of Fabrics
Textile factory, first in America, 54
Thackeray, 160
The Adelphi, 76, 145, 147
The American Builder's Companion, 149
The Cabinet-Maker and Upholsterer's Drawing Book, Sheraton, 80
The Gentleman and Cabinet-Maker's Director, Chippendale, 70, 71, 74
The Golden Age of Furniture, 75
The Land of the Pueblos, Mrs. Lew Wallace, 95
The Salem Frigate, Jennings, 134
"Thornbacks," 108
Thornton, Dr. William, 148
Tier table, 204
Tilt-top table, 75
Toiles de Jouy, fabric, 60, 201, 203, 207; wallpaper, 171, 191
Tontine Franklin Crescent (Bulfinch), Boston, Massachusetts, 147
Tories, 117, 118, 135
Tours of old houses, 131
Townsend, Job, 72
Townsend, John, 72
Tradition, 118
Trestle table, 20, 69, 176, 179, 184
Triad harmony, 30, 31, 32
Trim and woodwork, 23, 103, 124, 127, 128, 129, 130, 147, 148, 157, 162
Tripod table, 75
Trollope, Mrs., 155
Trumbull, John, 117

Tudor furniture, 61, **62**

Tufft, Thomas, 71

Tulipwood, 78

Turkey work, 53, 55, 56

Tuscan architectural order, 126

Value, color, 29, 31

Vanity Fair caricatures, 182, 214

Vassall, John, house (Longfellow), Cambridge, Massachusetts, 123, 125, 127

Velvet, 133, 203

Veneering, 64, 69, 152, 182, 203

Venetian blinds, 133, 192

Vermont, 97

Victorian architecture, 159-64; Victorian Gothic, 161-62

Victorian chair, 87, 216

Victorian mansion, Portland, Maine, 135

Victorian period, 26, 27, 61, 159-64; colors, 162; fabrics, 163; furniture, 61, 87, 163; houses, 159-62; interiors, 162-64; rugs and carpets 162; wallpapers, 163. Victorian today, 212-17; colors, 212-17; curtains, 214-17; fireplace, 214-216; furniture, 212-17; interiors, 213-17; lamps, 214-17; rugs and carpets, 214-17; wallpapers, 213-17; woodwork, 213-17. Country rooms: bathroom, 186; bedroom (man's), 214; bedrooms, 215-16; dining room, 216; living room, 216. Suggested decorated rooms town house: bedroom, 217; dining room, 217; living room, 216

Virginia, Monticello, 123; Governor's Palace, Williamsburg, 112, 123; University of Virginia, 123; Westover, 123; Williamsburg, 112, 120, 121, 130; State Capitol, 153

Voile, 203, 207

Wainscot, 151, 197; chair, 63

Wallace, Governor General Lew, 95

Wallpapers. how to hang, 47; how to patch, 49; how to use, 45; reproductions of tapestry and leather, 27, 163; wallpaper chart for quantity, 50; in Early American home, 106; in Colonial, 133; in Federal, 151; in Victorian, 163. In today's interiors: Early American, 168-87; Colonial, 190-201; Federal, 203-11; Victorian, 213-17. Types of: American, 44-45; architectural, 24, 191; Chinese, 24, 25, 40, 44, 133, 151, 191, 203; English, 43, 44; flock, 40, 211, 216; floral, 24, 190; French, 40-43, 151, 203; landscape, 25, 43; scenic, 24, 25, 43, 133, 136, 151, 191; toiles de Jouy, 171, 191

Walls and wall treatment in Early American home, 20; in Colonial, 24; in Federal, 25; in Victorian, 26, 27, 163. In today's interiors: Early American, 168-71; Colonial, 191; Federal, 203-11; Victorian, 213-17; stenciled, 24, 51, 52, 169, 175, 195; painted, 51, 130, 175

Walnut, 23, 37, 132, 189; black, 87, 162, 163, 185

Walnut, age of, in England, 23, 68, 190; in America, 23, 190

Walpole, Horatio (Horace), 160

War of 1812, 26, 79, 141, 152, 204

Ward, John, house, Salem, Massachusetts, 102, 103

Warm colors, active and advancing, 32

Warner house (McPhedris), Portsmouth, New Hampshire, 123, 125, 135

Warren, Russell, 148, 152

Washington, D. C., National Capitol, 147, 148

Washington, George, 53, 114, 115, 136, 192

Washington Hall, Salem, Massachusetts, 143

Weavers, emigration to America, 54

Weaves, early pattern, 55

Weaving, 53, 55, 108; silk, 55

Welsh dresser, 179, 181

Wentworth-Gardner house, 136, 195

Wentworth, Governor Benning, 136-39

Wentworth, Lady (Longfellow), 136-39

Wentworth, Governor John, 136

Wentworth, Madam Mark Hunking, 136

Westover, Virginia, 123

William and Mary, 43, 65

William and Mary College, Williamsburg, Virginia, 121

William and Mary furniture, 61, 65-67, 131, 176; characteristics, 66, 189-91; in America, 23, 65

Williamsburg, Virginia, 130; care of possessions, 120, 127, 189; Governor's Palace, 112, 123; Royal Colony of, 112; William and Mary College, 121

Wilton, English rug, 204

Window trim, Colonial, 124, 128, 129, 147; Federal, 130, 203; Greek Revival, 157

Windows: taxed, 20.   In Early American house, 20, 102; Colonial, 23, 124, 127, 133; Federal, 151; Greek Revival, 156, 157; Victorian, 27, 161.   In today's Early American, 174-75; Colonial, 192, 194; Federal, 203; Greek Revival, 205,

208; Victorian, 214-17

Windsor chairs, 20, 22, 69, 108, 176, 179, 181, 197, 200

Witch House, Salem, Massachusetts, 103

Wood. *See* under various names

Woodbury, Connecticut, 54, 57, 103, 106, 128, 168

Woodwork in Early American house, 20, 103; in Colonial house, 24, 130, 133; in Federal, 25, 151; in Greek Revival, 157; in Victorian, 162.   In today's Early American, 168-71; Colonial, 191; Federal, 203; Victorian, 213-17

Wren, Sir Christopher, 120, 121, 145, 153, 154

Yale Museum of Fine Arts, Garvan Collection, 73

Zuber, Jean, 43